THE

CIVILIZATIONS OF THE EAST

India

THE

CIVILIZATION OF INDIA

By René Grousset

TRANSLATED FROM THE FRENCH
BY CATHERINE ALISON PHILLIPS

With 249 Illustrations

TUDOR PUBLISHING COMPANY

NEW YORK

Originally Published as
TOME II — L'INDE
LES CIVILISATIONS DE L'ORIENT

Tudor Publishing Company 1939

MANUFACTURED IN THE UNITED STATES OF AMERICA

TABLE OF CONTENTS

The Civilization of India

CHAPTER I

BUDDHIST AND BRAHMAN INDIA

CHAPTER II

FARTHER INDIA AND THE MALAY ARCHIPELAGO

CHAPTER III

MOSLEM INDIA

INTRODUCTION

The Civilization of India

THIS VOLUME IS THE SECOND OF THE SERIES PLANNED AS AN INtroduction to the study of the arts in Asia, and is devoted to the Indian world, both Muḥammadan and non-Muḥammadan, including Farther India and the Malay Archipelago, but excluding Kashgaria and Tibet, which will find a place, with China, in Volumes III and IV of this series.

The fact is that India, with the cultures which trace their origin to it, is a world apart, one of the three or four great centres of human thought. There have been an Indian æsthetic ideal and an Indian humanism of equal value to the world at large with the æsthetic ideal and the humanism of either the Mediterranean countries or China.

To convey an idea of what this centre of culture was, I have given copious illustrations and quotations from texts, as in the previous volume, or even more so. The mere juxtaposition of a page from the *Lalitavistara* with a relief from Amaravati, or of a stanza of the *Gita Govinda* with a Rajput miniature, will create the atmosphere and suggest the surroundings in which they came into being better than any dissertation. By such means as these I have attempted to call up a picture of Indian civilization, while referring my readers to another of my works for a history of facts and ideas.

This volume could never have appeared but for the kindness of

MESSRS. VICTOR GOLOUBEW, FINOT, PARMENTIER, AUROUSSEAU, G. COEDÈS, HENRI MARCHAL, ANDRÉ GODARD, FOUCHER, HACKIN, HENRI VEVER, STOCLET, DOUCET, LOO, PHILIPPE STERN, JEAN BUHOT, MEHTA, ANANDA COOMARASWAMY, GANGOOLY, and the directors of the Archæological Survey of India and of the British Museum, to whom I owe the illustrations which lend interest to these pages. I offer them my thanks and hereby inform my readers that in order to study the subject more fully, they have only to refer to these gentlemen's published works or collections. For the rest, the author of the present sketch has had no other ambition than that of stimulating his readers to pursue their studies of Indian æsthetics further under the guidance of the masters mentioned above.

THE
CIVILIZATIONS OF THE EAST

India

CHAPTER I

Buddhist and Brahman India

ORIGINS OF INDIAN CIVILIZATION: PROBLEM OF THE RELATIONS BETWEEN INDIA AND CHALDEA

IN THE FIRST VOLUME OF THE PRESENT WORK WE MADE SOME reference to the prehistoric civilization of the Indus valley. This civilization, we may remember, goes back to the aeneolithic age — that is, to the time when copper, and afterwards bronze, were appearing side by side with stone. The two sites upon which remains of it are well vouched for, Harappa in the Punjāb and Mohenjo-Daro in Sind, would seem to go back as far as to the end of the fourth or the beginning of the third millennium, B.C. According to the first hypothesis of Sir John Marshall, director of the Archæological Survey of India, the three cities at Mohenjo-Daro, remains of which have been found one above the other, probably date, the first from about 3300, the second from about 3000, and the third from about 2700, B.C. The solid foundations of the two sites point to a people long since organized for purposes of town life.[1] This people bred cattle and produced cotton textiles, as well as a pottery with black paintings on a red ground, and a glazed blue and white faience, while copper utensils

[1] See *Archæological Survey of India, Annual Report*, 1923–4, Plates XVIII, XX: *Report* of 1924–5, Plates XVII–XXVI; *Report* of 1925–6, Plates XVII–XLVI.

and instruments have been found with its flint weapons. But what interest us most here are the stone, ivory, or earthenware seals which it has left behind it in hundreds, as well as others of bone and various compositions. These seals have inscriptions in a pictographic writing which is still very near to hieroglyph, together with figures of animals (Fig. 1).[1] These animal motives have been compared with those on the Chaldean cylinders. But, apart from the fact that the writing on them is different from the cuneiform script, the animals represented belong for the most part to the fauna of India: the zebu, the elephant, the tiger, and the rhinoceros. This alone would suffice to prove that, though it may have had some contact with the neolithic civilization of Mesopotamia — and, indeed, was bound to have done so — the civilization of Mohenjo-Daro was none the less an indigenous one. Possibly, however, we may try to explain the artistic affinities which have been pointed out between Mohenjo-Daro and Chaldea by certain previously existing racial affinities. Up till quite lately, we must admit, such a hypothesis would have appeared to be devoid of all foundation; but it may be less hazardous since Monsieur P. Rivet's recent theory of curious similarities of vocabulary between the Sumerian of primitive Chaldea, on the one hand, and the southern Asiatic (Austro-Asiatic) and

FIGURE 1

Seal from Mohenjo-Daro.

— Drawn by Jean Buhot after photograph by the Archæological Survey of India

[1] Ibid., 1923–4, Pl. XIX; 1924–5, Pl. XXII, XXVIII; and 1925–6, Pl. XXXII.

Oceanian languages on the other, to which latter group belongs the tongue spoken by the Muṇḍa, or primitive tribes of India — especially since Monsieur Przyluski inclines to regard these Muṇḍa as the former masters of the Indo-Gangetic region.[1]

We may further note that the discoveries of the last few years enable us to mark a series of stages on the way between the Indus and Mesopotamia. At the opening of Volume I we mentioned the painted vases with geometrical or leaf-shaped motives found by Sir Aurel Stein and Mr. Hargreaves in Baluchistan and Seistān,[2] and the affinities between these and the painted vases of Mohenjo-Daro on the one hand, and the pottery at Anau and Susa on the other. We have now to call attention to the rock-carvings found by Professor Ernst Herzfeld in 1928 at Kurangūn, in the district of Mamasēni, in the Persian province of Fārs, and at Sarpul-i Ẓohāb, near Qasr-i Shīrīn. These reliefs, one of which, in particular, represents a king and his attendants in an attitude of adoration before a pair of divinities, have a decidedly Sumerian appearance, and Professor Herzfeld has no hesitation in attributing them to the same date as that which Sir John

FIGURE 2
Capital at Sārnāth.
— *Photo, Archæological Survey of India*

[1] It should, however, be pointed out that the racial types in the sculptures of Mohenjo-Daro are not at all of the Sumerian type. See the excellent reproductions, in Philippe Vogel: *Annual Bibliography of Indian Archæology for 1925* (Leiden, 1928), Pl. III (stone bearded head, and stone bearded statue finished in stucco and painted).

[2] See Fred. H. Andrews: "Painted Neolithic Pottery in Sīstān Discovered by Sir Aurel Stein," *Burlington Magazine*, December 1925, p. 304 (with plates); H. Hargreaves: Memoirs of the Archæological Survey of India, No. 35, *Excavations in Baluchistan, 1925* (Calcutta, 1929); *Archæological Survey of India, Report, 1925-6*, Pl. XIII–XV (excavation at Nāl, Baluchistan, by Mr. Hargreaves).

Marshall suggested formerly for the palmy days of the civilization represented by Mohenjo-Daro: about 3000 B.C.[1] After such discoveries as these, the distance between the Sumerian world and the civilization of the Indus valley tends to diminish, at least spatially. They

FIGURE 3

Elephant from a capital at Sārnāth.

— From a photograph by the Archæological Survey of India

are no longer two isolated points. The gulf which used to separate them geographically is daily being filled up.

Again, in connexion with the comparison which has been instituted between the Sumerian and the so-called Austro-Asiatic languages, we may mention the discovery at Mohenjo-Daro of a charming cop-

[1] Herzfeld in *Illustrated London News*, November 19, 1927, pp. 905, 926; May 25, 1929, p. 892; June 1, 1929, pp. 942–5.

per statuette representing a nude dancing-girl, a work whose austere elegance and movement are not without some analogy with certain qualities of Melanesian art.[1]

Taking yet another point of view, perhaps it may be possible to establish a few points of similarity between the representations of animals at Mohenjo-Daro and those of the earliest school of Indo-Aryan sculpture — the Maurya school. The earliest specimens of this sculpture, as we shall see, are the capitals of Aśoka's pillars, among them that of Sārnāth, dating from the third century B.C. Now, if we compare the animals — zebu, elephants, etc. — of Sārnāth, or even those of the gates at Sāñchī, dating from the first century B.C., with the corresponding beasts at Mohenjo-Daro, it becomes hard to banish all idea of a distant relationship between them. Do not the seals of Mohenjo-Daro already display one of the essential merits of classic Indian art — that is, a naturalistic treatment of animals characterized by a wonderful breadth and flexibility? Similarly, an alabaster statue has been found on the same site, of a fabulous beast, part ram, part bull, part elephant, or an exquisite little earthenware statuette of a seated monkey, which may well foreshadow the whole art of Indian animal sculpture, from the capitals of Aśoka to the *ratha* of Māvalipuram. Or, again, what power of synthetic construction — another eminently Indian quality — is to be seen in two statuettes reproduced by Sir John Marshall: a terracotta buffalo and an earthenware mastiff![2] Lastly, the jungle life that we shall soon admire at Sāñchī is already apparent on the seals of Mohenjo-Daro, on which we see, now a huntsman stalking a tiger from a tree, with the beast turning on him, now a rhinoceros attacking two natives. It is true that if the chronology at present established is correct, more than fifteen centuries separate the aeneolithic age in India from Maurya art. But, though the intermediate links in the chain are

[1] See *Annual Bibliography of Indian Archæology for the Year 1927*, Kern Institute, Leiden, 1929, Pl. II.

[2] See *Archæological Survey of India, Report, 1925–6*, Pl. XXIX, XXXII, and XXXVIII.

FIGURE 4

Great *stūpa* at Sāñchī, north gate.
— *From a photograph in the archives of the Musée Guimet*

FIGURE 5

Great *stūpa* at Sāñchī, east gate.

— *Archives of the Musée Guimet*

missing, does it necessarily follow that all idea of relationship must be set aside? The technique of seal-engraving must have been lost after the arrival of the Aryans and the fall of the urban civilization of the Indus valley; moreover, no trace is left of the earliest works of Aryan India — the minor arts of the ivory- or wood-carver — so that, as soon as the Indians had learnt from the example of the Greeks how to render in stone the reliefs formerly carved in ivory or wood, we find works which attained perfection at a single bound. But this very fact, viewed in the light of the finds at Mohenjo-Daro or Harappa, prompts us to ask ourselves whether we are not here faced with a phenomenon similar to that which presents itself in the Ægean region, where the ancient pre-Hellenic culture, destroyed by the Indo-European invaders, was afterwards incorporated by them in the Greek civilization.[1]

As for the dating of the antiquities of Harappa and Mohenjo-Daro, the essential piece of evidence is still the stone seal in the Baghdād Museum catalogued as No. 1822. This seal, which was found at Kish (Tell-el-Uhaimir), in 'Irāq, and bears an intaglio of decidedly " pre-Aryan " workmanship, representing an animal of the bovine tribe, together with pictographic characters which are likewise " pre-Aryan," was undoubtedly brought to Chaldea from the Indus. The ticket in the Baghdād Museum dates it " about 3200 B.C.," and the Museum officials remind us that this object was found in a very archaic deposit, belonging to pre-Semitic, Sumerian Kish. None the less, so experienced an archæologist as Monsieur Watelin wonders whether the seal was really found *in situ,* and had not slipped down from a more recent deposit and was not really brought from the Indus to Chaldea about the time of the third dynasty of Ur (between 2470 and 2360). And, again, Monsieur Alfred Foucher has judiciously observed that if, as is possible, the pre-Aryan civilization of the Indus

[1] Ramaprasad Chanda: *Survival of the Prehistoric Civilization in the Indus Valley,* No. 41 of the Memoirs of the Archæological Survey of India (Calcutta, 1929).

valley was destroyed by the arrival of the Aryans, it might perhaps be well to assign a later date to the later years, at least, of this civilization, bringing it down to the time of the Aryan invasion — that is, towards the beginning of the first millennium. Such a suggestion would enable us to explain, in case of need, the possible affinities between the pre-Aryan art of the Indus valley and archaic Indo-Aryan art.[1]

ARYAN INDIA: THE VEDIC POETRY

THE NEW-COMERS, THE INDIANS OF HISTORIC TIMES, FORMED, WITH their brothers the Iranians, a distinct group of the great Indo-European family — the Indo-Iranian or Aryan group. The language of the Indians and that of the Iranians in their most archaic form — that is, Vedic Sanskrit for the Indians and Avestic and Old Persian for the Iranians — had close affinities which permit us to assume a long period of existence in common between them.

When the Indians, to whom we shall now refer by their Sanscrit name of the Āryas, came down from Iran into the Indo-Gangetic plain at a date which has been approximately assigned to about the end of the second millennium B.C., they had to wrest the country from indigenous races still represented on Indian soil today and belonging to two races: the Dravidians, who continue to form a dense mass of population in the Deccan, and the Muṇḍas, who were subsequently confined to a few districts of central or eastern India. In these surroundings, which were so different from their Iranian fatherland, and in the midst of peoples of a different race, the Āryas seem to have formed an exclusive society. In spite of inevitable mixtures of race, the chief preoccupation in the Vedic texts seems to have been with that anxiety for racial purity which is no more than the instinctive

[1] Cf. Ramaprasad Chanda: *The Indus Valley in the Vedic Period,* No. 31 of Memoirs of the Archæological Survey of India (Calcutta, 1926); Ananda Coomaraswamy: "Archaic Indian Terracottas" (in the Museum of Fine Arts, Boston) in the review *Ipek,* 1928, pp. 64–76.

FIGURE 6

Sāñchī, north gate, detail.
— *Archives of the Musée Guimet*

defence of the conqueror against the slow process of retaliation on the part of the conquered masses. The three classes of Aryan society — the Brahmans or priests, the *Kshatriyas* or warriors, and the *Vaiśyas* or husbandmen — had to create an impassable gulf between themselves and the non-Aryan populations. Little by little an equally deep gulf was to appear within this Aryan society, too, with the creation of the exclusive castes. The Brahmanical caste in particular acquired a position of importance unknown to any sacerdotal class in the ancient world.

FIGURE 7
Sāñchī: *Jātaka* of the six-tusked elephant.
— *Archives of the Musée Guimet*

For material reasons, the sacred books of the Brahmans, or *Vedas,* which were handed down orally from generation to generation, could not have been written down before the sixth century, for writing in India was of Aramæan origin and was most probably introduced at the time of the domination of the Achæmenid Persians in the Punjāb. Nevertheless, in view of the archaic character of their language, it may be supposed that the Vedas, in the form of a mass of oral traditions, go back to the first half of the first millennium B.C. They are, in the first place, liturgical texts, collections of hymns, and sacrificial formulas — the sacrifice consisting of an offering to the gods of milk, honey, cakes, and a drink made of the fermented juice of the soma. This means that the Vedas are by no means lacking in arid liturgical formalism. None the less, passages are to be found in them of fine poetry — an ample poetry, full of colour, with a grand imagery like that of the Homeric poems.

The gods to whom these hymns were addressed, and whom the earliest Āryas brought with them from Iran, were, as might be expected of a pastoral and still half-nomad race, celestial or atmospheric divinities who are still somewhat vague in outline.

FIGURE 8
Sāñchī: adoration of the bodhi-tree by the animal kingdom.
— *Archives of the Musée Guimet*

In the first place, the sun under its different names — Āditya, Sūrya, Savitṛi, or Vishṇu. — "With thy light," runs one of these old nature hymns, "thou dost cover the earth which beareth mankind, thou dost flood the heavens and the vast air, and thou lookest upon all that doth exist. Seven tawny-haired mares draw thy chariot, O dazzling Sūrya; thy beautiful hair is crowned with rays of light, thou god who seest all things!" With Sūrya were associated Ushas, the dawn, and the Aśvins or celestial riders. The dawn inspired the Vedic bards with accents of a moving freshness: "She hath come, the white, the radiant one, with her shining calf, and the sable goddess hath yielded up her throne; Dawn and Night, the immortal sisters who follow one upon the other, proceed on their way, and the one doth extinguish the other. . . . The shining one who leadeth the glad songs of youth, she hath shone, the brilliant one, and thrown open to us the gates. She hath caused the changing world to rise, she hath found wealth for us. The dawn hath awakened all things that exist. She hath revealed herself, the daughter of heaven, radiant, young, and clothed in brightness. . . . Thou who dost reign over all the treasures of the earth, do thou, O Dawn, with thy rays bring us happiness this day! . . . They have gone hence, those mortals who saw the first glow of dawn, and, lo, they approach who shall see the shining of dawns to come! . . . The goddess Dawn hath shone for ever throughout the past and shall shine for ever upon the days that are to come. Immortal, ever young, she doth advance according to her own law. . . . Arise, the breath of life hath come to us: let the darkness retreat! The light doth advance. She hath yielded her path to the sun's course. We have reached the turning at which life is prolonged. Today, O generous one, bring with thee in thy rays life and prosperity to him who doth sing thee, and unto us all! " (*Ṛigvēda*).

Of a similar nature was Varuṇa, god of the heavenly ocean or starry firmament, who, as such, looks upon all human actions: " O Varuṇa," runs the hymn to this cosmic divinity, " the wind is thy breath, which stirs the air. In thee doth repose the immensity of the earth and of the heavens. O Varuṇa, in thee are all the worlds! Thy happy light doth see the lovely forms of heaven and of earth come into being around it." Indra, god of the thundering sky, who, hidden in the storm-cloud, commands the atmosphere, is more anthropomorphic in character: " He appears, and the mountains, sky, and earth have trembled with terror. All the forests shudder at his passage."

In fact, Indra soon became a warrior god, the protector of the conquering Āryas in their struggle against the natives of the country; he was the " King Indra " represented in Indian iconography as covered with jewels, wearing the royal turban or the tiara, armed with the thunderbolt (*vajra*), the disk (*chakra*), the ax (*taṅka*) and

FIGURE 9

Sāñchī, north gate, detail.

— *Archives of the Musée Guimet*

elephant-goad (*aṅkuśa*), and mounted on the white elephant. It was his victory over the serpents Ahi and Vṛitra, ravishers of the clouds and demons of drought, that restored the fertilizing rains to the parched earth: "Indra with his thunderbolt hath smitten Ahi," sings the Vedic hymn. "He hath poured forth the waters upon the earth and loosed the torrents of the celestial mountains. He hath smitten Ahi, and the waters, like cows running towards their byre, are returning to the river." And elsewhere, addressing the sacred Gangetic rivers, the poet cries: "Indra hath granted unto you the rushing movement that ye did desire, and ye advance towards the great reservoir as though borne on a car; side by side, rolling your swollen waters, each of you, O beautiful ones, doth address the other. . . . I will proclaim for ever the great feat of Indra; he hath cloven the serpent in twain, his lightning hath burst the dikes, and the waters have poured down, eager for flight!"

Among the companions of Indra should be mentioned the Maruts and Rudra, gods of the whirlwind and dispensers of rain: "The Maruts press the clouds like a breast, they milk them amid the roar of the thunderbolt. . . . Like wild elephants they uproot the forests when their ruddy steeds are harnessed to their chariot." And in another passage: "The bellowing bull of the flood pours forth the seed of life to the plants. He blasts both trees and demons; the universe trembles beneath his heroic arm, and the innocent man shudders as the roaring giant smites the sinners. As the horses bound beneath the whip which guides them, lo, his moist messengers announce his coming, and he is heard afar off, like the roaring of a lion, as the god takes form in the rain-bearing cloud. The winds rush forth, the lightnings fly, the plants upraise their heads, the sky is swollen. Abundance pours forth for all living creatures when the god sheds his sap upon the earth. . . . Roar, O god, thunder and engender life, drive across the heavens in thy chariot heavy with downpours, drawing the open water-skin whose mouth is hanging over us, level

Figure 10

Sāñchī, north gate, detail.
— *Archives of the Musée Guimet*

the slopes and the hollows. Tip up the great bowl; let it be emptied out in torrents unrestrained, flood both heaven and earth with rich moisture, and make a good watering-trough for the kine " (*Ṛigvēda*). This powerful nature-poetry, rich with the sap of the tropical earth, explains by what process Rudra, the father of the Maruts, and god

Figure 11
Sāñchī, west gate: sermon in the Deer-park.
— *Archives of the Musée Guimet*

Figure 11b
Sāñchī, west gate: adoration of the bodhi-tree by the elephants.
— *Archives of the Musée Guimet*

of the forests, afterwards, under the name of Śiva, became the symbol of cosmic force, of tellurian and generative forces, the animating principle of Hindu pantheism.

Even the gods of the sacrifice, the sacerdotal gods, assumed a naturalistic aspect under the breath of the Vedic poetry. For such was the importance of the Vedic sacrifice that its elements were proclaimed divine and adored in themselves. This is what happened to Agni, the altar fire, and Brahma, the magic formula recited by the officiating priest. It is true that the sacrificial origin of Agni was never to be entirely forgotten, for the iconography of later days represents him with two heads, symbolizing the Brahmanical fire and the fire of the domestic altar, and with four arms, bearing the sacrificial implements — the ax for cutting the wood, the torch for kindling the fire, the fan for fanning it, and the spoon for casting the offering upon it. None the less, this god, whom the Brahmans had raised to a position of equality with the atmospheric divinities, ended by becoming confused with them, and in the first place with the divine fire. Does not the flame of the morning sacrifice seem to call for the return of light and the awakening of nature? "Agni has awakened to meet the dawn, the glittering one, the priest and guide of great sages. Kindled by pious hands, sending forth his light to a distance, he has thrown the gate of darkness open wide. Agni, the object of our worship, has grown in stature through the praises, the poetry, and the melodies of the singers; delighting in the thousand aspects of the eternal order, he, our messenger, has shone at the break of dawn" (*Ṛigvēda*).

A little later, in the *Sāmavēda*, Agni, the fire, was to be celebrated as the essential principle of the universe, by the same process of reasoning as that of the old Ionian philosophers: "The god with the golden germ appears. He is new-born, and already he is master of the earth. He fills both heaven and earth. To what other god should we offer sacrifices? He gives life and strength. All beings, all gods, are subject to his law. Immortality and death are but his shadow. His greatness is in these snow-covered mountains, this ocean with its waves; and the heavenly regions are his two outstretched arms. By him heaven and earth, the whole of space, the whole firmament, have been firmly established. It is he who has poured forth the waters through the air. Earth and heaven, made stable by his care, have thrilled with the desire to look upon him, while Sūrya is shining in the east. When the great waters came, bearing in their womb the germ of universal life and giving birth to Agni, then did the soul of the gods, the one and only soul, come to life. He sees them with pride

FIGURE 12
Sāñchī: capital from the east gate.
— *Archives of the Musée Guimet*

round about him. He alone is god above all gods! " The *Mahābhārata* was afterwards to address the sacrificial fire, now become the universal force, in like terms: " O Agni, thou art the soul of the winds, thou art the substance of the young growing shoots; the waters are thy seed. Immanent in all things, and ever growing with them, thou dost bring them to maturity. In thee the all doth live. Clothed in the form of the sun, thou takest up the waters of the earth with thy beams; then, by the rains which thou dost pour forth in their season, thou restorest life to all things. Then are all things born of thee anew: the twining plants, the green foliage, the lakes, the favoured reservoir of the waters, the whole of that moist palace subject to Varuṇa."

FIGURE 13
Sāñchī: *yakshiṇī* from the east gate.
— *Photo, Archæological Survey of India*

Innumerable secondary gods throng about these principal divinities. In the first rank come the *asuras,* a very ancient category of divinities, once the equals of the *dēvas* enumerated above, but now reduced to the position of Titans hostile to the gods, and soon to assume the character of demons. Next come the *apsaras,* the changing clouds who developed into celestial courtesans, prompt to serve the secret designs of the gods by their charms. In the same category is Kāma, the god of desire and of love, who is represented as armed with flowery arrows and riding on the back of a parrot. In a different class are the four Lokapālas or kings of the heavens and guardians of the world, with their tribe of genii, among whom are Kuvēra or Vaiśravaṇa, king of the region of the North, having under his command the *yakshas,* good or bad genii endowed with wonder-working powers;[1] Virūdhaka, king of the South, having under his orders the pot-bellied gnomes called *kumbhāṇḍa;* Dhṛitarāshṭra, king of the East, reigning over the *gandharvas* or celestial musicians; and lastly, Virūpāksha, king of the West, ruling over the *nāgas,* or genii with magical powers, who live in watery palaces in the depths of lakes and appear sometimes in the form of serpents, sometimes as men whose heads are crowned with a hood of cobra's heads (cf. Fig. 62 and 65).[2] In Indian mythology the legendary adversaries of the *nāgas* are the *garuḍas,* gigantic birds which are generally represented with human heads, having the beak of a bird: the subject of a *garuḍa* carrying off a *nāgī,* or female *nāga,* occurs repeatedly in Buddhist and Brahmanic sculpture.[3] Lastly we may mention the *kiṃnaras,* who are genii of a different class, often represented in the form of sirens.

FIGURE 14
Sāñchī: *yakshiṇī* from the east gate: back view.
— *Archives of the Musée Guimet*

In spite of the poetic attractiveness of these divinities, the time soon arrived when they no longer satisfied Indian thought, and at a very

1 See Fig. 147; also the *yakshiṇī* in Fig. 12. See also Ananda Coomaraswamy: *Yaksas,* Smithsonian Miscellaneous Collections, Vol. 80, No. 6 (Washington, 1928).

2 See P. Vogel: *Indian Serpent-lore, or the Nāgas in Hindu Legend and Art* (London, 1926), with a charming relief of a *nāgarāja* from Ajaṇṭā.

3 See Vol. IV of the present work, Fig. 183.

early date speculative ideas made their appearance, which had already reached full development in the Upanishads, a sort of philosophico-religious meditations appended to the sacred text of the Vedas towards the seventh and sixth centuries B.C. In these new religious works we find a dogma formulated which had hitherto been unknown, but was henceforth to dominate all Indian creeds without exception: the dogma of transmigration — that is, of endless reincarnations of living beings in fresh mortal forms, each time determined by the good or bad conduct of the dead man in the course of his last existence. At the same time the Upanishads developed a spiritualist monism in which the essence of the soul is taken as identical with the very essence of the universe — that is, of the Godhead. The term by which this universal divine substance is referred to is the word *Brahma,* applied in primitive times to the ritual words of the officiating priest at the sacrifice. From the same term was subsequently derived a special sacerdotal god, Brahmā, whom we shall find represented in Indian sculpture with the lock of hair and water-pot of the Brahmans.

As far back as this remote period, in fact, the Indian soul revealed its tendency towards mysticism. In the course of their speculations upon the conceptions of the Upanishads or kindred ideas a great number of Brahman ascetics, or yogis, as they were called, renounced the things of this world and retired to the depths of the forest, there to give themselves up to meditation and to find in the depths of their own hearts a means of escape from the endless vicissitudes of transmigration (cf. Fig. 63 and 149–150). It was such a state of mind as this that gave rise to Jainism and Buddhism.

We shall not dwell at any length upon Jainism here. The historic founder of this creed, Vardhamāna, known as Mahāvīra, the "Great Hero," seems to have lived in the eastern part of the Ganges basin between 600 and 528 B.C.[1] His doctrine was an ascetic one: the soul,

[1] See A. Coomaraswamy: *Catalogue of the Indian Collections in the Museum of Fine*

FIGURE 15

Sāñchī, east gate, detail.
— *Archives of the Musée Guimet*

defiled by contact with the world, can only attain salvation by turning in upon itself. The Jains formed a religious order practising poverty, chastity, and charity towards all beings. Their ethical code was characterized by a scrupulous respect for every form of life, however humble: this is the doctrine of "non-violence" or *ahiṃsā,* which is still found in our day — for instance, in the teaching of Gandhi — and that we shall also see developed in Buddhism.

THE LIFE AND LEGEND OF THE BUDDHA

THE BUDDHA ŚĀKYAMUNI LIVED IN THE EASTERN BASIN OF THE GANGES between about 563 and 483, B.C., according to the most probable approximate dates arrived at by present-day specialists; but his story has come down to us wrapped in a veil of legend. These legends are, however, most beautiful, so that we hardly know what to admire in them most — the outward poetry of the myths which form their subject, or the more intimate and tender beauty of the Buddha's own teaching. Now they relate the fabulous adventures of a charming prince, a being more than half divine, the hero of the most wonderful of Indian tales; now we hear the gentle, grave, and infinitely human words of a wise man very near to ourselves.[1]

According to this creed, Buddhas are men of more than human sanctity, who, by myriad acts of devotion performed during thousands of successive existences, have at last acquired merit to attain to the highest knowledge, as earnest of their definitive deliverance or *nirvāṇa.* Pending this time, they are *bodhisattvas,* or "beings of wisdom," candidates for Buddhaship, preparing in paradises of

---

Arts, Boston, Vol. IV, *Jaina Paintings and MSS.* (Boston, 1924), pp. 5–17, Life of Mahāvīra and other Jinas.

[1] For the iconography of the life of the Buddha, see: Foucher: *L'Art gréco-bouddhique du Gandhāra,* Vol. I, pp. 290–599; N. J. Krom: *The Life of Buddha on the Stūpa of Barabudur, according to the text of the Lalitavistara* (The Hague, 1926; with 120 reproductions).

FIGURE 16

Sāñchī, east gate, detail.
— *Archives of the Musée Guimet*

beatitude for their last incarnation. Thus the future Buddha Śākyamuni, while spending his transitory penultimate existence, "adored by those who are adored," in the heaven of the Tushitas, or blessed gods, one day became aware that the hour of his last transmigration had arrived. Before leaving heaven he summoned the assembly of gods and genii to instruct them in the Buddhist Law and present to them his successor among them, Maitrēya, the Buddha of the ages to come. As a result of the inquiries made by the gods with a view to a country and family for the Buddha's incarnation, their choice fell upon the family of King Śuddhodana, of the house of the Śākya, which reigned at Kapilavastu, on the borders of Oudh and Nepal. In all India there was no more valiant or wiser rajah than Śuddhodana. As for his wife, Queen Māyā, she was the incarnation of all the Indian canons of beauty (cf. Fig. 13, 33, 51, 54, 55, 70, 71, 78, 79, 85, 88, 89, 101): "Young and in the flower of her years," says the *Lalitavistara,* "her beauty was consummate. Her hair was of the lovely hue of the black bee, her feet and hands were delicate, she was soft to the

FIGURE 17
Buddha: schist relief from Gandhāra.
— *Louvre (Fonds Foucher). Archives of the Musée Guimet*

touch as a garment from Kāśilindi. Her eye was as limpid as the young leaf of the blue lotus. Her firm arms were arched like the rainbow. Her lips were red as the fruit of the *bimba*. Her teeth were white as the flower of the *sumanā* (jasmine). Her belly was curved like a bow, she had a deep navel, and her hips were softly spreading, firm, and rounded. Her thighs, smooth and well formed, were like the trunk of the elephant, her legs like those of the antelope. The palm of her hands and the sole of her feet were like the juice of the rosy lac. She was the pearl among women, singled out by her superior beauty."

FIGURE 18
Head of Buddha, *c.* first century A.D.
— *Musée Guimet, Clemenceau donation. Photo, Gauthier*

The moment the bodhisattva chose the house of King Śuddhodana and Queen Māyā for his reincarnation, the whole of nature made demonstrations of joy. Hundreds of birds settled upon the roofs and terraces of the palace, from which their song could be heard. The trees burst into bloom and the water-pools were covered with wondrous lotus-flowers. Queen Māyā, warned by a grave presentiment, retired to the women's quarters and abandoned herself to meditation. It was now that the bodhisattva

FIGURE 19

Bodhisattva of Shāhbāz-garhi.

— *Louvre, Fonds Foucher. Photo, Giraudon*

descended into her womb (Fig. 107), coming down in the form of a baby elephant (the baby elephant has the same position in Indian iconography as our *amoretti* and cherubs have in classical art) — a little elephant " as white as snow and as silver, having six tusks, a head the colour of cochineal, beautiful feet, a splendid trunk, and teeth like a line of gold, the most beautiful of all elephants, with a graceful gait and joints as firm as adamant." Sculpture was to popularize the scene of the descent of the elephant bodhisattva, borne in a palankeen by a throng of deities (Fig. 39), and the scene of the incarnation, with Queen Māyā stretched on her couch, surrounded by the four guardians of the heavens — the four Lokapālas (Fig. 37).

When the time for the birth of the bodhisattva arrived, his mother betook herself to the park of Lumbinī, at the gates of the city of Kapilavastu. And there, in the attitude popularized by sculpture, standing erect, and holding in her right hand the branch of an aśoka-tree, she gave birth to the bodhisattva, who issued forth from her right side and was received in the arms of the gods Indra and Brahmā, the supreme gods of the Vedic religion and of Brahmanism respectively, who had hastened to the spot to greet the infant.[1] Two *nāga* kings, Nanda and Upananda, showed the upper part of their bodies in the heavens and caused two streams of water to appear, one cold and the other hot, to enable Indra and Brahmā to give the new-born infant its ritual bath. The child took possession of the world by advancing seven steps towards each of the four cardinal points.[2] " At that moment all beings felt the pores of their skin thrill with pleasure. The musical instruments of both gods and men sounded without being touched, and trees of all seasons were covered with flowers. Gently caressing breezes began to blow, bearing perfumes of every kind from the country of the gods."

The young prince received the name of Siddhārtha. The chariot

[1] Cf. Vol. IV, Fig. 176. [2] Cf. Vol. IV, Fig. 177.

bearing him returned to Kapilavastu, drawn by a train of *apsaras*, but seven days after his birth his mother, Queen Māyā, died of happiness and departed to be reborn among the gods. Her place was taken by her sister Mahāprajāpatī, one of the most noble figures in Buddhist legend. A little while later the greatness of the new-born child was prophesied by the Buddhist Simeon — in this instance a Himalayan ascetic, the holy old man Asita, who prophesied for him the glory of a world-ruler (*chakravartin*), or, if he preferred the way of renunciation, the career of a Buddha. He pointed out to those present the physical signs by which a Buddha is known, which were already visible on the infant's body — the only ones that we need remember, on account of their iconographical importance, being the *ushṇīsha*, a protuberance of the skull (or, rather, a topknot of hair arranged for the convenience of wearing the royal turban), the *ūrṇā*, or tuft between the eyes of wool as white as snow, and the mark of the Wheel of the Law (*chakra*) on the soles of the feet (cf. Fig. 104). Indeed, when, in accordance with the customary

FIGURE 20
Head of a bodhisattva.
— *Louvre, Fonds Foucher. Photo, Giraudon*

usage, the bodhisattva was led to the temple by his parents, the statues of the Vedic and Brahmanical gods prostrated themselves before him, chanting the following verses: " It is not for the Mēru, the king of the mountains, to bow before the grain of mustard seed, it is not for the Ocean to bow before the water held in the hoof-mark of a cow, it is not for the moon or the sun to bow before the fire-fly: and how should he that possesses wisdom bow before the divinities? " Let us remember this last trait: though the Buddha is no god, though he is but a hero beyond compare, a " lion among men," the gods themselves are his inferiors and definitely subordinate to him.

FIGURE 21
The Buddha of the Great Miracle.
— *Musée Guimet; Hackin archæological mission to Pātāvā, 1924. Photo, Gauthier*

After the cycle of legends connected with his childhood come those relating to his youth. When Siddhārtha was taken to school, he astonished his master by his inborn knowledge. It seems, moreover, that, even as early as this, the bodhisattva had, as it were, a presentiment of the Illumination. One day, relates the poet of the *Buddhacharita*, while he was watching the husbandmen working in the fields, " as he saw the young grass torn up and scattered by the plough, covered with the eggs and young ones of the insects that had been killed, he was overcome by a deep sorrow, as though he had witnessed a massacre of his own people. And, seeing the husbandmen with their faces marred by the dust, the wind, and the scorching sun, this noblest among men was filled with the most profound compassion." He seated himself in the shade of a jambu-tree (rose-apple tree) and for the first time meditated upon the universal suffering. His father, however, sent to seek him, and at last he was found: the sun was now sinking towards the horizon, but the shadow of the rose-apple tree had not moved, and continued to protect the divine youth.

The time now arrived when a wife had to be found for Siddhārtha. They wanted one who should be perfect, "neither frivolous nor rash, clothed in the garment of modesty, doing good deeds, as kind to her slaves as to herself, knowing the sacred books as a courtesan does, the last to go to rest and the first to arise." All the young girls in the country were passed in review before the prince, but only one answered to the description quoted above: the beautiful Gopā. Gopā's father, doubting whether Siddhārtha, who had been softly bred in the life of the palace, possessed the virile qualities of a true *kshatriya,* insisted that he should be subjected to various tests of swordsmanship, boxing, archery, etc. From this contest Siddhārtha emerged victorious, having distinguished himself as being the only one capable of drawing the giant bow of his heroic ancestor (Fig. 108). The princess Gopā was therefore given to him in marriage, accompanied, according to the royal custom, by a numerous suite of secondary wives.

The life of the bodhisattva among the delights of the women's quarters is delineated for us with equal complaisance by the pious historians of the *Lalitavistara* and by the sculptors of Amarāvatī and Bōrōbudur (Fig. 29 and 109). "The young prince reposed upon his bed, while lovely women delighted him with strains of softest

Figure 22

Statuette from Haḍḍa.

— *Musée Guimet. Godard Mission. Photo, Pivot*

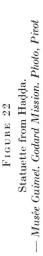

Figure 23

Statuette from Haḍḍa.

— *Musée Guimet. Godard mission. Photo, Pivot*

music played by instruments of every kind." But in the midst of this band of women the lion among men was pensive. The voice of the flutes and the lutes already said to him that " the union of the three worlds is an unstable one — unstable as the clouds of autumn; the birth and the death of living creatures are like scenes in a play. The life of a living being passes by like a mountain torrent, or like a flash of lightning across the sky." Warned of these thoughts, his father, King Śuddhodana, was careful that no spectacle of human sorrow should meet his eyes; and so, when one day Siddhārtha had to go to the royal park, the sick and the infirm were removed from his path. But such was the will of the gods that, lo, in despite of the royal command, the young man came upon a decrepit old man, a sick man, and a corpse, one after the other — all symbolical encounters which were a brutal reminder to him of the vanity of pleasures and the falseness of a princely life. The bodhisattva then went and besought his father to let him embrace the monastic life (Fig. 110). The monarch, who had based the hopes of his race upon Siddhārtha, had recourse to every means that might change the course of his thoughts.

FIGURE 24
Statuette from Haḍḍa.
—Musée Guimet. Godard mission. Photo, Pivot

"His orders to the women's apartments were as follows: never for an instant to cease the music and singing; all pleasures and sports were to be continued without a pause; the women must exert all their feminine seductions and enchain the young prince so that a spell

FIGURE 25
Greco-Buddhist plaster head from Haḍḍa.
— *Musée Guimet; Barthoux mission, 1924. Photo, Gauthier*

might be thrown over his mind and he should not depart as a wandering monk" (cf. Fig. 29). Thus speaks one of our sources, the *Lalitavistara*. But the poem of the *Buddhacharita* is better informed and tells us how Śuddhodana once again sent his son into the park, filled with dancing-girls: "Behold the god of love, behold Kāma in person," they murmured on seeing his arrival. Curious and with wide-eyed admiration they gathered round him, and saluted him with their smooth hands, like the cups of the lotus-flower. By the King's instructions, Udāyin, a friend of his childhood, encouraged them to exert all their fascinations. Some, wreathing their arms round Siddhārtha like twining plants, sought to hold him by force; others, whether carelessly or feigning to be almost carried away by their transports, allowed the gauzy draperies which veiled their youthful forms to slip aside; others swung their tempting forms on the branches of the mango-trees; and, lastly, yet another sang in the prince's ear the song of the forest, full of furtive desires and of the emanations of the spring. But his consciousness of the vanity of all things now rendered him insensible to these blandishments, and he returned to the palace, resolved to abandon the world.

FIGURE 26
Plaster head from Haḍḍa.
— *Musée Guimet; Barthoux mission. Photo, Gauthier*

One night, while the harem slept, Siddhārtha sat up on his bed and beheld all these women in the abandonment of sleep. Their limp bodies had lost their accustomed grace. "The sight of them lying strewn here and there, thus transformed, suggested to his mind the idea of a cemetery" (Fig. 30). He crept away stealthily, summoned his groom, Chandaka, and sent for his horse, Kaṇṭhaka, the finest charger in the royal stables. At this point the *Buddhacharita* places in the mouth of the bodhisattva the most touching address to his faithful steed; for a long time he stroked the noble beast, explaining to him what he expected of him, and the importance of the part that he called upon him to play in the salvation of the world. In vain did the groom, Chandaka, attempt to dissuade his master: "Whither goest thou, O lion among men, with the long lashes and eyes as lovely as the petals of the lotus — thou who art like unto the full moon in autumn, white lotus that delighteth in the moon's rays, with thy countenance as full of grace as the newly-opened flowers, thou who hast the brilliance of pure gold and of the luminary of night, of the diamond and of the lightning, thou who hast the gait of an elephant at play, thou who hast the bearing, the splendid bearing of the bull, and of the king of beasts and of the swan, — whither goest thou?" But the bodhisattva pointed out to him the necessity of his mission; and the gods, who abetted his designs, took care to put to sleep the guards who watched at the gates of Kapilavastu. These gates

FIGURE 27

Woman carrying a *chauri* (fly-fan). School of Amarāvatī, second century.
— *Musée Guimet. Archives of the Musée Guimet*

opened of their own accord before the divine company, while the four Lokapālas, or kings of the four regions of the heavens, laid their hands beneath the hoofs of the horses to deaden all sound.

Once outside the city, the good horse Kaṇṭhaka devoured the miles. Once they had passed the frontiers of the kingdom, the bodhisattva dismounted at the edge of a forest. He handed over to Chandaka his gold necklaces and ornaments; then he bade farewell to the weeping groom and also to the horse, which licked his feet, overcome with the same emotion. Taking a sword, he cut off his hair and threw it up into the air, where it was gathered up by the gods (Fig. 111).[1] All that the bodhisattva now lacked was the garment of a hermit: so a god appeared, disguised as a wild huntsman, and exchanged his poor rags for the fabrics of Benares worn by the fugitive. The prince Siddhārtha had disappeared, and all that remained was one anchorite among the many anchorites of the forest — the monk Gautama, as he was henceforth to be called, or Śākyamuni, " the ascetic of the tribe of Śākyas."

The bodhisattva lived in several hermitages, one after the other, and especially in one near the town of Vaiśālī, with the anchorite Arāta, whose disciple he became. But the teaching of this master did not satisfy him, so he once more started out on the eastward road, and arrived at the land of Magadha (southern Behar). He visited the capital of the country, Rājagṛiha, where he begged alms like the mendicant monks, and where the king, Bimbisāra, did homage to him and assured him of his protection. He next arrived at the village of Uruvilvā, and beheld the river Nairañjanā, " with its pure waters and fine flights of steps, adorned with trees and groves and surrounded on all sides by pastures and villages." The bodhisattva was pleased with this landscape with its absence of extremes. " In truth," the texts represent him as saying, " this spot upon earth is level and pleasing and tempts one to linger; it is well suited to a king's son desirous of

[1] See also Vol. IV, Fig. 178.

FIGURE 28
The assault of Mārā. School of Amarāvatī, second century.
— *Musée Guimet. Photo, Gauthier*

renunciation" — remarkable words which seem to reveal a sense of moderation in the historical Buddha and a subtle communion with the beauty of things which is more akin to the mentality of a Socrates or a Plato than to certain excessive conceptions of the Hindu mind. . . .

Yet it was here that the bodhisattva, surrounded by five disciples, set to work to practise terrible austerities for six years. Seated motionless with crossed legs, and having reached the last degrees of exhaustion, he was like a skeleton. The gods themselves feared for his life, and his mother, Māyā, hastened down, weeping, from heaven. But the bodhisattva set her mind at rest, for he had now realized the fruitlessness of these austerities and knew that the way of salvation was not to be found in them. Renouncing asceticism and the mechanical practices of yogism, he resolved to pursue truth by means of the intellect, by restoring to his mind the physical support which was indispensable to it. He therefore took the milk and rice prepared for him by a pious young girl named Sujātā in the neighbouring village (Fig. 114), and refreshed his weary limbs in the Nairañjanā (Fig. 115); upon which his five disciples were scandalized and left him. For his part, he wended his way towards Bodh-Gayā, where grew the Tree of Wisdom (*bodhidruma*), the sacred fig-tree beneath whose shade was to be enacted the vital scene of the Buddhist gospels.

The bodhisattva — and with regard to the following events the documents are particularly precise — seated himself at the foot of the tree on a handful of freshly mown herbs (Fig. 116) strewn upon a seat which had miraculously risen from the ground in this spot. And now began the sublime meditation, the issue of which was to be the salvation of the world. The Buddhist devil Mārā (a form of Kāma, the god of love and of death) tried to prevent the happening of that which was to bring about the ruin of his own power (Fig. 28 and 117–118). Accompanied by all his hosts, he attacked the bodhisattva as he sat meditating beneath the Tree of Wisdom. The *Lalitavistara*

FIGURE 29

Scene in the women's quarters. Marble relief of the school of Amarāvatī, fourth century.
— *Musée Guimet. Photo, Gauthier*

lingers lovingly over the description of these hideous monsters, which the Buddhist monuments of India and Turkestan were to reproduce faithfully in accordance with its accounts.[1] Gathered in a howling rout round the Blessed One, they hurled at him a cloud of missiles, including even whole mountains, but as these approached him, they were transformed into celestial canopies and garlands of flowers. The demons also darted forth jets of poison and flame from their eyes and mouths, but this ring of fire was checked in its course and hovered like a crown of light round the bodhisattva, who now called heaven and earth to witness the excellence of his effort by the act known as the *bhūmisparśa,* or touching of the earth: immediately the ground opened and the Earth appeared down to his middle and did solemn homage to him.

Terror having proved fruitless, Mārā had recourse to other weapons. He sent his daughters, who tried all their seductive wiles upon the bodhisattva, singing to him as follows: " Friend, let us rejoice. Lo, the time has come of the most lovely, the most charming of seasons, the season of spring, the joy of both women and men, when the trees are in bloom, and everything is filled with flocks of birds. Behold these flowering trees with their young branches, upon which the kokil-birds sing and the bees hum. Come, abandon thyself to pleasure upon the earth, where grows the greensward, soft, rich, and thick, in the woods haunted by a host of fairies. . . . Thy body is fair and graceful, and we were created to give pleasure to gods and men: to this end do we exist. Arise now swiftly and enjoy thy fair youth." Their silky hair, the *Lalitavistara* goes on to say, was drenched with heavy perfumes, their faces were artfully painted, their eyes were lovely and as large as the petals of a full-blown lotus. And the tempting voice went on: " Behold them, lord, they are lovely and have no thought save of love. Behold, O lord, their firm breasts, high-placed and rounded, the three captivating creases at their waist, and their

[1] Cf. Vol. III, Fig. 220; Vol. IV, Fig. 27.

FIGURE 30

The sleep of the women. School of Amarāvatī, fourth century.
— *Musée Guimet. Photo, Gauthier*

broad hips with the graceful contours. Their thighs are like the trunk of the elephant, their arms cannot be seen for their bracelets, their waist is adorned with a glittering girdle. Look upon them, O lord, they have the grace of the swan and sweetly speak the language of love which goes to the heart, and, more than all this, they are most expert in divinely voluptuous pleasures. Look upon them, O lord, they are thy slaves. . . ." The bodhisattva triumphed over this attack, as over the rest, and a little while afterwards, when the three daughters of Mārā made a last effort to seduce him, he turned them into three decrepit old women.

Having triumphed over temptation, the motionless bodhisattva, still seated at the foot of the tree, concentrated his thoughts upon universal suffering and the means of abolishing it. His glance embraced the whole universe. He beheld the endless cycle of rebirths, prolonged to infinity, from the infernal regions and the world of animals up to the gods themselves, throughout all eternity. And all birth, all life, all death was pain. " Then, while his thought was thus concentrated, in utter purity, in the last watch of the night, when the dawn appears, at the moment of the beating of the drum," the bodhisattva attained to the possession of wisdom. Going back over the chain of causes, he discovered that the cause of all suffering is the longing for existence, which is based upon our false conceptions of thought, the ego, and the material world. Hence, to do away with the longing for existence, by abolishing its intellectual causes, would mean the abolition of suffering. . . . Such was the inward Illumination, the revelation of perfect wisdom (*bodhi*), by which the bodhisattva at last became a supreme Buddha.

After the Illumination the Buddha remained by the tree for yet another four weeks. During the fifth week a terrible storm devastated the country. But a king of the Nāgas, Muchilinda, appeared in the form of a giant serpent and coiled his body beneath that of the Buddha, thus raising him above the flood, while with his hood, formed

FIGURE 31

Marble relief of the school of Amarāvatī, fourth–fifth centuries.

— *Musée Guimet. Archives of the Musée Guimet*

of seven heads, he sheltered the head of the Blessed One against the hurricane — a scene which we shall often find reproduced on Buddhist monuments, especially in the Khmer art of Farther India (Fig. 152 and 153).

The Buddha was now in possession of the treasury of truth; but his consent was necessary that it might be poured out upon the world. The gods Brahmā and Indra came and begged for it in the name of all creatures. He therefore started upon his preaching, or, to use the words of the records, "he set in motion the Wheel of the Law (*dharmachakra*)." He first betook himself to Benares, where, in the Deer-park (*Mṛigadāva*), he found the five disciples who had once abandoned him, and converted them (Fig. 11). It was before them that he delivered the "Sermon of Benares," which has been called the Buddhist Sermon on the Mount. The Master's words were as follows: "There are two extremes, O monks, which should be avoided: there is the life of pleasure, which is base, ignoble, opposed to the intelligence, unworthy, and vain. And there is the life of austerities, which is miserable, unworthy, and vain. The Perfect One, O monks, has remained far from these two extremes and has discovered the way which passes in the midst, which leads to rest, to knowledge, illumination, and *nirvāṇa*. . . . Behold, O monks, the holy truth about pain: birth, old age, sickness, death, and separation from that which one loves — these are pain. And behold the origin of pain: it is the thirst for pleasure, the thirst for existence, the thirst for that which is evanescent. And behold the truth about the abolition of pain: it is the extinction of this craving by the annihilation of desire."

Here we undoubtedly have one of the discourses which can be attributed to the Blessed One with the greatest probability. In other *sūtras* of the same order the Buddha further said: "I have come to satisfy the ignorant with wisdom. Alms, knowledge, and virtue — behold the possessions which do not fade away. To do a little good is of more worth than to accomplish difficult works. If one desired to

FIGURE 32

Miracle of the infuriated elephant. Amarāvatī, *c.* third century.
— *Madras Museum. Photo, Goloubew*

understand how great is the fruit of alms-giving, one would not eat one's last mouthful of food without having given of it to others. The perfect man is nothing unless he spends himself in benefits to living beings, unless he consoles those who are abandoned. . . . My doctrine is a doctrine of pity; that is why the happy ones of the world find it hard. . . . The way of salvation is open to all. The Brahman came forth

FIGURE 33
Scene of adoration. Amarāvatī, *c.* third century.
— *Madras Museum. Photo, Goloubew*

from the womb of a woman even as the *chaṇḍāla* (outcast) to whom he closes the way of salvation. . . . Annihilate your passions as the elephant overturns a hut made of reeds; but know that he who believes that he can flee from his passions by establishing himself in the shelter of a hermitage is deceiving himself. The only remedy against evil is sane reality."

This doctrine was really that of universal charity. In it charity

FIGURE 34

Relief from Amarāvatī.

— *Madras Museum. Photo, Goloubew*

took the place of the complicated practices of Brahmanical ritualism. It took the place of everything and was everything: " There is a sacrifice," said the Master, " that is easier than milk, than oil, and than honey: it is alms-giving. Instead of slaughtering animals, let them go free. May they find grass, water, and cool breezes! " For Buddhist pity embraced the universe. It brooded over all suffering: " More tears have been shed than the waters that are in the great ocean." And later: " Just as the great sea, O disciples, is filled with one savour alone, that of salt, so this doctrine is filled with but one savour, that of deliverance." There is a charming parable attributed to the Buddha which is symbolical of this " *misereor super turbas* (My heart is filled with pity for the multitudes) ": " Imagine, O disciples, in the forest, on the flank of a mountain, a great hollow and a pool near which live a great herd of wild beasts. And, lo, a man comes seeking to harm these beasts. He closes up the way by which there is a good, safe passage and in its stead opens up a marshy path. And thus, O disciples, the troop will perish. But, O disciples, a man is coming who seeks the good of the herd. And he is opening up the way of safety." This man was none other than the Buddha himself.

The first five disciples of the Deer-park did not long remain the only ones. They were soon joined by sixty monks, and thus the Buddhist Order was founded. The monks wore the yellow robe and the tonsure. They observed the vows of obedience, poverty, and chastity. Distinctions of caste were abolished among them: " Just as the rivers, O disciples, on reaching the ocean, lose their former names and now bear but one name, that of the ocean; even so, O disciples, the four castes now bear but a single name within the Community." They had to practise patience and preserve their cheerfulness under the worst insults. If evil persons insulted a monk, he was to say: " They are good, they are very good, for they do not strike me." If they struck him, he was to say: " They are good, they are very good, for they do not kill me." And if they killed him, he was to say: " They

FIGURE 35
Viśvantara *jātaka* (?). School of Amarāvatī.
— *Madras Museum. Photo, Goloubew*

are good, they are very good, for they are only delivering me from this painful life, without harming my salvation."

Soon came the dispersion of the brothers: "Start out upon your way, O disciples," said the Buddha, "for the salvation of many, for the happiness of many, for pity of the world, for the good of both gods and men." As for the Blessed One, having thus set on foot the evangelization of India, he returned to Uruvilvā. There he met three Brahman anchorites, the brothers Kāśyapa, whose sacrifices were being disturbed by a demon in the form of a serpent. The Buddha exorcized the serpent, and the three Brahmans were converted. The eldest, Mahā Kāśyapa, was to become one of the leaders of the Community. The Buddha and his new converts next betook themselves to the capital of the Magadha, Rājagṛiha, where King Bimbisāra became a lay member of the Community and presented the Blessed One with the site of the first Buddhist monastery, the Park of Bamboos (*vēṇuvana*), at the gates of his city. This was the prototype of the monasteries described in the Buddhist Scriptures: "Not too far from the city and not too near to it, easily accessible, not too full of stir by day, silent at night, far from the tumult and press of men, places of retreat and resorts propitious to solitary meditation." Here the Blessed One was joined by two new and famous disciples, Śāriputra and Maudgalyāyana.

Their pure hearts were filled with a tranquil kindliness and a childlike joy: "We live in perfect joy, without enemies in a hostile world. In perfect joy do we live who own no property. Gaiety is our food, as it is that of the radiant gods." This state of mind was accompanied by a deep feeling for nature: "Sure of my goal, without haste, I mean to enter into the charming forest, the haunt of fiery elephants. In the blossoming forest, in a cool mountain grot, I mean to bathe my body and to walk alone, with no companion, in the vast and charming forest. . . . When the storm clouds beat their drum in the heavens, when torrents of rain fill the ways of the air, and the monk

FIGURE 36
"The young rajah." School of Amarāvatī.
— *Madras Museum. Photo, Goloubew*

in a hollow of the mountain abandons himself to meditation, there can be no higher joy. On the banks of the rivers decked with flowers and crowned by the variegated garland of the forests, he sits in joyous meditation. There can be no higher joy." And later on, apropos of the same theme, comes the following call to solitude: "When, ah,

FIGURE 37
Conception of the Buddha. School of Amarāvatī.
— *Madras Museum. Photo, Goloubew*

when shall I live in a cave and be filled with the intuition of the instability of all existence? When shall I live in joy among the mountains, a sage in my garment of rags, in my yellow robe, calling nothing my own, devoid of desires, annihilating both love and hate? The places that are crowned with the thorn-bush of the *karēris* and filled with the pattering of the rain, where the elephants lift up their voice, the peacock's cry resounds, and the wise men wander, these charming spots fill me with contentment. . . ."

FIGURE 38

Relief representing a *stūpa*. School of Amarāvatī.
— *Madras Museum. Photo, Goloubew*

While the Buddha was going from town to town and from monastery to monastery organizing his Community on the banks of the Lower Ganges, far away in his native city, near the *terai* of Nepal, his father, old King Śuddhodana, sent him message upon message asking to see him once more before he died. Now that his work was secure, the Buddha acceded to this request. He went to Kapilavastu and saw his family again. At Kapilavastu, indeed, as everywhere else, he insisted upon begging his food. He treated his father with infinite gentleness, and his own wife Gopā too, whose praiseworthy behaviour since their separation was thus rewarded.[1] He made the acquaintance of his son Rāhula, who had grown up in his absence and was now admitted into the Community. Nanda, the brother of the Buddha, also became a monk, though a little against his own inclination. The Buddha lured him to his abode by a pious stratagem, kept him there, and gave him the tonsure, in spite of his memories of his charming wife. Nanda's regrets and the consolation, both affectionate and ironical, which were lavished upon him by the Buddha form one of the most lively displays of wit in the Scriptures. The Buddha was afterwards to return once more to Kapilavastu, this time through the air, to be with his father when he breathed his last. Nor did he forget the mother who had died in giving him birth, but transported himself to the heaven of the thirty-three gods in order to teach her the Law. On this occasion he remained for three months in heaven. His return to earth down a staircase of precious stones has frequently been represented on Buddhist monuments, and notably in the paintings of Tibet.[2]

After his journey to his native city the Buddha had returned and taken up his residence in Magadha, where he received a visit from a celebrated figure in the Scriptures, the rich merchant Anāthapiṇḍika, a native of Śrāvastī in the kingdom of Kosala (Oudh).

[1] See the delightful fresco of the Buddha's return to his home, from the antechamber to Cave XVII at Ajaṇṭā, in Havell: *Indian Sculpture and Painting*, Pl. XLVI–XLVIII.
[2] Vol. IV, Fig. 182.

FIGURE 39

Descent of the bodhisattva from heaven. School of Amarāvatī.
— *Madras Museum. Photo, Goloubew*

Anāthapiṇḍika offered the Community the Park of Jētavana in this city, whose limpid pools, luxuriant verdure, and countless flowers Chinese pilgrims were still to admire many centuries later. It was at Śrāvastī that the Buddha worked what is known as the " Great Miracle ": Prasēnajit, king of Kosala, had organized a contest of miracles between him and three hostile ascetics, a scene which ended in the apotheosis of the Blessed One. He rose up into the air, " attained the

FIGURE 40
Aihoḷe. Vishṇu-Nārāyaṇa (who moves on the waters).
— *Photo, Archæological Survey of India*

region of light, and had no sooner reached it than lights of many colours issued from his body; flames leapt forth from the upper part of his body, and a shower of cold water rained down from the lower part of it" (*Divyāvadāna*). Shortly afterwards he was seen seated upon a lotus created by the *nāga* kings, with Brahmā on his right hand, and Indra on his left; next, by the magic of his omnipotence, he caused more lotuses to appear in incalculable numbers, which filled the heavens, each of them bearing within it a magic Buddha like unto himself. . . . This too is a scene which frequently occurs, from the sculptures of Gandhāra (Fig. 21) down to the paintings of Tibet.[1]

Among the disciples who devoted themselves to the Buddha about this time should be mentioned three of his fellow-countrymen, three young Śākya noblemen who left Kapilavastu and joined him at Magadha: Ānanda, Anuruddha and Dēvadatta. Ānanda, who was his cousin, became his most intimate companion — the "Beloved Disciple" of Buddhism. On the other hand, the envious and perfidious Dēvadatta was to become its Judas Iscariot. With these young nobles there arrived a simple barber, Upāli, who afterwards showed himself one of the lights of the Church. At the instance of Ānanda, and in spite of his own repugnance, the Buddha ended by admitting nuns into the Community. The first of these was his aunt and mother by adoption, Mahāprajāpatī. We may also mention another

FIGURE 41
Buddha of Sārnāth, fifth century.
— *Photo, Archæological Survey of India*

[1] See Foucher: "The Great Miracle of Śrāvastī," in *Beginnings of Buddhist Art* (London, 1917), pp. 184–204; J. Hackin: *Sculptures gréco-bouddhiques du Kapiśa* (Paris, Monuments Piot, XXVIII, 1926).

holy woman, Prakṛiti the Mātaṅgī, whose story begins like that of the Woman of Samaria. She was the daughter of a pariah and was at a fountain when Ānanda, the Beloved Disciple, asked her to give him some water to drink. She rightly objected, saying that she was an untouchable: "I am the daughter of a pariah, reverend Ānanda!" "I do not ask thee what is thy family or birth, my sister; but if thou hast water remaining, give me some that I may drink." The story, it is true, turned out otherwise than in the Gospel, for the Mātaṅgī fell in love with Ānanda. She sought to draw him to her by spells, till one day the Buddha intervened and diverted the passion of the young girl towards spiritual ends, so that she became a nun. For the rest, though the Buddha preached chastity, we can find no trace of bigotry in him in this respect. Thus he accepted in a kindly spirit the offering of Āmrapālī, the Hindu Magdalen, a pious courtesan who presented the Community with the Park of Āmravana in her city of Vaiśālī.

Thus the Buddha travelled through Oudh, Behar, and Bengal, preaching his doctrines and converting the masses. Genii and animals were as subject to him as men, and before the might of his benignity the malice even of the most evil creatures gave way. The *nāga* (or dragon-king) Apalāla was causing cruel floods in a valley of Gandhāra, so the Buddha betook himself to that region, forced the dragon to come out of the lake where he concealed himself, and converted him. There was an even more cruel *yaksha* which was tormenting the city of Āṭavī, levying upon it a yearly tribute of human beings, which it devoured. The Buddha transported himself to Āṭavī through the air and reduced the monster to a gentler frame of mind (cf. Fig. 147); the monuments of the school of Gandhāra delight in showing the children who have been miraculously delivered from the power of the *yaksha* and are thanking their saviour. In the same way the Buddha converted the *yakshiṇī*, or female monster, Hāritī, which devoured little children, by hiding one of the ogress's offspring in his alms-bowl, so that she at last understood the sufferings of a

FIGURE 42

Gupta Buddha from Mathurā, *c.* fifth century.
— *Mathurā Museum. Photo, Archæological Survey of India*

mother, renounced her taste for human flesh, and became a sort of Madonna and protectress of childhood (cf. Fig. 84).[1]

Dēvadatta, the Buddha's cousin, became jealous of his fame and plotted against his life in concert with Prince Ajātaśatru, the unworthy son of the pious king Bimbisāra of Magadha: at the moment when the Buddha was passing by with his disciples, an elephant, infuriated with alcohol, was let loose upon them, but the raging beast was cowed by the gentleness of the Blessed One, stopped before him, and worshipped him (Fig. 32). The same thing happened to an infuriated buffalo in similar circumstances.

FIGURE 43
Buddha from Dong-du'o'ng.
— *Photo, Goloubew*

On another occasion a monkey appeared one day and offered a bowl of honey to the Buddha. In his joy at seeing his offering accepted, the animal cut such a caper that it killed itself and was immediately reborn in the body of a saint. Another time a child, who had nothing else to offer the Blessed One, innocently presented him with a handful of dust, a touching gesture which brought him such merit that in later days he was reborn in the body of the great Indian emperor Aśoka.

[1] See Foucher: "The Buddhist Madonna," in *Beginnings of Buddhist Art*, pp. 272–92.

The King of Magadha, Ajātaśatru, who, by the advice of Dēvadatta, had for a time adopted a hostile attitude towards the Blessed One, was also touched by grace in the end. One October night, at the time of the full moon, in the season when the lotus is in flower, the monarch was in a reverie on the terrace of his palace: "Of a truth," he thought, "this moonlight night is beautiful, of a truth this moonlight night is delicious. What *śramaṇa* (Buddhist monk) or what Brahman ought I to listen to, that my soul may be rejoiced?" He ordered the elephants to be got ready for himself and his queens, and paid a torchlight visit to the mango grove of Jīvaka, where he listened to the Blessed One and was converted.

FIGURE 44
Buddha from Dong-du'o'ng.
— *Photo, École française d'Extrême Orient*

By this time, however, the Buddha had reached the age of eighty and had been preaching his doctrines for forty years. Feeling his end approaching, he wished to see once more the monasteries that he had founded. He left Rājagṛiha and travelled northwards, followed by Ānanda alone: "I am old, Ānanda," he said, "an old man who has reached the end of his path. Do you be a torch and a refuge unto yourselves. Let truth be your only guide." He passed through Vaiśālī, where he begged alms in his accustomed fashion. In a solemn and noble discourse he announced to his disciples his approaching end: "My existence is almost at an end, the close of my life is at hand. I am going hence, but you will be left behind. Watch without ceasing and live always in holiness." Sick and weary, he at last reached the region of Kuśinagara, in the land of the Malla, where he had resolved to enter into *nirvāṇa.*

This sage, who desired the strings of the lute to be neither too slack nor too tightly drawn, expired gently. On the banks of the river Hiraṇyavatī, in a grove of sāl-trees, he caused a bed to be made ready between two twin trees, which immediately became covered with flowers. Ānanda was in despair. With infinite tenderness the Buddha consoled him: "Do not complain, do not despair. From all that man loves a parting is necessary. How could it be, Ānanda, that what is born and is subject to change should not pass away? But thou, Ānanda, hast for long honoured the Absolute by thy tenderness and kindliness, joyfully and without feigning, without reserve, in thought, word, and deed. Thou hast done what is good, O Ānanda!" Before taking leave of the world he once more addressed Ānanda, saying: "It might be that thou shouldst think in this wise: 'We have now no longer a master.' This must not be, O Ānanda. The doctrine that I have preached — behold your master when I shall have disappeared." And he repeated: "Of a truth, O disciples, all that is created shall perish. Strive without ceasing." These were his last words. "His spirit," says a Buddhist catechism, "plunged into the depths of mystical absorption, and when he had reached the point at which all thought, all ideas, die away and the consciousness of individuality ceases, he entered into the supreme *nirvāṇa.* Before the gate of Kuśinagara which opens towards the east, the nobles of the Malla burnt the body of the Buddha with royal honours."

Figure 45

Ajaṇṭā. Paintings from Cave XVII.
— Photo, Goloubew. By permission of Messrs. Van Oest

But the legend of the Buddha does not come to an end with his historic existence. Side by side with this, there is the whole cycle of his *jātakas* — that is, his "births" in the course of his previous exist-

FIGURE 46
Ajaṇṭā. Cave XVII.
— Photo, Goloubew. By permission of Messrs. Van Oest

ences.[1] The Buddhist Scriptures place the account of these *jātakas* in the mouth of the Blessed One himself, something in the fashion of the Christian parables. Certain of them should, moreover, be borne in mind, not only on account of their profoundly poetical character, but

[1] See Binaychandra Sen: "Studies in Jātakas," *Journal of the Department of Letters*, University of Calcutta, Vol. XX (1930).

also because a knowledge of them is necessary for the interpretation of Indian iconography.

One of the most famous is that of the elephant with the six tusks

FIGURE 46b
Ajaṇṭā. Cave XVII.
— *Photo, Goloubew. By permission of Messrs. Van Oest*

(*shaḍdanta jātaka*). In a previous existence the bodhisattva had been a king of the elephants, a white elephant with six wonderful tusks, " like unto the roots of a water-lily." One of his mates, being jealous of another female in the herd, longed for vengeance; she allowed herself to die of starvation and was born again in the body of a queen of Benares. This queen sent a hunter to slay the elephant, in order to gain possession of his tusks. The hunter, who had cunningly assumed the disguise of a harmless monk, discovered the divine elephant, " like a walking mountain," a little apart from the herd, near a pool covered with lotuses, and shot him with a poisoned arrow. The elephant's pain was so great that he was on the point of killing his enemy; but he restrained himself and even prevented his herd from trampling upon the hunter. On learning what mission had been entrusted to the latter, he tore out his own tusks with his bleeding trunk and, quivering with pain, offered them to his tormentor; at this moment he died, and was reborn in the body of the future Buddha (Fig. 7).[1]

The story of the king of the deer belongs to the same type. This animal lived on the slopes of the Himalayas and was the leader of a herd numbering five hundred. The King of Benares sent beaters to surround the whole herd. The king of the deer waited upon him and obtained the liberation of the captives, on condition that every day he should send one deer to the shambles at Benares. It so happened that a hind with young was chosen to go to the slaughter. Presenting herself before the king of the deer, she " prostrated herself before him, kneeling down upon her forelegs, and said: ' Only wait till I have fawned, and then I will give myself up without a regret.' " Touched with compassion, the king of the deer took her place and offered himself up to the King of Benares, who, touched at such magnanimity, renounced his cruel tribute. And the story, as related in the *Sūtrālaṃkāra,* ends with a few tender stanzas worthy of the legends of St. Francis: " All these forests and all these woods, all these springs and all these pools, I give them to the deer, and I forbid any man to do them harm."

[1] Cf. A. Foucher: "The Six-Tusked Elephant," in *Beginnings of Buddhist Art,* p. 185.

FIGURE 47

Ajaṇṭā. Cave I. Fresco of the "Beautiful Bodhisattva."
— *Photo, Goloubew. By permission of Messrs. Van Oest*

Further on we come to the story of the wise hare: "And in another life I was a hare and I lived in a forest on a mountain. I fed upon herbs and plants, upon leaves and fruits, and I did no harm to any creature. We lived together — a monkey, a jackal, a young otter,

FIGURE 48
Ajaṇṭā. Cave II.
— *Photo, Goloubew. By permission of Messrs. Van Oest*

and I. I instructed them in their duties and taught them what is good and what is evil." One day a Brahman, or, rather, Indra disguised as a Brahman, approached the hare and asked it to provide him with food. Upon which it replied: "'A noble gift, a gift such as has never been given before, see what I am prepared to give you today. Collect wood and light a fire! ' When the wood began to burn, I sprang into the air and cast myself into the midst of the flames. Just as cool water calms the torment of heat in him who plunges into it, so this flaming fire calmed all my torments. Skin and flesh, bones and heart, all my body with all my limbs, I gave it all to the Brahman." Another version presents this *jātaka* in rather a different form. The hare is the companion of an anchorite, when a year of drought comes. The springs are dried up, and, since the fruits which served as the anchorite's food fail, he is about to abandon his monkish garb and return to the world lest he die of starvation. In order to save his friend's body and soul at the same time, the hare then arrives at a heroic resolution. He salutes the anchorite and makes the following little speech to him: " We animals have neither sense nor judgment. Pardon me, great ascetic, if I have committed any offence against thee! " — after which he leaps into the fire. But in this version the anchorite lifts him out of the flames, and the gods are so touched that they send abundance of food to the two friends.

Or, again, we have the *jātaka* of the " great monkey " (*mahākapi jātaka*). In this the bodhisattva is a king of the monkeys. The neighbouring prince causes him and all his subjects to be cut off in a mango forest where they are disporting themselves. The beasts are soon driven back to the banks of the Ganges. In order to escape and enable his subjects to escape also, the monkey-bodhisattva crosses the river with a mighty bound, bearing a bamboo rope passed round his body. He is thus able to set up a hanging bridge by which all his subjects cross over, while he himself falls a victim to his own self-sacrifice, his back being broken by those whom he has saved.

The Śibi *jātaka* is equally touching. There was once a charitable king, the King of the Śibis. In order to test him Indra assumed the form of a falcon pursuing a pigeon, or, rather, pursuing another god disguised as a pigeon — " a pigeon with a body blue as the firmament, and eyes like ruddy pearls." Pursued by the falcon, the pigeon

FIGURE 49
Ajaṇṭā. Cave I.
— *Photo, Goloubew. By permission of Messrs. Van Oest*

took refuge in the bosom of the King of the Śibis. The falcon came and claimed his prey on the plea of his own right to live, or, failing his prey, he demanded an equal quantity of freshly slain flesh. The King, by a sublime act of sacrifice, himself cut off some flesh from one of his thighs. But, miraculous to relate, when the pigeon was placed in the balance, it always weighed heavier than the flesh in the other scale, so that the King was forced to put his whole body into the scale in order to save the animal. Then Indra revealed himself, and the King was afterwards reincarnated in the body of the Buddha Śākyamuni.

In the Viśvantara *jātaka* the spirit of self-sacrifice is again carried to the sublimest pitch. Viśvantara, or Vessantara, was a young prince in whom charity amounted to a passion. He possessed a white elephant endowed with the magic faculty of inducing rain. A neighbouring monarch, whose land was afflicted with drought, demanded the animal. Viśvantara gave it up, upon which his fellow-countrymen were enraged and demanded that he should be punished by his father, the King. The charitable prince was to be sent into exile with his wife Mādrī, who expressed a wish to follow him, and their two children (Fig. 6 and 35).[1] As they drove off on their way, two Brahmans demanded the horses which drew their chariot, and a third demanded the chariot itself; and he granted their request. By dint of endless trials the exiled family at last reached the foot of the Himalayas, where they lived in a hut, with the roots and fruit of wild plants for their food. Touched with compassion, the very trees bent down their branches and offered their fruits to the two children of Viśvantara and Mādrī. But another Brahman presented himself and asked the father to give him his children as servants; and in spite of his own misery and their terror he gave them up. Next Indra, disguised as an anchorite, came and asked his wife of him as a slave; and again he consented. At last Indra revealed himself and

FIGURE 50

Ajaṇṭā. Cave I.

— Photo, Goloubew. By permission of Messrs. Van Oest

[1] Cf. Sir Aurel Stein: *Serindia*, I, Fig. 134, p. 517.

FIGURE 51

Ajaṇṭā. Pair of lovers from Cave I.
— *Photo, Goloubew. By permission of Messrs. Van Oest*

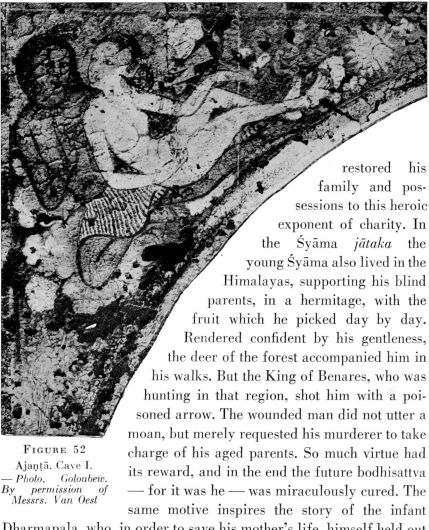

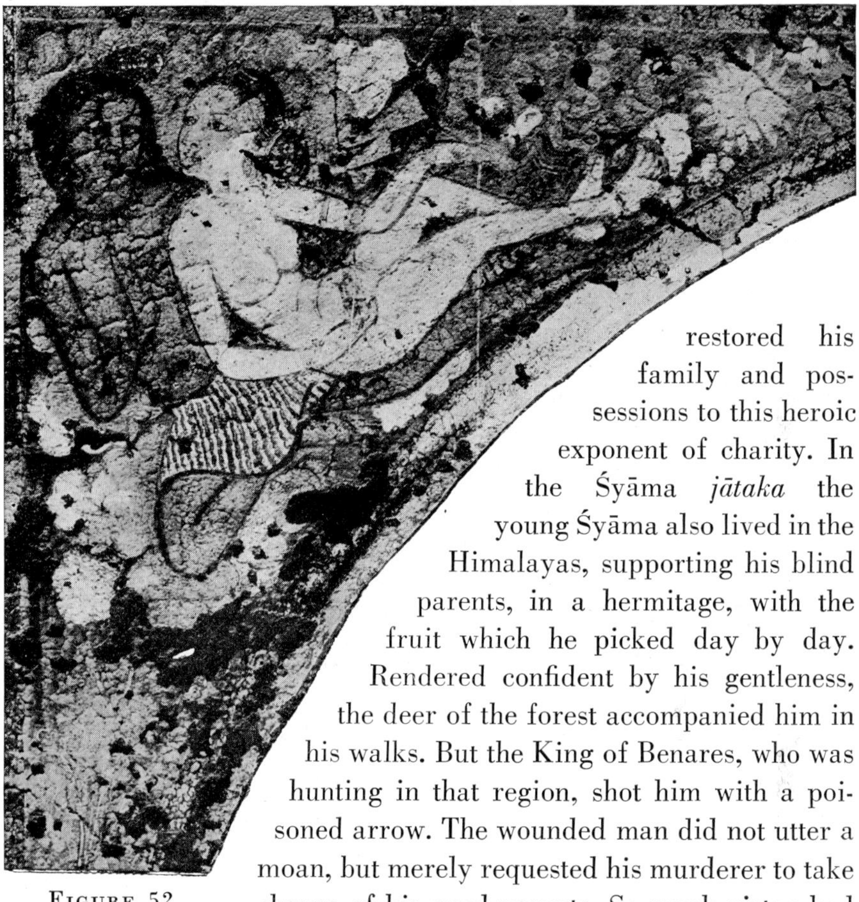

FIGURE 52
Ajaṇṭā. Cave I.
— *Photo, Goloubew. By permission of Messrs. Van Oest*

restored his family and possessions to this heroic exponent of charity. In the Śyāma *jātaka* the young Śyāma also lived in the Himalayas, supporting his blind parents, in a hermitage, with the fruit which he picked day by day. Rendered confident by his gentleness, the deer of the forest accompanied him in his walks. But the King of Benares, who was hunting in that region, shot him with a poisoned arrow. The wounded man did not utter a moan, but merely requested his murderer to take charge of his aged parents. So much virtue had its reward, and in the end the future bodhisattva — for it was he — was miraculously cured. The same motive inspires the story of the infant Dharmapala, who, in order to save his mother's life, himself held out his little arms to the executioner. And the story of the *nāgarāja* Chāmpēya belongs to the same category. This serpent-king, instead of living out his life in the depths of his lake-palaces as a genius of

Figure 53

Ajaṇṭā. Cave I. The "Beautiful Bodhisattva."
—*Photo, Goloubew. By permission of Messrs. Van Oest*

the waters, returned into the world of men in order to work out his salvation. He endured the tortures inflicted upon him by an ant-hill full of angry ants, and also those to which he was subjected by a serpent-charmer, until the day when his wife, the *nāgī*, or water-

FIGURE 54
Fresco from Sīgiriya.
— *Copy in the Musée Guimet. Photo, Pivot*

fairy, revealed his identity to the King of Benares, when the future bodhisattva recovered his form as a young god.[1]

These are but a few examples out of a thousand from this Asiatic Golden Legend, the most poetic, tender, and moving that could be imagined. No better example could be found of that purely Indian sentiment of universal brotherhood, that fervour of humanitarianism

[1] See a beautiful relief at Amarāvatī, the *jātaka* of the *nāga* Champaka in Vogel: *Indian Serpent-lore*, Pl. VII b.

which extends even to animals and plants. It will be no surprise to us to find such a literature inspiring the tender naturalism of Sāñchī and Ajaṇṭā.

FIGURE 55
Fresco from Sīgiriya.
— *Copy in the Musée Guimet. Photo, Pivot*

During the last existence of the Buddha, during his actual historic life, we can, moreover, distinguish a certain number of mythical personages who were subsequently to play as great a role as Śākyamuni, especially in China.[1] First of all we have the familiar genius Vajrāpaṇi, a *yaksha* who devoted himself to Śākyamuni and constituted himself his faithful guardian from the time of his "depar-

[1] Cf. A. Foucher: *Étude sur l'iconographie bouddhique de l'Inde*, École des Hautes Études, Sciences Religieuses, Vol. XIII, Pt. 2, 1905, pp. 22–102; Miss Alice Getty: *The Gods of Northern Buddhism*, Oxford, Clarendon Press, 1914, 2nd ed. 1928.

ture from home" to that of his entry into *nirvāṇa*. He is easily recognized on the monuments by his thunderbolt (*vajra*). In the Middle Ages he too was to become a bodhisattva — that is, a future Buddha.

For Śākyamuni, the historical Buddha, was not to be the last of the Buddhas, any more than he had been the first of them. We know the name of him who was to succeed him after this cosmic cycle: the bodhisattva Maitrēya, the Messiah of Buddhism. We also know that instead of being born, like Śākyamuni, of a *kshatriya* house, Maitrēya was to become incarnate in a Brahman family: hence the fact that his hair is braided into the Brahmanical lock and that he carries a water-pot, the insignia of the sacerdotal caste.[1]

Other figures in the Buddhist heaven are the Dhyāni-Buddhas — that is, the contemplative, or, if we prefer so to call them, the celestial Buddhas. The best known of these is Amitābha ("Infinite Light"), who reigns over a paradise of marvels, the "Land of the West" or "Blessed Land" (*Sukhāvatī*), a resort of beauty and virtue which the elect only leave to enter at will into *nirvāṇa*.[2] Among the Dhyāni-bodhisattvas surrounding Amitābha, the first place belongs to Avalokitēśvara, who is, moreover, a spiritual emanation from him (Fig. 126). Avalokitēśvara, "he who looks down from on high" — also called Lokēśvara, "the lord of the world," or Padmapāṇi, "the lord of the lotus" — is, as his name indicates, a sort of pitying and compassionate Providence.[3] A single invocation of him, coming from a pure heart, would save those shipwrecked in a storm, or travellers attacked by brigands or wild beasts. He is represented as a charming prince, wearing a high tiara-shaped headdress, adorned with a figure of his spiritual father, Amitābha, and holding in his hand a pink lotus and a rosary. From Avalokitēśvara is in turn derived his "Śakti" — that is, the feminine embodiment

1 Cf. Vol. IV, Fig. 32.
2 Cf. Vol. IV, Fig. 33, 58.
3 Cf. Vol. III, Fig. 204, 208, 209, 229, 235; Vol. IV, Fig. 26.

of his energy — the Buddhist goddess Tārā, the queen of pity, who is never called upon in vain.[1]

We may also mention the bodhisattva Mañjuśrī, the lord of transcendent wisdom, whose legend seems to be connected with the sub-

FIGURE 56
Temple of Liṅgarāja at Bhuvaneśvara, ninth–thirteenth centuries. West view.

Himalayan region (Fig. 53).[2] We read of a descent which he made into the palaces of the Ocean, during which he converted the race of the *nāgas*. His attributes are the sword, the lance, and the blue lotus, and he rides upon a lion. Side by side with these truly divine beings, Buddhism has also a number of demi-gods: one of these is

[1] Cf. Vol. IV, Fig. 166, 168, 169.
[2] Cf. Vol. III, Fig. 224; Vol. IV, Fig. 9–10, 175 b.

Pāñchika, the King of the *yakshas*, who in the popular form of the cult developed into the genius of riches, with the money-bag and the pike as his attributes; another is the corpulent Jambhala, also a god of wealth, whose attributes are the citron and the mangosteen fruit.[1]

In the long run the historic Buddha was almost thrown into the background by this tribe of bodhisattvas and saints. A whole mythology was built up, which the Master, perhaps, had not foreseen, but which should not be undervalued, for it provided the Oriental genius with delightful themes — motives of love and consolation, a whole world of dreams of unexpected æsthetic value, new sources of inner life, and mystic nutriment for the loftiest souls. A great hope ran through the Far East, no longer based upon the almost Socratic wisdom of the Buddha Śākyamuni, but on the certainty of a radiant after-life, the " Paradise of the West," or Land of Purity, where souls of an unsullied white will be born again after death in the mystic lotus. Beyond the confines of reality, tender, wondrous images appeared in a luminous atmosphere of fine gold, images which still move us when we think of all the human dreams and indomitable hopes for which they stand.

THE EARLIEST BUDDHIST ART: MAURYA AND ŚUṄGA ART

IN 326 B.C., A CENTURY AND A HALF AFTER THE DEATH OF BUDDHA, Alexander the Great, having subdued the Persian Empire, entered India and conquered the Punjāb. The conquest was merely ephemeral, but had as its result one of the most important events in the history of India: the political unification of the country by the first great native dynasty, that of the Mauryas (322).

Until about 185 B.C. the Mauryas reigned over the whole of the Indo-Gangetic plain, together with a part of the Deccan. The seat

[1] See Foucher: "The Tutelary Pair," in *Beginnings of Buddhist Art*, pp. 146–84.

of their rule was the land of Magadha (southern Behar), the land of Buddhism *par excellence*, for with it were connected most of the memories of the monastic life of Śākyamuni. The first two Maurya emperors, it is true, Chandragupta and Bindusāra, remained strangers to Buddhism, but their successor, Aśoka Priyadarśin (274–237 or 268–232), was converted to this religion and became a royal

FIGURE 57
Ratha of Māvalipuram, seventh century.
— *Photo, Goloubew*

saint. This was an event of capital importance for the history of Indian civilization, for in the pursuit of religious propaganda Aśoka, being master of almost the whole of India, from Kābul and Nepal to Mysore, ordered the construction of the first specimens of Indian epigraphy and art which have come down to us: in order to preach the Buddhist morality to his peoples, he caused a host of edicts to be hewn in the rock or inscribed upon pillars from end to end of his empire, which enable us to form an idea of his moral qualities. They show us that the pious monarch succeeded in extracting from Buddhism a practical morality of value for humanity in general and acceptable to all. Without entering into the question of dogma he enjoined upon his subjects the domestic and social virtues, humanity towards all creatures, the giving of alms to monks and to the poor, and pity for animals. He was himself the first to set the example of these virtues. Thus he founded hospitals for both man and beast. "Every man," runs one of his edicts, "is my child. Just as I desire for my children that they may enjoy every kind of prosperity in this world and in the next, even so do I desire the same thing for all men. I have planted banyan-trees along the roads, that they may give shade to both man and beast. I have planted gardens full of mango-trees, I have had reservoirs for water dug in a number of places, and caravanserais built for the enjoyment of both man and beast. I have also appointed supervisors of religions, to attend to the concerns of all the sects. I have equally at heart the interests of the Buddhist monks and that of the Brahmans and Jains." There was, in fact, no intolerance in this crowned monk. If he preached the Dharma, or Buddhist "Law," it was, so he himself tells us, in order to bring about the "kinship" — or, as we should say, the brotherhood — of all men. And his legislation may be summed up in the maxim, worthy of Marcus Aurelius: "One must be gentle to all living creatures."

He carried this apostolic mission into the sphere of art also. As we have said, India had certainly had its own architecture and schools of sculpture before the Mauryas, but no remains of them have come down to us, for both architects and sculptors used none but perishable materials, such as wood, ivory, or clay. Under the Maurya rulers the use of stone became general for columns and statues, the sort employed being sandstone, which was to survive the centuries. In agreement with Mr. Ramaprasad Chanda, superintendent of the Indian Museum at Calcutta, we have no hesitation in regarding this highly important innovation as the effect of Greco-Persian influence (see Ramaprasad Chanda: *Beginnings of Art in Eastern India,* Memoirs of the Archæological Survey, No. 30, Calcutta, 1927). As we know from the Greek historians and from Aśoka's own inscriptions, the Maurya sovereigns, Chandragupta, Bindusāra, and Aśoka, maintained regular relations of a diplomatic, commercial, and intellectual order with the great Seleucid kings who succeeded both Alexander and the Achæmenids in Iran. It is probable that these relations brought the Mauryas a knowledge of the art of Hellenistic Iran, which was still full of the grandeur of the Achæmenid period; and, as a matter of fact, Mr. Spooner has discovered at Aśoka's old capital of Pāṭaliputra (Bankipur, near Patna) the remains of a columned hall which seems to be more or less inspired by Darius's famous Hall of the Hundred Columns at Persepolis. "All Aśoka's monuments," notes Mr. Ramaprasad Chanda, "whether monolithic columns, rock inscriptions or sculptures, likewise bear witness to a happy adaptation of Achæmenid models." [1] We may further observe that, with this Achæmenid inspiration, not only was Persia to make her influence felt in India, but so, too, were the various types of art from which that of the Achæmenids had drawn its inspiration: firstly Assyro-Babylonian art,[2] which influenced the representation of animals, and afterwards Egyptian art, which affected the column, while even the Greek art of Ionia had its effect upon the technique of the bas-relief: the diluted Hellenism which is subtly evident in the sculpture of Aśoka may be traced to this indirect source, as well as to the coming of Seleucid workmen, which is equally possible.

The art of Aśoka is represented by *lāt,* or columns bearing inscriptions — monolithic pillars of polished sandstone with sculptured capitals. The finest of these pillars, that of Sārnāth, at the gates of

[1] Cf. Sir John Marshall: "The Storied Past of India: Chandragupta's Palisaded Capital," in *Illustrated London News,* March 24, 1928, p. 477 (with many illustrations).

[2] Cf. C. L. Fabri: "*Un Élément mésopotamien dans l'art de l'Inde,*" *Journal asiatique,* Paris, 1930.

Benares, was set up on the site of the famous Deer-park where Buddha preached his first sermon (Fig. 2).[1] It was surmounted by a richly decorated capital formed in ascending order: firstly, of a bell-shaped reversed lotus; secondly, of an entablature with a frieze on which

FIGURE 58
Temple on the shore. Māvalipuram, seventh century.
— *Photo, Goloubew*

are carved, in such high relief as to have all the qualities of sculpture in the round, an elephant, a galloping horse, a zebu, and a lion separated from one another by wheels (*chakra*), the symbol of the Buddhist Law; and, thirdly, on top of the capital, of three lions, or, rather, the forequarters of three lions standing back to back, which

[1] See *Archæological Survey of India, Report, 1904–5* ("Excavations at Sārnāth"), Pl. XX, p. 70.

once supported a great Wheel of the Law, crowning the whole design. According to the hypothesis of Vincent Smith, perhaps we ought to regard these four animals on the frieze as symbolic of the four cardinal points. Almost equally beautiful is the capital of one of the pillars of Rāmpurvā, the base of which is also formed of a bell-shaped lotus, while the entablature is adorned with a delightful floral frieze of lotus and palmette motives, crowned by a fine statue of a zebu carved in the round. There is another capital with a bell-shaped lotus at Rāmpurvā, crowned by a seated lion, and a lion also crowns the columns of Aśoka at Bēsarh, Bakhirā, and Lauriyā Nandangarh. In other places the terminal statue represents an elephant, as at Sankisa, or a horse, as at Rummindei, on the column erected by Aśoka in the ancient park of Lumbinī, the scene of the Buddha's Nativity. The frieze of the abacus is also different on the various pillars: we may mention among others the elegant friezes of geese on the capitals of Lauriyā Nandangarh and Sāñchī.

Mr. Ramaprasad Chanda wonders whether certain of these pillars — those whose capitals are surmounted by a statue of an animal treated by itself, without any Wheel of the Law — may not be due to Aśoka's father, King Bindusāra.[1] This king, it appears, was a Brahmanist by religion, so that, according to this theory, the animals in question would represent the symbolical beasts which bear the Brahmanical deities upon their backs: the bull of Śiva, the elephant of Indra, the lion of the goddess Durgā, and the *garuḍa* of Vishṇu (the last of which is to be found at Lauriyā Araraj). His suggestion is that Aśoka afterwards used these pillars for his Buddhist propaganda, or rather, in his broadly syncretistic spirit, associated these Brahmanical symbols with his preaching of the Law.

However this may be, the historian of art must pause before this school of animal-sculptors, which produced masterpieces from the very first. No doubt we are here dealing with masters familiar with

[1] Cf. Ramaprasad Chanda, op. cit., Pl. II and III.

Achæmenid technique: in the lions at Sārnāth the execution of the muscles in the treatment of the muzzle and paws is directly reminiscent of Khorsābād and Persepolis. But here the vigour and dignity

FIGURE 59
General view of the Kailāsa at Ellora.
— *Photo, Goloubew*

of Assyro-Persian tradition are found in combination with genuinely indigenous elements. The poetry of the *jātakas,* the Buddhist tenderness to our animal brethren, have effected a transformation in this art imported from the Middle East, by softening its Assyrian violence and at the same time restoring to the dry Achæmenid forms a new fullness and freshness of life. The harsh realism of Assur became a free and wonderfully flexible naturalism — and Indian art was born. We need only look at the elephant on the Sārnāth capital, at the easy gait of this huge, massive form, and the life which throbs in this quivering trunk: the whole art of Ellora and Māvalipuram is already contained in this short relief.

The representations of human figures in the Maurya period are far from possessing as much character as those of animals; but they should none the less not be ignored. The *yaksha* from Pārkham in the museum at Mathurā,[1] the *yakshiṇī* from Besnagar in the Calcutta Museum, the woman carrying the *chaurī* (fly-fan) from Dīdarganj in the Patna Museum,[2] have all the appearance of transitional works. In their cylindrical rigidity we are still conscious of the rudimentary technique of the old native artisans, accustomed to carving a human form out of a stump of wood. But here again the balance in the distribution of masses and a certain elegance in the treatment of the *dhoṭī* (loin-cloth) bear witness to a strongly artistic temperament; while in the beauty of the torso and abdomen and the fullness of the breast the *chaurī*-bearer of Dīdarganj even directly foreshadows some features of the Indian ideal of female beauty as it was to be developed at Bhārhut and Sāñchī.

Towards 185 B.C. the Maurya dynasty was replaced by that of the Śuṅgas, who occupied the throne of Magadha till about 73. But this new royal house reigned over the plain of the Ganges alone. The Punjāb, as we shall see, fell into the power of the Greeks, while the powerful kingdom of the Andhra was established in the Deccan, where it lasted from 200 B.C. till about A.D. 200 and was for a time the chief of the native states. Under the Śuṅga and Andhra dynasties the artistic evolution started by Aśoka was continued. It was now

[1] Ananda Coomaraswamy: *Yakṣas*, Smithsonian Miscellaneous Collections, Vol. 80, No. 6, May 1928, Pl. I.
[2] See Ludwig Bachhofer: *Early Indian Sculpture*, Vol. I (1929), Pl. 9.

that the earliest Buddhist art rose to its supreme achievements in the schools of Bhājā, Beḍsā, Bhārhut, Kārlī, Sāñchī, and Amarāvatī.

The typical architectural forms in which this art was expressed and with which we shall henceforth have to deal in the course of this history fall under three categories: the *stūpa*, the *vihāra*, and the *chaitya*. The essential feature of the *stūpa* is a hemispherical dome,

FIGURE 60
Temple at Elephanta.
— *Photo, Goloubew*

built of brick or stone, and called in Sanscrit *aṇḍa*, or the egg; this dome is raised upon a terrace (*mēdhī*) and surmounted by a kiosk (*harmikā*), as in Fig. 38.[1] It is surrounded at a certain distance by a stone railing or balustrade (*vēdikā*), often adorned at the four cardinal points with a corresponding number of porticoes (*toraṇa*), which constitute the work of art properly so called. The *stūpa* doubtless drew its inspiration from the ancient tumuli and was theoretically

[1] Cf. Foucher: *L'Art gréco-bouddhique du Gandhāra*, I, 45.

intended to contain the relics of the saints. The pilgrimages which were made to these shrines ended in a procession round the edifice (*pradakshiṇa patha*). The *vihāra* is a monastery,[1] and the *chaitya* an underground monastery, or crypt, which often contains a small *stūpa* known as a *dāgaba* (dagoba), forming a sort of altar.

According to the works of Sir John Marshall, director of the Archæological Survey of India, and Mr. Ramaprasad Chanda, superintendent of the Calcutta Museum, the earliest works of art belonging to this period are the sculptures of the enclosure of the *stūpa* at Bhārhut in Baghelkand, which may, in their opinion, go back to the middle of the second century B.C. At any rate, on one of the jambs of the east door of this *stūpa* appears an inscription mentioning the Śuṅga dynasty, which dates from the time when the old wooden door was replaced by a stone *toraṇa*. The treatment of the human figure on the reliefs of this building is still somewhat primitive and gives us the impression of being the work of ivory-carvers. It might have come out of a workshop for turning out religious images wholesale, so stumpy and crowded are the figures, as though the old masters, accustomed to the limitations of working on their small slabs of ivory, did not as yet venture to avail themselves of the liberty afforded by the size of the stone. All the same, these are singularly interesting scenes, owing to the naïveté and fidelity with which the story of Buddha is treated. Yet the Buddha himself is never represented here; in accordance with a convention which was to last for the whole duration of the earliest Indian school, he was never represented in person, but only suggested by a certain number of easily interpreted symbols. We may note that this prejudice had a logical explanation: it was not fitting to give *new life* to the features of him who had entered into the final *nirvāṇa*. But in default of the Buddha himself, there were all the traditional scenes connected with him;

[1] In early times the *vihāra* was the habitation of a single monk only. The monastery was called *saṅghārāma*. But nowadays such a monastery is commonly known as a *vihāra* (Foucher: *L'Art gréco-bouddhique du Gandhāra*, I, 99).

and, above all, there were the *jātakas,* his previous lives, in which the human or animal form of the future bodhisattva could be shown without sacrilege. As a matter of fact, as Monsieur Foucher has pointed out the scenes illustrating the *jātakas* constitute the chief

FIGURE 61
Tanjore. The Great Pagoda, ninth–twelfth centuries

interest at Bhārhut.[1] Artistically this is all to the good, for many of the *jātakas* are concerned with animal subjects: and though the human figures at Bhārhut are, as a rule, rather poor, the animal ones, on the contrary, in spite of a certain awkwardness of technique, give evidence of a charming truth to nature. The figures of monkeys, for instance, are often singularly amusing, while the elephants' heads

[1] See A. Foucher: *The Beginnings of Buddhist Art* (London, 1917), p. 29 ("Representations of Jātakas on the Bas-reliefs of Bhārhut"); L. Bachhofer: *Early Indian Sculpture,* I, Pl. 23–33.

display an intelligence worthy of the masters of Sārnāth (Fig. 3). We may also note that occasionally, by way of exception, we find at Bhārhut a few magnificent native " portraits," such as the medallion in the Calcutta Museum, with the turbaned head of a rajah — a racial type of an astonishing intensity of expression (see Bachhofer: *Early Indian Sculpture*, I, Pl. 32).

The Buddhist monuments of Bhājā and Beḍsā seem to belong to the same period. At Bhājā near Poona in the Mahratta territory, there is a *vihāra* of the second century B.C., and a *chaitya* the architecture of which once again points to a rendering in stone of the technique of construction in wood. Quite near by, at Beḍsā, the *chaitya* seems to date from about 175 B.C. That at Nāsik, in the same region, is later, belonging to the middle of the first century B.C. And lastly the great *chaitya* of Kārlī, the fourth of these ancient monuments in the Mahratta territory, seems to belong to the early years of our era.[1]

The best-known as well as the finest of the monuments of the Śuṅga period is the Great Stūpa, or " Stūpa I," at Sāñchī, near Bhopal, in Malva.[2] According to Sir John Marshall and Mr. Ramaprasad Chanda, the nucleus of the dome goes back to the time of Aśoka, in the middle of the third century B.C., but in its present form the dome, as well as the four doors, is of the Śuṅga period. The most ancient of these doors is the southern one, which an inscription tells us was presented as a votive offering by a certain Ānaṃda, " chief of the artisans," in the reign of Śātakarṇi, king of Andhra from 75 to 20 B.C. Another inscription informs us that one of the jambs of this door is due to the ivory-carvers of the city of Vidiśā (Bhilsā) in Malva; and, as a matter of fact, both here and at Bhārhut there is more than one detail — for instance, the conventional mode of repre-

[1] See Gangoly: *Indian Architecture* (Rūpam, Calcutta), Pl. XII, XVII.

[2] See Sir John Marshall: *A Guide to Sāñchī* (Calcutta, 1918); Foucher: *Beginnings of Buddhist Art*, p. 61: "The Eastern Gate of the Sāñchī Stūpa"; Sir John Marshall: "The Monuments of Sāñchī," *Archæological Survey of India, Report, 1913–14*, pp. 1–40.

Figure 62

Descent of the Gaṅgā, Māvalipuram.

— *Photo, Goloubew*

senting a town — that reminds us of the technique of ivory-carving in all ages. Next in chronological order come the north (Fig. 4), the east (Fig. 5), and the west doors. We may note in passing that there is a third inscription indicating that one of the jambs of the east door was presented by the banker Nāgapiya.[1]

Here again it is easy to detect a certain influence coming from Achæmenid Persia; indeed, there are belated specimens of the Achæmenid style to be found in India in the first century B.C., just as there were "belated antiques" (*Spätantike*) in Kashgaria in the Middle Ages. The winged lions (Fig. 6), the winged griffons, the columns in the style of Persepolis, with their bell-shaped capitals, honeysuckle motives, and dentils or serrated motives, are all borrowings from Persepolis or Susa on the part of Sāñchī; the lions on the south door, in particular, are directly reminiscent of the Achæmenid lions on the capital of Aśoka at Sārnāth, though inferior to these. We may also divine a certain infiltration of Hellenic influences, though these are less direct; but, as Monsieur Foucher points out, there are certain foreshortenings, certain three-quarter-face figures on the reliefs at Sāñchī, which can only be explained by a knowledge of Greek technique. And in this connexion he recalls that, quite close to Sāñchī, at Vidiśā (Bhilsā), was a pillar set up in honour of Vishṇu by Heliodorus of Taxila, ambassador of the Greco-Indian king Antialkidas.[2]

We have purposely referred to these foreign influences only that we may proceed to maintain with still greater force that the art of Sāñchī none the less remains specifically Indian in type. It is Indian in its general inspiration, which is entirely Buddhist, as well as in the majority of its floral or animal motives, from the wonderful wreaths of lotus to the swans, peacocks, and elephants which

[1] See Ramaprasad Chanda: *Dates of the Votive Inscriptions on the Stūpas at Sāñchī*, Memoirs of the Archæological Survey of India, No. 1 (Calcutta, 1919).

[2] See Ramaprasad Chanda: *Archæology and Vaishnara Tradition*, Memoirs of the Archæological Survey of India, No. 5 (Calcutta, 1920).

here serve as the chief decorative motives. Equally Indian, and Buddhist too, is the convention by which, at Sāñchī as at Bhārhut, the person of the Buddha is replaced by a certain range of symbols. Thus the young elephant suggests, or rather represents, the Conception; Māyā seated upon the lotus and surrounded by young elephants pouring water over her represents the Nativity; sometimes even a single lotus suffices to symbolize this scene; the riderless horse represents the Great Departure; the demons or courtesans before the tree and the empty seat are emblematic of the Assault of Mārā and the Temptation; the tree and the seat alone stand for the Illumination (*Bodhi*); the Wheel of the Law (or *dharmachakra*) for the preaching of Buddha; the throne and the parasol for the general scenes in which the Buddha figured; the way through the air, the aerial journey to Kapilavastu; the *stūpa*, the *nirvāṇa* of the Blessed One. Similarly the emblem of the *trisula* represents the "three jewels" (*triratna*):

FIGURE 63
Māvalipuram. Ascetic prostrating himself.
— *Photo, Goloubew*

that is, the Buddha, his Law (*dharma*), and his Church (*saṅgha* or *saṃgha*). What is more, this symbolism is not peculiar to the historic Buddha: at Sāñchī each of the Buddhas of the past may be recognized by the particular variety of tree which stands for him: hence a row of seven trees with an equal number of *stūpas* will signify the seven Buddhas of the past who have entered in glory into *nirvāṇa* (Fig. 6). Indeed, nothing could be more remarkable than the ease with which the old masters of Sāñchī manage to relate the life of Buddha without ever representing him, thanks to these conventions which they adopted once and for all. This constitutes a *tour de force* in the sphere of iconography which has not been sufficiently appreciated.

The half-secular, half-religious subjects which give us glimpses into the life of the nobles of Śuṅga India have a savour all their own. Whether the subject be King Bimbisāra leaving Rājagṛiha on a visit to the Blessed One, or King Śuddhodana leaving Kapilavastu to go to meet his son, we see before us a faithful portrayal — complete with thronging chariots, elephants in state trappings, and mounted troops — of one of those " Indian kings " whose ancestors had held their own against Alexander and whose peers were still checking the Greek reconquest by Menander on the Ganges. A similar scene, full of authentic local colour, is that of the curious " War of the Relics," which, on the morrow of the death of the great embodiment of pity, almost ended in a conflict between the neighbouring kings over his mortal remains. Still more definitely historic are the scenes of the visit of Aśoka to the *stūpa* of Rāmagrāma and the sacred tree of Bodh-Gayā; this last scene in particular is of inestimable value to the historian, not to speak of the great artistic charm with which it represents the pious monarch, who, aided by a dwarf and surrounded by his women, is gracefully dismounting from his kneeling elephant (Fig. 15–16). In spite of their religious character we may compare with this series the two figures of Lokapālas, or kings of the

FIGURE 64
Māvalipuram. Descent of the Gaṅgā.
— *Photo, Goloubew*

heavens, which support the jambs of the eastern gate: with their puffed turbans and profusion of jewels, their elegant *dhoṭī* and close-shaven faces (such as are always found in India down to the time of the Indo-Scythians), these figures are still eminently representative of aristocratic fashions among the Indians of the *kshatriya* caste about the beginning of our era.

But, as might be expected, what constitute the chief charm of Sāñchī are still the *jātakas,* or "birth stories," with their subjects drawn from forest and animal life, which are so well suited to the Indian genius. Whether we are dealing with animal stories, such as that of the elephant with six tusks (*shaḍdanta jātaka*) (Fig. 7), or of the king of the monkeys (*mahākapi jātaka*), or with human stories having the jungle as a setting, such as the story of the *ṛishi* or unicorn saint (the simple-minded anchorite who was the son of a hind and was powerless to defeat the wiles of a courtesan), or the dramatic legend of Prince Viśvantara (Fig. 6), or the equally touching story of Śyama, we feel that the masters of Sāñchī are far more at home in all these scenes than in those from the life of the historic Buddha. What love of nature is to be seen in them, what an understanding of floral and animal forms! Just as our cathedrals are encyclopædias in stone, so the gates at Sāñchī unroll before our eyes the marvellous poem of Indian nature, a very *Jungle Book.* We need only mention, on the east gate, the adoration of the tree by the animal kingdom—buffalo, animals of the feline tribe, serpents or serpent deities (*nāga*) and *garuḍa,* antelope and wild elephants, all offering the homage of creation to the symbol of *Bodhi* (Illumination) (Fig. 8); or, on the same gate, the adoration of the *stūpa* by wild elephants (Fig. 9 and 11 b), like the dream of some St. Francis of Assisi who had been through the experiences of a Mowgli; or, on the north gate, the splendid peacocks which adorn the projecting end of the central lintel (Fig. 10 and 15); or the splendid tame elephants, carved half in the round, which serve as capitals to the east and north gates (Fig. 9, 12,

FIGURE 65

Descent of the Gaṅgā: *nāga* and *nāgī*.

— *Photo, Goloubew*

and 15): not even the modelling of Aśoka's sculptors at Sārnāth was more powerful. We may also notice the charming little elephants to which is allotted the part played by our angels in the scenes of the Conception or the Nativity (Fig. 6 and 15). And lastly we may specially mention the admirable scene of the elephant-bodhisattva in the forest, surrounded by his herd, in the *shaḍdanta jātaka* on the central lintel of the south gate (Fig. 7). As we stand before these scenes, with their delicate and tender feeling for nature, Assyrian bas-reliefs seem very conventional, and even Greek bas-reliefs almost strike us as cold.

In this connexion we may note what it is that distinguishes the Indian animal-sculptors from those of classical art: it is precisely this brotherly sympathy with all living beings, a sentiment having its source at once in the dogma of transmigration and in that tenderness towards the whole universe which is distinctively Buddhist and Jain, or, in later days, Krishnaite. Filled with the spirit of the *jātakas*, the jungle became an earthly paradise.

On the whole, as Mr. Ramaprasad Chanda has recently pointed out, this Buddhist art expresses, not so much the ideal of renunciation and extinction which was that of Buddhist theory, as the freshest, most naïve and pagan love of life. All that is left of the Buddhist religion here is its gentleness and simplicity, and we find the naturalistic spirit at its height. Never, even in the Greece of the classic age, has the innocent and spontaneous joy of life been so happily expressed. Never has the poetry of the female form been rendered with a more sensuous power than in the statues of female genii (*yakshiṇīs*), carved in the round, which form a link between the jambs and the end of the lower lintels of the east and north gates. These figures are to a certain extent the equivalents of the Greek caryatids. But the caryatid was always a human column, immobilized by her architectural role, while the *yakshiṇī* of Sāñchī swings freely outwards from the structure as a whole. Under her canopy of foliage she sup-

Figure 66
Māvalipuram. "The ascetic cat."
— *Photo, Goloubew*

ports herself by her elbow and back against the mango-tree which climbs upwards at the end of the lintel on the north gate; or else, as on the east gate, she leans outwards from the branches of the tree, hanging by both her arms, like some living liana, in a curve of infinite grace, so that the "golden bowls" of her full bust, all the

FIGURE 67
Māvalipuram. Detail.
— *Photo, Goloubew*

blooming flesh of her young body, seem to sway forward into space (Fig. 13 and 14).[1]

Such forms as these, at once strong and voluptuous, are often to be found at this period, notably in the two rock-carvings of two almost wholly nude couples clasped in each other's arms, which guard the entrance to the *chaitya* at Kārlī. The two male figures, with their turbans in the same style as those of the medallions of Bhārhut and Bodh-Gayā, and their athletic muscles, and the two nude female fig-

[1] See also the wonderful female torso from Sāñchī, recently acquired by the Museum of Fine Arts, Boston (Ross collection). Cf. Coomaraswamy: "A Yakshī Torso from Sāñchī," *Bulletin of the Museum of Fine Arts, Boston,* Vol. XXVI, No. 164 (December 1929), pp. 90–4.

Figure 68

Māvalipuram. Rock-carving, seventh century.
— *Photo, Goloubew*

ures, which are almost as powerfully built and at the same time as sensuous as the *yakshiṇī* of Sāñchī, represent splendid types of humanity.[1] The same may be said of the figures of male and female donors on the veranda of the *chaitya* of Kanhēri, dating from the second century of our era. In spite of the fact that it is used for Buddhist purposes, this might well be called the pagan art of India (Fig. 84–85).

The Great Stūpa or Stūpa I is not the only monument of this kind at Sāñchī. More than ten of them may be counted in the same locality. Stūpa III doubtless also belongs to the first century B.C. Its southern door, which is the latest in date and is richly decorated, seems to Sir John Marshall to have been added at the beginning of the first century of our era. As for Stūpa II, side by side with some rather primitive reliefs, it displays certain details belonging to a far more advanced art — for instance, a delightful nude female figure among lotuses in a medallion on the balustrade, in which Sir John Marshall thinks he sees traces of a certain Greek influence.[2] But it may be objected that the feminine types in which Hellenistic influence is admitted, such as those we know at Gandhāra, are far from presenting the same grace. It is true that the nude figure on Stūpa II at Sāñchī is more supple and elegant, less heavily sensual than those of Bhārhut, Kārlī, and Stūpa I, but this happy transformation may well be specifically Indian, merely heralding the art of Amarāvatī.

The enclosure at Bodh-Gayā may possibly date from about 100 B.C. The medallions which once adorned it are of considerable interest, both for their æsthetic value and for the happy blend of influences which is revealed in them. The Indian elements are of the same quality as at Bhārhut and Sāñchī; moreover, the medallions of ele-

[1] L. Bachhofer: *Early Indian Sculpture*, I, Pl. 19, 20 (Bhārhut); II, Pl. 67, 68 (Kārlī), and 92–93 (Mathurā).

[2] Sir John Marshall: *A Guide to Sāñchī*, Pl. XIII, C; Codrington: *Ancient India* (1926), Pl. 17 A.

phants, winged elephants, buffalo, and bulls are almost identical at Bodh-Gayā and at Bhārhut, bearing witness to the same feeling for nature in both places; while the *kshatriya* in the rich turban which we admired just now at Bhārhut is also found on a medallion at Bodh-Gayā. But at the same time Bodh-Gayā has motives of Hellenic origin: the quadriga of Sūrya, drawn by a team of horses, each pair of which is rearing in a contrary direction, is certainly of Greek inspiration, and so is the centaur on one of the medallions. But these Hellenic borrowings never appear here in an unassimilated state, as we shall find them at Gandhāra; they have become assimilated and Indianized. It is this happy combination of Greek infiltration and native tradition which has produced, for instance, the delightful winged elephants, or the charming cows with the bodies of sirens, which we shall find persistently appearing, from Bodh-Gayā to Ajaṇṭā. We might almost apply the same praise to the frieze of Kaṅkālī, near Mathurā, dating from the beginning of our era and showing *suparṇas*, or mythical birds represented under the form of harpies, and *kinnaras* in the form of centaurs.[1] But the imitation was already becoming more direct: we are verging on the art of Gandhāra.

THE GREEK BUDDHA

WHILE THE NATIVE GENIUS WAS DEVELOPING FREELY IN THE SCHOOLS of the Ganges region and central India, north-west India had fallen into the power of the Greek princes established in Bactria, the last heirs of Alexander in these regions. The Kābul valley — or Gandhāra, as it is sometimes called, from the ancient name of one of its districts [2] — and the Punjāb [3] thus became Hellenic soil, and

[1] Cf. Coomaraswamy: *Bulletin of the Museum of Fine Arts, Boston*, Vol. XXV, No. 150 (August 1927), p. 51.

[2] The Kābul valley included, from east to west, the ancient districts of Gandhāra proper (Peshawar), Nagarahara (Ningrahar), Lampaka (Lamghān), and Kapiśa (the region to the north of Kābul, towards Kohistan).

[3] Western Punjāb (Taxila) and eastern Punjāb (Sākala, modern Sialkot).

remained so for the whole of the second century and the first third of the first century B.C. The beautiful Greco-Bactrian and Indo-Greek coins in the British Museum and the Cabinet des Médailles, Paris, show us the pure profiles of these adventurers of genius, Demetrios, Eukratidas, Apollodotos, and Menander, who, a century and a half after Alexander, enacted a sequel to the Macedonian epic in India. One of these Greek kings, Menander — the Milinda of Indian tradition — who reigned from about 170 to 150 B.C., even carried his arms as far as the Ganges. This prince, whose conquests in the Indus valley thus exceeded those of Alexander and left a more lasting memory there, seems to have shown some curiosity to become acquainted with the wisdom of the East. There is a Palī work, the *Milindapañha,* in which he appears as one of the interlocutors in a philosophic dialogue with a Buddhist doctor. Further, a coin of Menander has been found bearing the Buddhist sign *par excellence,* the Wheel of the Law (*dharmachakra*).

The Greeks were expelled, first from Bactria, about 135 B.C., and afterwards from their Indian possessions, between 75 and 58 B.C., by various Scythian peoples who descended upon them from central Asia. The chief of these peoples, known to the Romans in later days by the name of Indo-Scythians,[1] founded a great empire in eastern Iran and north-west India, which the Indians called the Empire of the Kūshāns (Kūshāṇa) from the name of the reigning dynasty. The Kūshān emperors, the most famous of whom was Kanishka, held northern India under their domination during the second half of the first century and the whole of the second century of our era. But the seat of their power was still the former Greek kingdom, the more or less Hellenized land of Gandhāra and the Punjāb. It is, moreover, worthy of note that they carried on the traditions of the Greek rulers to a very great extent and also played the part of protectors of Hellenism in these regions. Their coins, like those of their Greek prede-

[1] Called by the Chinese Yue-chi.

FIGURE 69

Māvalipuram. Sculptured monolith, seventh century.
— *Photo, Goloubew*

cessors, continued to be bilingual and frequently bore Greek inscriptions. Like the later Greek kings and like Menander several of them protected or even adopted Buddhism. The Buddhist Scriptures are full of the praises of King Kanishka. Moreover, in 1908 a Buddhist reliquary, bearing the name and portrait of that king, was found at Shāh-jī-kī-dhērī, near Peshawar, which was the work of a Greek or Eurasian named Agesilaus (in Prakrit Agiśala). And, lastly, we have a coin of Kanishka bearing a standing Buddha with the aureole and nimbus and draperies in the Greek fashion, and the word *Boddō* in Greek characters as its legend — a coin proclaiming the birth of Greco-Buddhist art.

The Greco-Buddhist school, also known, from the name of one of its principal centres, as the school of Gandhāra, is the easternmost school of Greco-Roman art in Asia, working in the cause of Buddhism. According to Monsieur Foucher, it must have taken shape in those sheltered communities of Kābul in which Hellenism had taken root so firmly, and hence at a period when it was already well acclimatized there — that is, towards the later days of the domination of the Indo-Greek kings. This school was to reach its highest point about the first century of our era, at which period the fine Greco-Roman art of the Cæsars and of the Flavian dynasty exerted a considerable influence over the taste of the Kūshān sovereigns. In the second and third centuries it was to follow the general tendency by which Hellenistic art, hitherto so supple and free, was to become transformed into an art which was specifically Roman — even Gallo-Roman in the west and Palmyrene in the east — a graver, heavier, more squat type of art. Greco-Buddhist art held its own, none the less, through the fourth century and well on into the fifth. Towards the middle and end of the period during which it flourished, in the third, fourth, and fifth centuries, it even gave rise to a style of profound originality, revealed to us by the fine school of Haḍḍa, which we shall describe below. This school was at the height of its achievement when, like the other

FIGURE 70

Māvalipuram. Arjuna-ratha.

— *Photo, Jouveau-Dubreuil*

"Gandhārian" schools, it was practically destroyed by the Hun invasions at the beginning of the sixth century.

FIGURE 71

Māvalipuram. Gaja-Lakshmī (Lakshmī with the elephants) from the cave of the *Varāha avatāra* (boar-avatar), seventh century.
— *Photo, Goloubew*

The essential innovation of the Gandhāra school is that of representing in sculpture the figures of Buddha and of various Buddhist saints which the old native school at Bhārhut and Sāñchī represented only by symbols. For the first time we see the legend of Buddha represented on the bas-reliefs in its entirety: the cycle of the Incarnation, with our bodhisattva descending into his mother's womb in the form of a young elephant; the cycle of the Nativity, in which Queen Māyā is standing beneath the tree in the garden of Lumbinī, with the child springing forth from her right side and being received by the gods Indra and Brahmā; the scene of the Seven Steps and the bath of the new-born child, in which, by a curious coincidence, we see the Greeks creating for the Buddha the same type of divine infant, or "*sacro*

FIGURE 72
The Kailāsa at Ellora. Battle of elephants.
— *Photo, Goloubew*

bambino," with its charming nudity and aureole of gravity, as Christian art was to discover for the child Jesus. Again, in the same vein, we have the horoscope uttered by the anchorite Asita, as he holds the child upon his knee in homely fashion in the presence of the King and Queen.[1]

All the scenes in the life of the bodhisattva follow in like fashion, so impossible was it for the Greeks, with their instinctive anthropomorphism, to understand the scruples of the earliest Indian sculptors against representing the life of the Blessed One. And so we see the youthful bodhisattva at school, astonishing his master by his knowledge — a reminiscence, in a provincial style, of some Roman fresco.

[1] See A. Foucher: *L'Art gréco-bouddhique du Gandhāra*, Vol. I (Paris, 1905), pp. 290–599.

Or we see his future wife, Gopā, being presented to him — a beautiful lady in Roman costume with a certain Asiatic languor. The contest in swordsmanship and boxing to which the bodhisattva was forced to submit before his betrothal was to provide the Greek artists with

FIGURE 73
Śiva and Pārvatī, Kailāsa.
— *Photo, Goloubew*

themes after their own heart. The first meditation of the young man beneath the jambu-tree and the country scenes are less happily treated, for the animal sculpture of the Gandhāra school, unlike that of native artists, was but poor. Among much that is commonplace, the Sleep of the Women was to suggest some scenes of women's life that are quite correct in style. The Great Departure and the farewell to the good horse Kaṇṭhaka are likewise treated with great truth to nature, but here again it is unfortunate that, nine times out of ten, the artists responsible for these bas-reliefs were only mediocre artisans, with no talent whatever for animal sculpture. There is undoubtedly a greater realism in the meetings with the Brahman anchorites and the representations of Buddha as an ascetic (the "austerities of Gautama"), for in these the Hellenizing sculptors were dealing with a subject already classic in the West — the commonplace theme of the bearded philosopher, which they had merely to repeat here. Besides which their knowledge of anatomy had free scope in the treatment of the shrunken bodies of the ascetics.

Starting from the scene of the Illumination, the Gandhāra artists created the traditional type of Buddha as repeated from that time onwards: as a Greek sage, standing or seated in the Indian fashion, draped in the ample monastic cloak, or *saṃghāṭi,* which is here treated like a toga (Fig. 22); the head is that of an Apollo, distinguished merely by the topknot of hair for the traditional turban of the nobles, or *ushṇīsha,* by the mark of wisdom between the eyes, or *ūrṇā,* the lengthening of the lobes of the ears (caused by the heavy ear-rings worn by the former Prince Siddhārtha), and, in case of need, by the aureole, an Oriental invention with which Greco-Levantine art was to endow the Buddhist saints in the East and those of Christianity in the West (Fig. 17–18).[1]

Round this type of Buddha, this figure of a Greek philosopher with the head of an Apollo, were grouped all the scenes of the Buddhist canon, from the Illumination to the *nirvāṇa:* the attack of Mārā, with monsters which are here rather lacking in character, the preaching to the five original disciples, the conversion of the Kāśyapa anchorites (miracles of the fire and serpent), the forced ordination of

[1] Cf. A. Foucher: "The Greek Origin of the Buddha Type," in *Beginnings of Buddhist Art,* p. 112; Foucher: *L'Art gréco-bouddhique du Gandhāra,* II, 278–362. An opposite view is expressed by Ananda Coomaraswamy in "The Origin of the Buddha Image," *Art Bulletin,* Vol. IX, No. 4 (Washington, 1927).

Nanda; next come the conversion of the ogre of Āṭavī, the monkey's offering, and the submission of the serpent divinity (*nāga*) Apalāla — three scenes in which, by the way of exception, the reliefs at Gandhāra succeed in presenting certain picturesque features. The same picturesqueness, and the same naturalistic treatment of animals — qualities all the more remarkable here because they are so rare — appear in the scene of the visit of Indra to Buddha during his meditations, with the monkey, which is also meditating, the birds, the lion, and the antelope, in a bas-relief from Loriyān Tangai in the Calcutta Museum. On the other hand, the great miracle of Śrāvastī, by which water and flames were produced at the same time, is rendered with the greatest fidelity, though coldly, too, in the manner of the miracles of Christ in Byzantine art. As for the *nirvāṇa,* this is naturally one of the scenes most frequently represented: the Buddha is at rest, lying on his right side, with his head supported upon his right hand; though in this position, the garments have preserved the same folds as in an upright posture; around him are disciples and holy women in lamentation; next come scenes representing the burial, the placing on the bier, and the cremation, in the presence of the same figures: scenes which are on the whole fairly analogous with those of our *Pietàs* and Entombments of Christ. Last come the "War" and the removal and veneration of the relics, completing the Gandhārian cycle of the life of Buddha.

As we turn over the reproductions of this series of bas-reliefs in Monsieur Foucher's volumes,[1] if we forget for a moment the strictly Buddhist subjects which inspire them, we obtain an impression as of a sort of life of Christ related by Greco-Roman artists — and Roman rather than Greek. A person knowing nothing of history might imagine that a form of Christianity had conquered the Roman Empire as early as the first century, so that Romanesque and Gothic art had thus been preceded by an official Christian art in the Rome of the Cæsars.

[1] *L'Art gréco-bouddhique du Gandhāra,* Vol. I (bas-reliefs), etc.

Christianity was to base its iconography upon the models of the classic Olympus. On the same principle, the figures of the Buddhist pantheon are here rendered by their equivalents in the Greco-Roman pantheon. The Buddha, as we have seen, is an Apollo with the addition of the insignia of the Buddha; and the same type, with a different

FIGURE 74
Dance of Śiva at Ellora.
— *Photo, Goloubew*

head-dress and attributes, was to serve for the six Buddhas of the past who preceded Śākyamuni and for his presumed successor, the future Buddha Maitrēya. It is the Apollo type, again, which served for the bodhisattvas, but this time it is an Indianized Apollo, transformed into a young rajah, with the full costume of the Punjabi or Awadhi nobles of the Kūshān period; a rich, puffed turban enriched with jewels, if the figure is of Prince Siddhārtha, or the Brahman top-knot, more or less adorned, if it is a figure of Maitrēya; the drapery of the *dhoṭī*, leaving the bust, or at least the right-hand side of the breast, uncovered; and, over all, a profusion of jewels, necklaces, bangles, and bracelets both above the elbow and at the wrist, pendants, neck-chains, ear-rings, etc. And finally, to complete the distinction between the Buddha and the bodhisattva, we find the moustache, a new fashion, it would seem, for it was unknown to the *kshatriyas* of Bhārhut and Sāñchī and would seem to have been brought into north-west India by the Scythian conquerors (Fig. 19–20).[1] This same royal type, directly copied from the society of the day, was also used to represent the Brahmanical gods who were concerned in the life of Buddha — Indra and Brahmā.

On the other hand, the heads of demons and *yakshas* were for the most part borrowed from the types of bearded genii usual in Greek sculpture, from the grotesque figures of the Kerameikos to the heads of Zeus, Hephæstus, Herakles, or Poseidon. The familiar genius Vajrapāṇi, with his thunderbolt, was often copied from a Zeus, if he was not rendered in the style of a Herakles, an Eros, a Hermes, or a Dionysos. Certain *yakshas* became *atlantes* (i.e., male figures analogous to caryatids). The Indian theme of a *garuḍa* carrying off a *nāgī* is interpreted in terms of the Alexandrian motive of Ganymede carried off by the eagle of Zeus, and some *nāgīs* are represented as bacchants. The genius of wealth, Pāñchika or Kuvēra, king of the *yakshas,* will be sometimes an Indian rajah of the type mentioned above, sometimes an Alexandrian youth.

And now what judgment are we to pass on all these works? From the iconographical point of view their interest can hardly be exaggerated, for, thanks to the fidelity with which they follow the accepted Buddhist traditions, they enable us to follow step by step, without symbols or puzzling enigmas, the legend of the Buddha, as

[1] Cf. Foucher: *L'Art gréco-bouddhique du Gandhāra*, II, 210–43.

related, for example, in the *Lalitavistara.* But from the æsthetic point of view the position is very different. It is obvious that the Gandhāra school, with its faces which are often weak and lacking in character, its conventional motives adapted to order, and, we may add, its commonplaces, cannot possibly be compared to the school of Sāñchī in sincerity of faith and emotion or spontaneity of inspiration, still less with the later schools of the Gupta and Pallava periods. But it would be a false interpretation of its nature to class it with the Indian schools. On the other hand, if we set it in its legitimate place, among the Hellenic schools, it cuts a most honourable figure there. Instead of putting the Gandhāra school in the shade by contrasting it with Gupta art, we should compare it with that of Alexandria, Pergamon, and the various schools of Romano-Asiatic or Romano-Syrian art, when it will assume its full value (Fig. 22, 23, 24). And, better still, the Indian characteristics of this sculpture, which were hardly discernible before, will be thrown into relief

FIGURE 75
Relief known as the "Nuptials of Śiva and Pārvatī" (in reality a *Gaṅgād haramūrti*), Elephanta.
— *Photo, Goloubew*

by this contrast. Then what we shall often find is no longer a commonplace copy of a decadent Apollo, but, beneath his flowing Greek draperies, a youth with a strange charm, like the new gods who were at that time conquering the West — some Mithras or Adonis. And when the type becomes still more Indian in the rendering of the bodhisattva princes, with their moustaches, turbans, nude torsos, necklaces, and bracelets, we shall find the proud face of a true rajah — as in the bodhisattva of Shāhbāz-garhī, brought back to the Louvre by Monsieur Foucher (Fig. 19; cf. Fig. 20), and the similar bodhisattvas of Bunēr or Sahri-Bahlol reproduced in Vol. II of Foucher's *L'Art gréco-bouddhique du Gandhāra.*

Moreover, in speaking of Greco-Buddhist art it is no doubt necessary to distinguish between the different periods. If we take the works of the first century — for instance, the profile of Buddha presented to the Louvre by Monsieur Foucher, or the head of Buddha with wavy hair treated in the Greek style, presented to the Musée Guimet by M. Georges Clemenceau (Fig. 18) — we shall find the true Hellenic characteristics to which we drew attention above, in all their freshness: the profile, in particular, has still its Apollo-like pride. The same quality is to be seen in the bas-reliefs included in the Clemenceau donation to the Musée Guimet, with their Buddhas, their bodhisattvas, and their *dēvatas* (divinities) nobly draped in the *himation,* which has now become the monastic cloak or *saṃghāṭi.* We shall still find these noble draperies even much later, in the terracottas turned out in quantity, as is proved by the charming figurines brought back in 1924 from Haḍḍa in Afghanistan to the Musée Guimet by Monsieur and Madame André Godard, or sent to the museum by Monsieur Barthoux from the same spot in 1928 (Fig. 22–26).

If, on the other hand, we pause before the relief of the Buddha of the Great Miracle (Miracle of Śrāvastī) brought back by Monsieur Hackin from Pātāvā in Afghanistan in 1925, we shall find signs of

FIGURE 76
So-called "Relief of the kiss," Kailāsa.
— *Photo, Goloubew*

profound development. This is a magnificent work, but in quite a different style (Fig. 21). Whereas the Clemenceau Buddhas have an affinity with the art of the Julio-Claudian and Flavian dynasties, the relief brought back by Monsieur Hackin reminds one of the art of the later Roman Empire, with the rather squat forms of the time of Diocletian. The treatment of the drapery is a sufficient illustration of this difference: in the Clemenceau figures it is still classical, but in the Buddha of Pātāvā it has become conventionalized and clings to the body as though wet, thus furnishing us with the transitional stage between the draped figures of the Gandhāra school and the nude forms of Gupta art. Thus we may draw a double lesson from the study of these works: on the one hand a sure conviction that the Greco-Buddhist art of Gandhāra, a provincial school of Greco-Roman art, followed the general evolution of this art from the age of Augustus down to the Tetrarchy; and on the other hand the conclusion that the art of Gandhāra gradually lost ground before an "Indian revival" which leads us on by an imperceptible transition to the native classicism known by the name of Gupta art.

Lastly, a new piece of evidence has just been provided by the stucco figurines, no doubt of rather a late date, between the third and the fifth centuries, discovered at Haḍḍa, near Jelālābād, by Monsieur Godard's and Monsieur Barthoux's archæological missions and sent by them to the Musée Guimet in very large numbers. The first thing that strikes us — and we need only pause before the first cabinet of stucco figures arranged by Monsieur Hackin at the entrance of the new room — is the purity of the classical tradition. As a matter of fact, while in its native country the tradition of Hellas froze into the art of the ages of Diocletian and Constantine, at Haḍḍa Alexandrian, Ephesian, and Pergamene Greece and the Greece of Antioch continued to live on, revivified by the Buddhist influence grafted on to them. On Buddhist soil Greece remained Greece, while in Christian

FIGURE 77

Śiva, Pārvatī, and Rāvaṇa, Kailāsa.

— *Photo, Goloubew*

countries it was becoming Byzantium. If, as Monsieur Hackin thinks, the stucco figures from Haḍḍa date for the most part from the period of the third to the fifth centuries, is it not permissible to state that the Hellenic genius, as a creative force and principle of renewal, took refuge and survived at Kābul? In several works in this set of figures we find a departure from the too often conventional, commonplace, and insipid Greco-Buddhist style as we had hitherto known it. Side by side with the everlasting Buddhas of the Apollo type, which deserve to be so characterized, we are surprised to find among the representations of subsidiary divinities, such as Vajrāpaṇi, *yakshas,* barbarians, and demons, figures of a rich intensity of feeling and a powerful realism which were curiously unexpected (Fig. 26). Instead of the conventional figures of barbarians which were all that Gandhāra had to offer so far, we have here real racial types full of character, speaking portraits of Aryan Scythians of the Gaulish type, Persians like those of the mosaic at Arbela, or flat-nosed Mongols. But above all, this creative force shows itself in the creation of what we may call a " Gothico-Buddhist " art. Every visitor who passes by the stucco figures of the Musée Guimet utters the same exclamation: " Gothic! " There are bearded heads of divinities among them which recall the fine figure of God at Amiens or the saint on the south-west portal at Reims; there are demons in scenes of the Assault of Māra which no longer have any affinity with Greek art, but are akin to the devils — whether decorative heads, caryatids, or gargoyles — of Reims, Amiens, and Notre-Dame, Paris. There is a tiny terracotta head here, with a smile like that of the angels at Reims, spiritual, penetrating, and acute. And there is another large figure bringing flowers in a fold of its garment to cast beneath the feet of the bodhisattva, which is again almost like an angel from Reims. Here are some curious beardless heads whose solid construction, intense expression, and value as portraits — not to speak of their head-dress, a sort of cowl or hood — no longer have any kinship with the antique, but proclaim themselves definitely mediæval: they might be pages or clerics of the Burgundian school. We find here troopers with moustaches, or, again, an *écorché* (study of muscles) worthy of Ligier Richier. Thus the plaster figures from Haḍḍa already foreshadow and herald the whole of the Christian sculpture of France, including the realistic school of fourteenth-century French Gothic. Christs in glory or Christs in judgment, apostles and King Davids, angels and youths, figures in hats recalling our pages and fools, caryatids, faces of demons and gargoyles — the statuettes of dried clay from Haḍḍa, as they appear in the second cabinet at the Musée Guimet, seem like anticipations of all our mediæval types — a Gothic dating from a thousand years previous to our own, which could have had no influence on ours either geographically or in point of time, and whose development can only be explained by some philosophical theory, as illustrating some law of the human mind! [1]

In our opinion, we have here a fact whose import goes beyond the domain of Greco-Buddhist art and is of exceptional importance for the general history of art. We may state it as follows: as the Middle Ages drew near, the *Greco-Roman art of the Far East,* when left to its own devices and evolving in accordance with its own traditions, was busy, at the very moment when it was brutally destroyed by the invasion of the Huns, in inventing the very formulas towards which the Greco-Roman art of western Europe was to work its way some centuries later — the Romanesque and the Gothic.

This law may perhaps be explained as follows: given, both in the West and at Gandhāra, the purely formal conventions of Greco-Roman art as a basis — Gallo-Roman in the West, Greco-Buddhist at Gandhāra — we next see the rise of two great world religions — Latin Christianity in the West and the Buddhism of Mayhāyāna on the Indo-Afghan frontier — which upset the general conception of life and

[1] See Sir John Marshall: *Excavations at Taxila; the Stūpas and Monasteries at Jauliān,* Memoirs of the Archæological Survey of India, No. 7 (1921); J. J. Barthoux: *Les Fouilles de Haḍḍa, Mémoires de la Délégation Archéologique Française en Afghanistan* (Paris, 1930).

FIGURE 78
The river-goddess Yamunā, Kailāsa.
— *Photo, Goloubew*

FIGURE 79

The river-goddess Sarasvatī, Kailāsa.

— *Photo, Goloubew*

raise the mind above itself. These two religions, though of course differing in their dogmas, are each inspired by a similar idealism and mysticism, a poetical type of piety and sensibility which had much in common. Under the influence of these two higher types of idealism we may see the Greco-Roman substratum undergoing two parallel processes of transformation, which follow similar laws in almost identical fashion. Without any possible geographical contact or any imaginable historical communication, Gothic was invented twice over at an interval of a thousand years — undoubtedly by no means the least curious of the adventures of the human mind. Let us hasten to add that this theory applies to the field of Gandhārian art, properly so called. It is a matter of fact that this Greco-Buddhist style existed in Afghanistan and was carried farther and farther afield by the missionaries of Śākyamuni, century after century, across central Asia; and that from it, as we shall show in the third volume of this work, was to be derived the great Wei art of China in the fifth and sixth centuries.

We might attempt to establish a similar connexion between its ideals and those of Byzantium. A fresco from Haḍḍa at the Musée Guimet, representing a standing Buddha with nimbus and aureole, with his hand in the *abhaya mudrā* (a Christian benediction!), is an anticipation of the Romano-Byzantine Christ in its attitude, its theological spirit, its pictorial technique, and its general convention.

Another conclusion to be drawn from the Afghan finds is that of the importance of the Iranian element in the formation of this Buddhist art on the frontier of central Asia. The old Bactrian province must have been subdued about 230 by the great Sāsānian king Ardashīr; about 303–310 we even see the Sāsānid Hormizd II becoming the father-in-law, and doubtless the suzerain, of the last Kūshān king of Kābul. From that time until the fifth century Bactria was a dependency of Persia; after which it was invaded by the horde of the Ephthalite Huns. It was next conquered by the Sāsānid king Khosrau I about 566, and it was not till the end of that century that it was definitely wrested from Persia by the Turks.

The long association of a Sāsānid viceroy with the Buddhist church in Bactria explains the correspondence revealed by the frescoes at Bāmiyān (Afghanistan). The celebrated frescoes studied in 1924–5 by Monsieur and Madame André Godard and Monsieur Hackin, and in 1929–30 by Messieurs Hackin and Carle, show us Gandhārian Buddhas and Indo-Gupta genii side by side with Sāsānid kings and equally Iranian lords.[1] The Sāsānid kings, bearded and wearing tiaras, are certainly those of the reliefs of Naqsh-i Rustam and Naqsh-i Rajab, and form an exact transition between the Mazdean of Iran and the hitherto inexplicable Sāsāno-Buddhist of the Khotan (Dandān-uiliq) region, brought by Sir Aurel Stein to the British Museum. But it is the beardless Iranian lords at Bāmiyān who give us the most delightful surprise. At the very first glance we feel convinced that they are the prototypes of the famous horsemen, showing Persian influences, discovered by Von Le Coq on the frescoes at Qizil, near Kūcha in the Gobi region. In this connexion nothing could be more significant than a comparison between the solar and lunar genii of the niche of Buddha, some 180 feet in size, at Bāmiyān, copied by Madame André Godard for the Musée Guimet (fifth century), and the elegant young men who painted their own portraits in the "Grotto of Paintings" at Qizil, fragments of which were brought to Berlin by Herr Von Le Coq (sixth–seventh centuries). We can feel no further doubts on the subject: these slender noblemen of Kūcha, tightly wrapped in their long, wide-flapped tunics, standing tiptoe upon the walls of the Museum für Völkerkunde, are certainly the direct heirs, both in type and in costume, of the genii of the Irano-Buddhist princes whose image has been yielded up to us by Bāmiyān — until we come to Dukhtar-i Nūshirvān. The same

[1] A. Godard, Y. Godard, and J. Hackin: *Les Antiquités bouddhiques de Bāmiyān*, with notes by Professor Pelliot (Paris, Van Oest, 1928).

chivalrous aristocracy, with the same arts and fashions, is to be found in Greater Iran from Afghanistan to the remotest oasis of the desert of Gobi.

Thus the Greco-Buddhist (or Gothico-Buddhist) art and the Irano-Buddhist art of the Punjāb and of Afghanistan appear as the antechamber to the art of central Asia. It was in them that the schools took shape which we shall afterwards see developing in Khotan, Kūcha, and Turfān and as far afield as Tun-huang. The latter can show no faces which do not already appear — down to the square construction and central Asiatic impasto — in certain Haḍḍa figurines and frescoes of Bāmiyān, in some of the many heads of Buddhas, bodhisattvas, and flying genii.

But here we are departing from the subject of the present volume. In order to follow out the history of "Buddhist Gothic" we should have to leave India and transport ourselves to the China of the Wei period in the fifth century — the transition to which is, moreover, provided by a little slate relief from Haḍḍa with a bodhisattva seated in European fashion — that is, with crossed legs — in his niche, which has obvious analogies with the reliefs photographed by Chavannes in the Wei grottoes of Yun-Kang (see Vol. III of the present work, chapter ii, and Fig. 103–170).

In India, however, Buddhist art had followed an entirely different development.

GUPTA ART: THE FORMATION OF THE INDIAN ÆSTHETIC IDEAL

The domination of the various foreign dynasties which had so long held sway over northern India at last came to an end in the third and fourth centuries of our era, when a great national empire, that of the Gupta dynasty, was founded in the eastern part of the Ganges basin in the former land of Magadha (Behar and Bengal), and ruled over northern and central India during the whole of the fourth century and three-quarters of the fifth. After the fall of the Gupta Empire another great Indian empire arose, again on the Ganges, in the first half of the seventh century, under King Harsha of Kanauj. As for the Deccan, it had preserved its independence under a number of native dynasties, the chief of which was that of the Andhras, lasting from about 200 B.C. to A.D. 200 and succeeded by that of the Pallava, lasting from the third to the eighth centuries.

It was under these various national dynasties that an æsthetic ideal which may properly be called Indian took definitive shape, by developing the indigenous elements existing at Bhārhut and Sāñchī and adapting the foreign elements of Gandhāra.

This æsthetic ideal is already present in the earliest art of Mathurā, which was contemporary with that of Gandhāra, since both of them flourished during the first two centuries of our era, under the rule of the Indo-Scythian or Kūshān kings. The Buddhas of the Mathurā school, which are fairly well represented in the museums of Mathurā and Sārnāth-Benares, are definitely distinct from those of Gandhāra.[1] Mr. A. Coomaraswamy, who has made a special study of them, notes their distinguishing characteristics as follows: the head is shaven, with no curls; when necessary, the *ushṇīsha* is in the form of a spiral; there is no *ūrṇā* between the eyes; the right shoulder is always bare; the chest is very full; the drapery clings closely to the body, so closely that its conventionalized folds give the impression of a wet garment; the general expression is vigorous rather than gentle. Mr. Coomaraswamy thinks that this style (which was also used at Mathurā for Jain statues) owes nothing to Greco-Buddhistic models, and that it is this school far more than the Greco-Buddhist one which created the first representations of Buddha. We must admit that, in spite of this eminent archæologist's arguments, we adhere to

[1] See Philippe Vogel: *La Sculpture de Mathurā*, Collection *Ars Asiatica*, Vol. XV (Paris, Van Oest, 1930), Pl. XXVI; Coomaraswamy: "Sculptures from Mathurā," *Bulletin of the Museum of Fine Arts, Boston*, Vol. XXV, No. 150 (August 1927), pp. 50–4.

the old theory, held by Monsieur Foucher, which, on the contrary, regards the Buddhas or Jinas of Mathurā as an Indian adaptation of the art of Gandhāra. Here again the transition from the heavy draperies of Gandhāra to the " wet " garments of Mathurā seems to us to be logically a step in the direction of the " Gupta nudes " of the next period (cf. Fig. 42). Similarly, the exaggerated force which characterizes these works seems to us to reveal a certain awkwardness on the part of the Indian sculptors who had inherited the plastic traditions of Gandhāra, until the time when they found their perfect expression in the melting softness of Gupta art. For the rest, this " Indian revival " finds free scope in the nude female figures of the Kūshān period in the museum at Mathurā, and especially in the group of the woman and child, which seems to have been a particular favourite of this school. We still find here the same ideal of feminine beauty as at Bhārhut and Sāñchī, the full bust and the heavy breasts contrasting with the slender waist, and the sideward thrust of the hip elevated into an æsthetic canon.[1] But, while losing none of its intoxicating charm, this voluptuous style of Indian beauty now gained in refinement. Its proportions became more harmonious, its seduction more sophisticated. We are on the way towards Amarāvatī and Māvalipuram. There is a statue in the Musée Guimet (Fig. 84–85) which, well on in the Middle Ages, seems to be in harmony with the tradition of these studies of motherhood at Mathurā.

At Amarāvatī the artistic evolution is more continuous.[2] This city of the eastern Deccan, between the mouths of the Godāvarī and the

[1] Philippe Vogel, op. cit., Pl. XVIII–XIX.

[2] Cf. A. Foucher: "*Les Sculptures d'Amarāvatī,*" *Revue des arts asiatiques*, V, i, 9; A. Coomaraswamy: "*La Sculpture buddhique,*" ibid., V, iv, 244–52; L. Bachhofer: *Early Indian Sculpture*, II, Pl. 108–131; Codrington: *Ancient India* (1926), Pl. 27; T. N. Ramachandran: "Buddhist Sculptures from a Stūpa near Goli, Guntur District," *Bulletin of the Madras Government Museum*, I, i (Madras, 1929); M. S. Dimand: "Two Indian Reliefs of the Amarāvatī School," *Bulletin of the Metropolitan Museum of Art, New York*, No. 10 (October 1928), p. 238; M. S. Dimand: "A New Indian Relief of the Amarāvatī School," ibid., Vol. XXV, No. 5 (May 1930), p. 131.

Kṛishṇā, was for a time the capital of the powerful kingdom of the Andhras — the Andaræ of Pliny — which lasted, as we have said, from the second century B.C. till the third century of our era and constituted what was in many respects an "Indian India," a refuge

FIGURE 80
Vishṇu as the lion-king, Ellora.
— *Photo, Goloubew*

for the national genius, as opposed to the Greco-Scythian governments established in the north.[1] The art of the region of Amarāvatī (Fig. 31), as we can admire it in the Madras Museum, and now in the Musée Guimet as well, forms a peculiarly precious link between the ancient schools of Bhārhut and Sāñchī and mediæval Hindu art. The breach of continuity caused in the north by imitation of the

[1] See Devaprasad Gosh: "Development of Buddhist Art in South India," *Indian Historical Quarterly*, 1928, pp. 724–40.

Hellenistic style did not occur here, where the Indian genius pursued its development freely, with nothing to thwart its tendencies. In fact, such a figure as the woman carrying a *chaurī*, or fly-fan, on a relief in the Musée Guimet, from the region of Amarāvatī, is, both in costume and in physiognomy, a racial type in the earliest Indian manner which might have come from Sāñchī (Fig. 27). Similarly, in the fine marble relief of the Temptation of Māra from Nāgārjunikoṇḍa, which seems to date from the second century of our era (Fig. 28), the Buddha, in accordance with the manner of the early school, is represented only by his traditional symbols: the bodhi-tree, the empty seat, and the footprints. In the figures of his temptresses, too, we may admire some nude female figures which have still some affinity with the *yakshiṇī* of Sāñchī, while the elephants of the demon army and the various animals in the lower frieze likewise display the vigorous and supple realism and the synthetic power which were to remain the heritage of Indian animal-sculptors from Aśoka's pillar at Sārnāth down to Māvalipuram.[1]

On the next relief, which, though belonging to the same group, is of a later date — the fourth century — and represents " The Life in the Women's Quarters " (Fig. 29) and " The Sleep of the Women " (Fig. 30), we still see the same naïve paganism and innocent delight in the nude as were revealed to us by the masters of Bhārhut and Sāñchī. Here, indeed, thanks to the more perfect technique, we even find a more refined sensuality and a still more delightful freshness. Has the chisel ever been wielded with a more caressing touch, or expressed such love of life, as in the group of the little seated queen being helped to her feet by a dwarf or a little child — or is the child teasing her? The fact is that a profound change has meanwhile taken place: the bodhisattva, who had hitherto been indicated merely by allusive symbols in the scene of the Temptation, is now represented.

[1] The same naturalistic style inspires the animal reliefs on the well-known moonstones of Ceylon.

For in the mean time the example of Gandhāra had spread as far as the Deccan. Moreover, on a fourth relief, which shows us the Buddha surrounded by praying figures, we find a true Buddha of the Gan-

FIGURE 81
Mahēśamūrti (triple image of Śiva) of Elephanta.
— *Photo, Goloubew. By permission of Messrs. Van Oest*

dhāra school, which is all the more striking because the scene immediately below it on the same slab shows us types which are more specifically Indian. We may add that, not far from this scene, Monsieur Jouveau-Dubreuil has also discovered, and sent to the Musée Guimet, a curious head of Buddha which is not Greco-Buddhist, but "Romano-Buddhist," the lower part of the face being of a curiously Neronian type. This should not surprise us too much when we remember that close at hand was found a coin of the Cæsars — an obvious piece of evidence, as Monsieur Jouveau-Dubreuil remarks, of the maritime relations which formerly existed between Roman Egypt and the Andhra kingdom.

This group of scenes from Amarāvatī is, moreover, remarkably varied, without losing any of its obvious unity. There are as many styles as there are scenes. After the figures in the relief of the "Life in the Women's Quarters," which are so sensual as to seem almost melted into softness by their own ardour, we find in a fifth relief of a later date — the sixth or even the fifth century — figures of princes or women whose slender and almost Botticellian elegance foreshadows the frescoes of Ajaṇṭā.

The school of Amarāvatī can show many a scene which is a veritable picture in stone, perfect in its composition, by some very great, though unknown, artist. We need only look at the medallion containing the story of the infuriated elephant, now in the Madras Museum (Fig. 32). Drugged by the treacherous Dēvadatta, the beast is let loose in the Buddha's path, and charges the crowd, overturning everything. We can see it on the left seizing an unfortunate man and hurling him away. The impetus of the charging beast, the terror of the crowd, the gesture of the two lovers who cast themselves into each other's arms in the face of death — this whole scene of panic forms a striking contrast to the sequel as shown on the right-hand side of the medallion, where the beast, tamed by "the power of Buddha's kindliness," prostrates itself before the calm and smiling Blessed One.[1]

[1] The same scene is represented on a sculptured stone recently found at Nāgārjuṅikoṇḍa, near Amarāvatī. See P. Vogel: "Further Discoveries on the Site of Nāgārjuṅikoṇḍa," *Annual Bibliography of Indian Archæology* for 1927, Kern Institute, Leiden, 1929, Pl. V.

We have mentioned the elegance of the nude figures in the second Amarāvatī manner. Some of the nude female figures are real *tours de force* — for example, those in the scene of the women prostrating themselves at the feet of the Buddha (Fig. 33).[1] Further on we are shown some handsome young prince, in the midst of his court of servants and undressed women, clad in nothing but a light waist-cloth, and leaning on his elbow upon his throne of state in a pose of ineffable pride (Fig. 36).[2] Or, again, in the Adoration of the *stūpa* (Fig. 38) and in the descent of the elephant of the Conception, whose miraculous shrine is borne by the gods (Fig. 39), we may observe the nude figures of very elongated proportions hovering in the air or dancing, and the extraordinary elasticity of their movements, which are characteristic of one whole side of the art of Amarāvatī and foreshadow that of Aihoḷe and Māvalipuram (Fig. 40).[3] By this time we have travelled far from Sāñchī. Or, rather, the purely naturalistic art of Sāñchī has now become spiritualized by a higher influence, which has raised life to a higher plane and attained an idealism of the highest order. And so we come to Gupta art.

[1] Among the most delightful works of the school of Amarāvatī treated in this way, I would draw particular attention to the two nude female figures seated in postures of amazing freedom, with crossed or bent legs, one on each side of a prince on his throne, which form part of a carved stone recently found at Nāgārjunikoṇḍa. I know few studies of the nude so moving in their slender grace. Even the nudes of the Alexandrian school would almost seem cold by comparison. This scene is reproduced by P. Vogel in the *Annual Bibliography of Indian Archæology* for the year 1927, Kern Institute, Leiden, 1929, Pl. V. The same remark applies to the circular relief at Amarāvatī showing serpent deities (*nāgas*) in attitudes of adoration round the Buddha's alms-dish (reproduced in particular by P. Vogel, in *Indian Serpent-lore*, Pl. X, Fig. b). The same elasticity of movement may be noted in the early reliefs at Aṇurādhapura, Ceylon. See the "Annunciation," in the Colombo Museum, reproduced in the *Ceylon Journal of Science*, Section G, Vol. I, Pt. 3 (edited by M. Hocart), Pl. XLII. The connexion between Ceylon and Amarāvatī is equally evident in the "Miracle of Śrāvastī" in the Colombo Museum (ibid., Pl. XLIII), in two pillars from the northern tope, Aṇurādhapura (ibid., Pl. XLIV), and in the charming *nāgarāja* of the eastern tope, Aṇurādhapura (ibid., Pl. XLV).

[2] Cf. the *nāgarāja* from Goli in the same style, reproduced by Ramachandran in the *Bulletin of the Madras Government Museum*, New Series, I, i, "Buddhist Sculptures from Goli" (1929), Pl. IV, J; also W. Cohn: *Indische Plastik*, Pl. 18.

[3] See Henry Cousens: "The Ancient Temples of Aihoḷe," *Archæological Survey of India, Report, 1907–8*, p. 189, Pl. LXXVI, Fig. 6.

Gupta art, so called because it took shape in the Gangetic region under the reign of the great Gupta dynasty in the fourth and fifth centuries of our era, gave those tendencies which were becoming apparent in the later days of the school of Amarāvatī their supreme expression. The Gupta schools carried on and used for their own purposes both the plastic traditions of Amarāvatī, which were characterized by the utmost elegance, and the lush sensuality of Mathurā. But, in spite of the spirituality of its latest works, Amarāvatī was still, as a rule, too mundane and restless; the artists of the Gupta school were to enrich its style with a greater spirituality and tranquillity. Similarly, the pagan full-bloodedness of Mathurā, a survival from the old schools of Bhārhut and Kārlī,[1] could no longer suffice for an age so profoundly and subtly metaphysical as the Buddhist fourth century: the Gupta artists recast it in the mould of a new canon of beauty — and thus was born the æsthetic ideal of India.

FIGURE 82
Mahēśamūrti of Elephanta, detail.
— *Photo, Goloubew. By permission of Messrs. Van Oest*

[1] See P. Vogel: *La Sculpture de Mathurā*, Collection *Ars Asiatica*, Vol. XV (Paris, Van Oest, 1930), Pl. XVIII and XIX (pillars of Bhūtesar, Museum of Mathurā).

We say designedly a new *æsthetic ideal,* and not merely a new *art.* We may note that this Indian æsthetic ideal presupposes a philosophy familiar with the Greek æsthetic canon, but which no sooner became familiar with it than it emancipated itself from it and created for itself a canon of equal value. In thus shaking itself free from Greek classicism, which had degenerated at Gandhāra into the commonplace, Gupta art gave birth to a new classicism, and this time a living one, for it was conditioned by its own surroundings. Gupta art based its plastic conventions not only upon a knowledge of Indian costume and of the conditions of subtropical life, but also upon an understanding of the Indian body itself.[1] It did away with the draperies which cumbered these bodies accustomed to transparent muslins: drapery was henceforth indicated merely by the liquid undulations — one might almost call them ripples — of a diaphanous garment which seems to cling to the limbs as though wet; till the time came when even these undulations disappeared and the garment was indicated only by a restrained use of intersecting terminal lines.

At the same time Gupta sculpture restored to the Indian form its native softness and suppleness. In expressing the proportions of the body it took its measurements, not from the geometrical criteria of the Greeks, but from the living curves found in nature — in the habit of growth of a flower, in the flowing movement of the animal form beneath its fur or hide. The face was now to have the oval form of a finely shaped egg, till, in the Pāla art of Bengal, it came to follow the more nervous lines of the betel-leaf. The forehead, between the hair and the eyebrows, had to have the lines of a drawn bow. The regular line of the eyebrows had also to resemble a bow or the leaves of the neem-tree. The darting glance of a woman's eyes was compared to the wagtail, and their soft glance to the eyes of a roe, while the eyes of divinities were like the lotus. A woman's nose was like a sesame-flower, the "moist, soft, red" lips were comparable to the

1 See Abanindranath Tagore: *Some Notes on Indian Artistic Anatomy*, published by the Indian Society of Oriental Art, Calcutta, 1914.

red fruit of the bimba-tree. The form of the chin was expressed by the simile of a mango-stone, the line of the neck by that of a shell; the softness of the body was like the muzzle of a cow, and the hero's breast like the body of a lion. The shoulder and forearm were curved like an elephant's trunk, while the forearm was also compared to the bole of a banyan-tree, and the fingers had the fullness of a bean-pod; the calf of the leg swelled like a spawning fish, and the hands and feet were two lotus-flowers.

FIGURE 83
Mahēśamūrti, central face.
— *Photo, Goloubew*

As to the favourite pose of the body, and especially of the feminine body, it was that of " the three bendings (*tribhaṅga*) " — that is, with the head inclined towards the right (in female statues), and the bust turned towards the left, while, thanks to the Indian predilection for a sideward thrust of the hip, the legs would again turn towards the right. The pose of male statues would be the exact opposite, the head being inclined towards the left, and so forth. (See Abanindranath Tagore, op. cit.)

This care to imitate the curves of flowers and animals, this predilection for " compensating " attitudes, which cause the body to yield the utmost plastic effect of which it is capable and seem to offer it to one like some great drooping flower, infused fresh life into the Indian æsthetic ideal. From this time onwards, for ten centuries to come, it was to be inspired by a supreme sense of rhythmic beauty. In future nothing abrupt survived in it. The contours of the limbs were softened into a melting line of ineffable suavity. Thus was produced a composite, flexible, simple, and harmonious art in which, since no secondary detail was allowed to interrupt the general line, earthly beauty was to be the direct expression of the highest spirituality. Thus, although from this time onward the nude predominated, no nudity could be more chaste than that of Gupta art. Thus in the period between the naïvely pagan art of Sāñchī and the heavily sensual art of the southern Deccan in later days, we reach the highest flights of the Aryan soul.

The two most felicitous specimens of Gupta statuary are the Buddha of the museum at Sārnāth, seated in Indian fashion and making the gesture of preaching, known to Indian critics as the *dharma-chakra mudrā* (gesture of moving the Wheel of the Law), a brilliant sandstone figure some fifty-four inches in height (Fig. 41),[1] and the standing Buddha, about seven feet high, from Jamalpur, now in the museum at Mathurā (Fig. 42), the former of which is almost nude, the latter attired in a transparent drapery, while both are surrounded by the huge circular aureole of the Gupta school, and date from the fifth century of our era.[2] We may also mention the colossal copper Buddha of Sultānganj, now in the Birmingham Museum, a marvellous young Indian body living and breathing beneath the transparent muslin.[3] The limbs are pure and harmonious, the faces have a tranquil suavity, and it is inspired by an art so steeped in

1 Cf. Nanda Lal Bose: "A Stone Image of the Buddha in the Sārnāth Museum," in *Rūpam* for October 1925; F. O. Obertel: "Excavations at Sārnāth," *Archæological Survey of India, Report, 1904–5*, p. 84, Pl. XXIX; H. Hargreaves: "Excavations at Sārnāth," ibid., 1914–15, p. 97, Pl. LXIII.

2 Cf. P. Vogel: *La Sculpture de Mathurā, Ars Asiatica*, XV (1930), Pl. XXXII; and in the same work, three other beautiful Buddhas, of the Gupta school, now in the museums of Lucknow and Calcutta (Pl. XXXI).

3 Cf. Arunsen: "Bronze Buddha from the Birmingham Museum," in *Rūpam*, January 1925.

intellectualism as to be a direct expression of the soul through the purely ideal beauty of form. Perhaps we shall understand the character of these works better if we consider that they are contemporary with the luminous and fluid metaphysics of the great Indian idealists of the fifth century, an Asaṅga or a Vasubandhu. To adopt the term coined by V. Goloubew, we are here dealing with an art which is no longer Indo-Greek, but, having eliminated Greece and the West, is henceforth *Indo-classical.*

The art of Ceylon, Farther India, and the Malay Archipelago is also akin to the art of Amarāvatī and the Gupta art of the Ganges. A curious proof of this has recently come to light: there is a beautiful and well-known Buddha from Amarāvatī in the Madras Museum, attired in a monastic cloak hanging in small folds, and with the hair in close curls in the Gupta fashion. Now a replica of this figure has been found in Annam, among the Cham works at Dong-du'o'ng, and has been identified by Monsieur Victor Goloubew as coming from Ceylon (Fig. 43–44).[1] "The history of sculpture in Ceylon," says Monsieur Hocart, "begins with the school of Amarāvatī." Two works of that school, executed at Amarāvatī, one representing a Buddhist Annunciation, the other the Great Miracle, were found in a ruined building south of the Aṇurādhapura-Trincomalee road and are now in the Colombo Museum.[2] "Another fragment of a square pillar from the northern tope at Aṇurādhapura is marked by that slimness and vivacity in which the Amarāvatī sculptors delighted (Colombo Museum, No. 30)."[3] Ceylon was afterwards affected by Gupta influence. The early Gupta period is represented by a rather pleasing bas-relief of a man and woman at Isurumuniya (Aṇurādhapura),

[1] See *Bulletin de l'École Française d'Extrême Orient*, XXI (1922), p. 72, Pl. XI; *Archæological Survey of India, Report, 1905–6*, "Excavations at Amarāvatī," Pl. LI; and the bronze statuette of a Buddha discovered at Kohat, Siam, reproduced by Coedès, *Indian Art and Letters* (1930), I, Pl. B ("Indian Influences upon Siamese Art").

[2] A. M. Hocart: "Archæological Summary," in *Ceylon Journal of Science*, Section G, Vol. I, Pt. 3 (January 13, 1927), p. 95, Pl. XLII, XLIII.

[3] Ibid., Pl. XLIV.

which " shows considerably more mastery and freedom than the previous examples " (Hocart).[1] The best of the Sinhalese " moonstones " — that is, circular stones with processions of animals — belong to the end of the Amarāvatī school and the beginning of Gupta influences properly so called: for example, the celebrated moonstone of the so-called Queen's Pavilion at Aṇurādhapura, " a work executed in a very hard stone, with a care and delicacy which in no wise hamper the vitality; the elephants, as usual in Indian art," says Monsieur Hocart, " are much better understood than the other animals and would be hard to surpass; yet even the least real of the animals (bullock, lion, horse, goose) have considerable artistic merit." [2] But purely Gupta influence is evident in the splendid great Buddha of Aṇurādhapura, making the gesture of meditation (*dhyāna mudrā*), more than two yards in height, and dating from the fourth or fifth century, which Mr. A. Coomaraswamy justly admires as one of the masterpieces of Indian art — own brother to the Buddha of Sārnāth! At the end of the thirteenth century Sinhalese sculpture was still capable of producing masterpieces, such as the famous standing bearded statue of Potgul-Vihāre, at Poḷonnāruva, known as the statue of King Parākrama Bāhu I, represented reading a book, in an attitude of amazing dignity and calm majesty.[3]

In the course of the foregoing paragraphs we have alluded to certain finger-gestures (*mudrā*) or seated attitudes (*āsana*) of Buddhist statues. For, just as the art of Gandhāra stereotyped once and for all the traditional scenes in the life of Buddha, so Gupta art, with the Pāla art which was its continuation, established once and for all the religious and artistic canon of Buddhist gesture and attitude.

1 Ibid., Pl. XLVIII.
2 Ibid., Pl. LII B.
3 Cf. Hocart, op. cit., Pl. LVI. For Sinhalese art in general, see Coomaraswamy: *Mediæval Sinhalese Art* (London and Broad Campden, 1908).

In accordance with the sacred texts, the Buddha is generally represented as seated upon a lotus throne (*padmāsana*). In this pose of the *padmāsana* he is seated in the Indian fashion, with the legs crossed in such a way that each foot is made to lie upon the opposite thigh, with the sole upwards. One variant of this pose was that of the *vīrāsana,* " the pose of the hero," in which the right foot is hidden beneath the left leg instead of lying upon it. A second variant is the *yogāsana,* or seated pose of meditation, in which the knees are a little raised, and supported by a band, according to the custom of the yogis.

FIGURE 84
Relief called "Maternity" (perhaps a Hāritī), northern India, *c.* ninth–tenth centuries.
— *Musée Guimet. Photo, Gauthier*

In addition to these almost hieratic attitudes, which denote the sublime immobility of the Illumination or, at the very least, the majestic calm of preaching, we find various attitudes of " pastime " or " ease " (*lalitāsana, sukhāsana*), the line of which is more flexible, one leg being bent and even raised and the other hanging down. The best-known of these poses, which is also the most elegant, is that of " royal pastime " or " royal pleasure " (*mahārāja līlāsana*), in which the left leg is bent and the right knee raised to support the right arm, while the right hand hangs down from the knee, the torso leaning slightly backwards and being supported by the left arm, which is propped against the throne.

As for the standing statues — for instance, the Buddha of Mathurā — either they are in a rigid and strictly frontal position or else, as in the Sultānganj Buddha at Birmingham, there is a slight sideward sway of the hips, so that a line drawn through the centre of the head, body, and legs is not a straight one, whether the head be erect (*samabhaṅga*) or inclined to one side (*tribhaṅga*), or erect or inclined indiscriminately (*ābhaṅga*); here we have the first beginnings of those drooping attitudes — so harmoniously rhythmical, if sometimes a little precious — that were so much beloved of the Śivaite sculptors of southern India later on, in the Middle Ages.[1]

Like these seated postures, the finger-gestures, or *mudrā*, have also been the object of a learned classification. The one most frequently met with in Buddhist statues is the gesture of meditation (*dhyāna mudrā*), which occurs in association with the attitude of the *padmāsana*, and in which the hands of the Buddha rest upon his lap, one upon the other, with the palms upwards and the fingers outstretched. Next comes the gesture of giving or charity (*vara mudrā, varada mudrā*), with the hand drooping, the open palm downwards, and the fingers outstretched and bent forwards. Next comes the gesture of "fearlessness" — that is, the gesture of reassurance (*abhaya mudrā*), with the hand open, on a level with the shoulder, the palm being turned frontwards and the fingers raised — one of the tenderest and most spiritualized gestures of the Buddhist canon. From this gesture is derived that of discussion (*vitarka mudrā*), which is the same, except that the index or the middle finger and the tip of the thumb are touching. Another very frequent gesture

[1] Among the most happy specimens of Gupta art we should also mention several reliefs or statues in Ceylon. We may note in particular the delightful couple — a seated man and woman — with a charming pose of matchless mastery and liberty, from Isurumunya, Aṇurādhapura, reproduced especially by M. Hocart in the *Ceylon Journal of Science*, Section G, Vol. I, Pt. 3 (January 13, 1927), Pl. XLVIII.

is that of the starting of the Wheel of the Law (*dharmachakra mudrā*) — that is, of preaching: the two hands are placed before the chest, " the right hand turned outwards, with the thumb and the forefinger meeting, and the left hand turned inwards, with the thumb and forefinger touching the two fingers of the other hand " (Fig. 41). As for the gesture of " touching the earth (*bhūmisparśa mudrā*)," it refers to the scene in which Buddha, when assailed by the Evil One, called the Earth to witness: the Buddha, seated in the *padmāsana* attitude, lets his right hand hang down over his right knee, palm downwards, in such a way that the fingers touch or brush against the ground. And, lastly, we have the gesture of adoration, which is also that of salutation (*añjali mudrā*), with the two hands raised and pressed palm to palm.

These ritual gestures are too often studied solely from the point of view of religious symbolism. But it is worth while to linger over them for the sake of their essentially æsthetic quality as well.[1] Never, indeed, has the spiritual value of the hands — those flowers of the flesh, which hold within their chalice the whole of human tenderness and thought — been comprehended with such mystical insight. The whole of the great peace of Buddhism is contained in the gesture known as *dhyāna mudrā*. The whole of the Blessed One's " power of gentleness " is revealed in that *abhaya mudrā*, in which, for twenty-four centuries past, half humanity has found a refuge. On the other hand, what calm assurance in the gesture by which he takes the earth as his witness; what supreme elegance — the finished grace of reason in the perfect sage — in the gestures of discussion and of the *dharmachakra*! And, as though to prove the universal value of these sacred gestures, are not the *añjali* and *vara mudrā* Christian symbols too, in which all pure hearts, from Fra Angelico to the masters of Ajaṇṭā, have joined in expressing their double ideal of faith and

[1] See Coomaraswamy and Duggirala: *The Mirror of Gesture* (Cambridge, Mass., 1917).

charity? When the Buddhist *mudrā* find interpreters worthy of them, they are, if we may be allowed to borrow the language of Ruskin, " gestures of the soul," transposing pure moral beauty into its direct æsthetic equivalent.

These principles find a peculiar application in Buddhist painting, and notably in the frescoes of Ajaṇṭā.

The chief group of Buddhist paintings in India is that at Ajaṇṭā.[1] This somewhat isolated spot, situated to the extreme north-west of the domains of the Niẓām of Hyderabad, in the direction of Khandesh, once contained a whole collection of *vihāra* and subterranean monasteries, adorned by the piety of the faithful with a large number of mural frescoes, dating from the second to the seventh centuries.

The earliest of these frescoes are those in caves 9 and 10, executed about A.D. 100 under the dynasty of the Andhras. We may remember that the Andhras, who ruled over the Deccan, were also the sovereigns of Amarāvatī. The earliest frescoes at Ajaṇṭā are thus in historic connexion with that art of Amarāvatī whose importance in the formation of the Indian æsthetic ideal we have seen above. In other words, the frescoes of caves 9 and 10 in no way represent a primitive art. On the contrary, as Mr. Percy Brown observes, here, as at Amarāvatī, we are concerned with an art which has already reached maturity and commands attention by its bold style and singularly vigorous drawing. The scenes are in general well-balanced, the figures skilfully drawn; and the treatment of the hands already reveals that mystic feeling which is the secret of the masters of Ajaṇṭā.

After a gap of two and a half centuries we arrive at a new period

[1] See Victor Goloubew: "*Documents pour servir à l'étude d'Ajaṇṭā. Les Peintures de la première grotte*," Collection *Ars Asiatica*, Vol. X (Paris, Van Oest, 1927); Griffiths: *Paintings in the Buddhist Cave-temples at Ajunta* (London, 1896–7); Lady Herringham: *Ajanta Frescoes* (India Society, 1915); Foucher: "Preliminary Report on the Interpretation of the Paintings and Sculptures of Ajaṇṭā," *Journal of the Hyderabad Archæological Society*, 5, 1919–20, and *Journal asiatique*, Paris, 1921, I, 201–45; Marcelle Lalou: "*Décorations des monastères bouddhiques*," *Revue des arts asiatiques*, V, 1928, p. 183.

of artistic bloom, represented by the pillars in cave 10. These paintings, which seem to date from about 350, under the Gupta dynasty, display a fairly considerable difference of style from the works of the second century. In the first place, here too, as at Amarāvatī, the Greco-Buddhist art of Gandhāra has made its influence felt in the mean time. The treatment of the Buddhist nimbus and that of the drapery, in particular, reveal unquestionable affinities with Gandhāra. On the other hand, as Percy Brown points out, though these works betray a certain conventionalism, the drawing of the figures shows a noble simplicity, a dignity and breadth of attitude, which mark a progress upon the previous series. Side by side with the influence of Gandhāra, this is, strictly speaking, the contribution of the Gupta period.

FIGURE 85
North-east Indian sculpture, perhaps school of Mayurbanj, Orissa, *c.* tenth century.
— *Musée Guimet. Archives of the Museum*

The third series is made up of the frescoes of caves 16 and 17, which date from about the year 500, under the reign of the little local dynasty of the Vākāṭakas, who were connected by blood with the Gupta emperors. The earlier in date, cave 16, is remarkable for the combination of the figures with architectural motives, " the buildings " being, moreover, " of a light and fanciful order " (Percy

FIGURE 85b

Liṅgodbhava, Dravidian sandstone figure from the Loo collection, tenth–thirteenth centuries.

Brown). As an example of this manner we may instance a fine Buddhist triad and an elegant " Sleep of the Women." In cave 17, moreover, Mr. Percy Brown draws attention to a " narrative style " which is rather striking: it is " literally a picture-gallery illustrating some of the most engrossing episodes in the birth, life and death of the Buddha. The conceptions of this group denote less idealism, and there is a decided feeling for the dramatic. They seem to have been selected with the object of attracting the observer by means of their direct humanitarianism." The " Return to Kapilavastu," the representation of the Seven Buddhas, and a variety of scenes of the Viśvantara *jātaka,* in particular, are treated in this spirit. But this popular — or comparatively popular — vein in no way detracts from the character of distinction possessed by the figures, as is proved by the elegant processions of *gandharvas* and *apsaras,* as well as by certain love-scenes (Fig. 45 and 46).

Cave 19, with its many Buddhas and its " Return to Kapilavastu," may date from about 550, so that it forms the link between this group and that of the seventh century.

The last group consists of caves 1 to 5 and 21 to 26. By far the most important are caves 1 and 2, which were decorated between 600 and 650, at the height of the Chālukya dynasty, which reigned over the Mahratta territory and held sway over the Deccan from 550 to 753. Cave 1 contains what are perhaps the most famous frescoes at Ajaṇṭā — for instance, the " beautiful bodhisattva " with the blue lotus (a Mañjuśrī or Avalokitēśvara, Fig. 47), the weighing of the flesh in the Śibi *jātaka,* and the banqueting-scene which was formerly supposed to represent Khosrau Pārvīz, king of Persia,[1] but, as Monsieur Foucher has established, really represents the god Pāñchika: it may be remarked that, even if it is not concerned with the famous Sāsānid monarch, as had been supposed, the group in question none

[1] Cf. "The Banquet of Persians," in the Japanese review the *Kokka,* No. 342 (November 1918). There are other coloured reproductions of frescoes from Ajaṇṭā in the *Kokka,* No. 323, 324, 325, 345, 355, 374.

FIGURE 86

Śiva. Art of the Carnatic, fifteenth century.
— *Property of Monsieur C. T. Loo*

the less points unquestionably to an Iranian influence: the scene of the banquet of Pāñchika in cave 1 should be compared with the figures at Dandān-uiliq, near Khotan, reproduced in Vol. III (Fig. 117) of this work, which show traces of Sāsānian influence and, what is more, belong to almost the same period as these figures at Ajaṇṭā — the eighth century. We may remark, in passing, that this should convince us of the enormous extent of the area over which Sāsānian influences were felt in Oriental painting, from Ajaṇṭā as far as Kashgaria, by way of Bāmiyān and Dukhtar-i Nūshirvān. But, together with these Indo-Iranian affinities, Mr. Percy Brown notes in this same cave 1 some curious resemblances both in style and in ideal with the Indo-Javanese art of the reliefs of Bōrōbudur, dating from the eighth century.

Cave 2 is the latest in date (Fig. 48) and exhibits two distinct styles, one of which, as Percy Brown notes, is broadly conventional, displaying a formalism analogous to that of the paintings at Dandān-uiliq in Kashgaria, mentioned above; while the same critic adds that, side by side with the central figures, which are still the work of very great artists, the accessory figures betray weaknesses of workmanship and, more generally, a lack of unity which is in contrast with the skilful composition of the previous groups. It should also be noted that, after the Persian influences, Mr. Percy Brown thinks he can here distinguish certain Chinese ones, which is not at all surprising if we recall the fact that Hiuen-tsang and other Chinese pilgrims of the T'ang age passed this way.

Every one of the chief subjects of the Ajaṇṭā frescoes is worthy of separate analysis. For instance, a study in itself might be made of the masculine types, from the elegant *kshatriya,* with the slight moustache, the transparent garments, and the almost feminine suppleness of body, to the more or less Iranian types mentioned above, with beards, conical caps, and thick garments. It would also be worth while to pick out all the scenes of court life: the train which follows

FIGURE 87

Statue of Brahmā. Art of the Carnatic, fifteenth century.
— *Formerly in the possession of Monsieur Loo. Photo, C. T. Loo*

the young prince riding on his elephant, in cave 1, as he issues forth from the palace with an escort of horsemen; the fine procession of richly caparisoned elephants with warriors on their backs and surrounded by horsemen, in cave 17 — a real scene of Indian epic, which Monsieur Foucher considers to be an illustration of the *Siṃhalāvadāna,* the story of the merchant Siṃhala, who became king of Ceylon. And, lastly, we really ought to enumerate all those scenes of jungle life in which unknown painters as powerful as the French artist Barye have brought to their direct observation of animal life a realism and fire worthy of the animal-sculptors of Sāñchī — and especially so in the combat of buffalo in cave 1, the *mêlée* of elephants in cave 19, and, in cave 10, the herd of elephants in the scene of the elephant with six tusks (*shaḍdanta jātaka*). In the same connexion we may note the charming elephants used as decorative motives on the panels of grotto 1, in the manner of Sāñchī and Bodh-Gayā. We should likewise observe the supreme elegance of the antelope in the scene of antelope adoring a *stūpa* in cave 17, the striking lifelikeness of the monkeys' gestures in cave 17, or of the figures of wolves, and the decorative splendour of the peacocks, which are again quite worthy of those at Sāñchī. For reproductions of these scenes we refer our readers to the splendid albums of Monsieur Victor Goloubew (*Ars Asiatica,* Vol. X).

Apropos of this point — and we purposely harp upon these comparisons — it is not without interest to recall the fact that Sāsānid Persia, on the very threshold of India, possessed an able school of animal-sculptors. We need only mention the relief on the right- and left-hand walls of the great grotto at Tāq-i Bustān, dating from about 620, and representing the great Khosrau II out hunting, which we reproduced in Vol. I of the present work; in addition to the local differences we shall distinguish several characteristics which the two schools have in common. The elephants in the boar-hunt, in particular, seemed to us, when we examined them afresh on the

FIGURE 88
The Seven Mothers. Art of the Carnatic, fifteenth century.
— *Property of Monsieur C. T. Loo*

spot, to have been greatly influenced, if not directly inspired, by Indian art.

To take another point, a whole study might be devoted to the survival of classical motives at Ajaṇṭā, where we find a sort of *amoretti*, or little genii, inciting cocks or kids to fight — a purely Greco-Roman theme that we are surprised to find occasionally associated with a Buddhist subject which is still specifically Indian (caves 1 and 17). The same might be said of the figures of the *kinnarīs*, which are copied from the monsters, half-bird, half-woman, of Greek mythology. A few scenes further on we may note how the Indian artist has adapted these classical motives. Side by side with the *nāgakanyā* (serpent maidens) in the form of sirens of a purely Greek type in cave 2, we see in cave 1 other fabulous creatures, having the tail and lower part of the body of a siren, but the head and forequarters of a buffalo, or even a cow — a typical creation of the Indian genius. Similarly, on the decorative panels we find classical Cupids mingled with an exotic flora, or even alternating with monkeys, buffalo, and charming young elephant-calves with all the grace of a child. Elsewhere on the same panels we find the Persian motive of heraldic animals face to face, which we shall find as far afield as Turfān in central Asia.

Nevertheless, the predominant factor is always the eternal naturalism of India. We have already found this inspiring the art of the great animal-sculptors, and we still find it as the vital principle of these beautiful human bodies moving freely in the light of the subtropical regions. But in the latter how greatly this naturalism is spiritualized in its tendencies and refined in its expression! To convince ourselves of this it is only necessary to recall all the nude female figures at Ajaṇṭā, with their flower-like grace, freedom of line, and variety of attitude, which make them, as it were, a poem of Hindu womanhood (cf. Fig. 49, 50, 51); for instance, in the scene of the Assault of Mārā in grotto 1, we may note the seductive wiles of the

FIGURE 89
Statue of a Mother.
— Property of Monsieur C. T. Loo

temptresses, and their enticements full of a wantonness at once childlike and sophisticated. We need only enumerate all the pairs of lovers in grotto 1 and recall their voluptuous languor and refined simplicity, the softness of their poses, and their chastely caressing gestures, and, above all, the abandonment of spiritual emotion and infinite tenderness, which prevent such motives from seeming out of place in a Buddhist sanctuary (Fig. 49, 51, 52).

All who adore pure art will find here a glimpse into the mysteries of another Quattrocento, another Florence or Umbria. Before these female faces, with their pure oval, their elongated eyes with an expression at once chaste, voluptuous, and melancholy, and their long, slender bodies in poses devised by a sophisticated æsthetic sense — before these supple figures with their innocent nudity, we involuntarily think of the women of Sandro Botticelli, such as his " Birth of Venus," and the divine pictures of the period of Italian art preceding Raphael. Indeed, the spirit which animated the artist of the Uffizi and that of the old masters of Ajaṇṭā are somewhat similar. Both of them celebrate, in a spirit of fervent neo-paganism, the artistic value of the lines of the female form and the pensive softness of lovely youthful bodies; while the Florentine master is just as mindful as his distant predecessors at Ajaṇṭā of the fact that these graceful creatures have to harmonize with the religious atmosphere of their surroundings. The treatment of the hands alone by the painters of Ajaṇṭā would be enough to express the almost Franciscan tenderness by which they are animated: what a spiritual quality there is in their slightest gestures, what mystical feeling in the most amorous caress! [1] Even in the idyllic scenes body and soul alike are instinct with an emotion of piety. Thus all this naturalistic art remains passionately mystical and is constantly lifted above itself by the most fervent *bhakti* (piety) as well as by the loftiest idealism.

[1] See Samarendranath Gupta: " The Hands in the Ajaṇṭā Frescoes," published by the *Modern Review*, Calcutta.

And, lastly, when its task is to clothe in a material form the ideal vision of Buddhas and bodhisattvas, Ajaṇṭā is the equal of Mathurā and Sārnāth. Indeed, the idyllic scenes of Indian life and the flowering jungle which form their setting are only there in order to throw the figures of the bodhisattvas into greater relief. But at Ajaṇṭā these supernatural apparitions are among the most moving visions that have ever haunted the dreams of man. We need only recall that supreme marvel in cave 1, the great picture of a bodhisattva — which, according to Monsieur Goloubew, represents Mañjuśrī, and, according to Mr. Coomaraswamy, Avalokitēśvara — dressed in transparent gauze, wearing on his head a high head-dress "on which lotus and jasmine flowers blossom in chased gold," and holding a blue lotus-flower in his right hand with an exquisite gesture (Fig. 47 and 53): a figure worthy of a place in the art of the world by the side of the sublimest incarnations of the Sistine Chapel, or of such drawings as that of Christ for the "Last Supper," in which Leonardo da Vinci has expressed the most intense emotions of the soul.[1]

To sum up these multifarious impressions in a single formula, we may say that the predominant feature of Ajaṇṭā is an intimate and harmonious fusion of the old Indian naturalism of Sāñchī, with its youthful freshness, and the infinite gentleness of Buddhist mysticism. And it is this which makes Ajaṇṭā a complete expression of every side of the Indian soul.

The frescoes of Sīgiriya, in Ceylon, are an offshoot of the same school.[2] The citadel of Sīgiriya, "the Lion's Rock," served as a refuge for Kāśyapa I, king of Ceylon (479–497). Here he built himself a palace the substructure of which has survived till our day, together with the rock-paintings with which it was decorated. These paintings are therefore almost contemporary with cave 16 at Ajaṇṭā. They consequently reveal an obvious affinity with Ajaṇṭā, though we may

[1] See also another bodhisattva from Ajaṇṭā reproduced in Vol. IV of this work, Fig. 22.
[2] Cf. Coomaraswamy: *Mediæval Sinhalese Art* (Broad Campden, 1923).

observe certain differences of technique between the two sites — for instance, the absence of blues at Sīgiriya. This affinity is all the more striking because the subject of the frescoes at Sīgiriya is a series of female figures tossing flowers, a subject quite in keeping with those canons of art of which we have just formed some impression. Whether these female figures represent the wives of King Kāśyapa, as Percy Brown would have it, or celestial nymphs, as Coomaraswamy thinks — and as a matter of fact they are represented as swathed in clouds up to the waist — they at any rate display the same characteristics: a pervading sensuality, which they inherit from the pagan art of Bhārhut and Sāñchī, together with a supreme elegance, a supreme æsthetic refinement of gesture and pose, and a Botticellian grace which are the artistic contribution of the Gupta and post-Gupta period, the distinguishing mark of the age of Kālidāsa (Fig. 54, 55).

A last centre of Buddhist painting is that of the grottoes of Bāgh, in the state of Gwalior, 235 miles to the north of Ajaṇṭā.[1] The frescoes of Bāgh, which may date from the close of the seventh century — and are consequently not far removed in date from caves 1 and 2 at Ajaṇṭā — display a strong resemblance in style to these, though they are distinguished from them by the fact that they no longer seem so exclusively Buddhist, but appear to be in great part entirely profane. Here the processions of horsemen and state elephants, which at Ajaṇṭā are lost in the religious inspiration as a whole, are treated for their own sake. Moreover, a whole section of the frescoes seems to be given up to representations of scenes from musical dramas accompanied by dances, known by the name of *hallīśaka*. This purely mundane influence proclaims the fact that, at the moment when the frescoes of Bāgh were painted, Buddhism was on the way towards vanishing from India. The hour of Hinduism had arrived.

[1] See *The Bāgh Caves*, by Sir John Marshall, M. B. Garde, P. Vogel, Havell, J. H. Cousens, and L. Binyon (The India Society, London, 1927); Sri Mukul Chandra Dey: *My Pilgrimages to Ajaṇṭā and Bāgh* (London, 1924).

THE RELIGIOUS REVOLUTION: RISE OF HINDUISM AND THE HINDU PANTHEON

FROM THE THIRD CENTURY B.C. TO THE SEVENTH CENTURY OF OUR era Buddhism exerted a profound influence upon the evolution of Indian civilization, and particularly upon the history of art; but it never obtained a hold upon the mass of the population. Even while it was at the height of its success, Brahman culture and the popular cults connected with Brahmanism had remained in favour, as Indian literature bears witness: the epics which are, as it were, the two bibles of Brahman legend seem to have assumed their definitive form at the very time when Buddhism was most in vogue, between the third century B.C. and the second century of our era, during the Maurya, Śuṅga, and Kūshān periods. And from the eighth century onwards the Brahmanic substratum rose to the surface and entirely eliminated Buddhism or else absorbed it. From the eighth century to the present day India has known no pantheon but that of Brahmanism, which developed in course of centuries into Hinduism.

Hinduism is the result of that process of religious syncretism by means of which the Brahmans brought all creeds and popular cults within the scope of their own orthodox religion. This process was based on the conception of the *Trimūrti,* the god in " three forms " or Hindu triad, Brahmā, Vishṇu, and Śiva — a convenient device, at once learned and popular, for harmonizing the three chief religions between which the land was divided: Brahmanism, or the religion of the sacerdotal caste, founded upon the Vedas; Vishnuism under its multifarious forms, such as Krishnaism, the cult of Rāma, etc.; and Śivaism.

Brahmā, a personal god derived from the metaphysical Absolute of the Upanishads, was, as such, the soul and creator of the universe. In traditional iconography [1] he is represented with four heads and four arms (Fig. 87 and 136); two of his hands bear the four books of the Vedas, and he is seated upon the back of the Indian swan (*haṃsa*). He is sometimes accompanied by his consort, Sarasvatī, the goddess of eloquence and music, who bears as her attributes the shell (*śaṇkha*) and the disk (*chakra*) and rides upon a peacock.[2] In spite of these personal characteristics Brahmā, by very reason of his origin, always remained too philosophic and abstract a divinity to play a very great part in worship, literature, and art. All the popularity and vigour of Hinduism continued to be attached to Vishṇu-Kṛishṇa and Śiva.

FIGURE 90

Śiva in the pose of the *jñāna* "*dakshiṇāmūrti*," as god of wisdom.

—*Musée Guimet. Archives of the Museum*

Vishṇu, also known as Hari and Nārāyana, is one of the most ancient gods of India, for, as a solar deity, he figures in the pantheon

[1] See O. C. Gangoly: "Some Images of Brahmā of the Choḷa Period," in *Rūpam*, July-October 1928; "A Stone Figure of Brahma" (South Indian, X–XIth century), *Bulletin of the Metropolitan Museum of Art, New York*, May 1927 (No. 5).

[2] See Krishna Sastri: *South Indian Images of Gods and Goddesses* (Madras, 1916), Fig. 6–9 (showing some very beautiful reliefs and statues from Māvalipuram, Kumbakānam, Tiruvādi, and Kandiyur).

of the Vedas.[1] His celestial character continued to be denoted by his colour, a dark blue, which is also the colour of his two incarnations, Kṛishṇa and Rāma. During the age of Hinduism, in the Middle Ages, he is represented with four arms, bearing respectively the shell (*śaṅkha*), the club (*gadā*), the lotus (*padma*), and the disk (*chakra*). He rides upon the giant bird *garuḍa* and has as his consorts Lakshmī, the goddess of beauty, and Bhūmi-dēvī, the goddess of earth.

According to the Vishnuites, Vishṇu, the preserver of the world, reposes, during the vast intervals between his acts of creation, upon the cosmic ocean, reclining upon the giant serpent (*nāga*) Śēsha, or Ananta, the serpent of eternity (Fig. 40).[2] During this state of sleep — that is, of beatific potentiality — which lasts for millions and millions of centuries, he contains within himself and broods over the world; then, as each cycle of creation comes round, he awakens and once more emits this universe — or, rather, a golden lotus issues from his navel, as though from a pool, and from it is born Brahmā, who creates the universe of him and for him.

A fresh *avatāra* of Vishṇu — that is, translated literally, a new " descent " of the god, a new incarnation which he accepts in order to save the world — coincides with each of these cycles. These various incarnations, the chief of which are ten in number, not to mention a multitude of others of a more secondary nature, have had too great an importance in the history of Hindu art for us to omit to give a short account of them here.

One of these avatars is that of the Brahman dwarf. At the time when it took place, the gods (*dēva*) were waging a fierce struggle against the Asuras or Titans, and, as happened in Indian mythology,

1 See Jouveau-Dubreuil: *Archéologie du sud de l'Inde* (Paris, Musée Guimet, 1914), Vol. II, "*Iconographie*," pp. 60–111 (Vishnuite iconography).

2 See Gopinatha Rao: *Elements of Hindu Iconography*, I, i, 263, Pl. XXIX, XXXI, and XXXII (Bhōgaśayanamurti, relief at Deogarh); Krishna Sastri, op. cit., p. 51 (Anantasāyin of Māvalipuram).

the gods had the worst of it. Bali, the proud leader of the Asuras, was on the point of grasping the domination of the world. But Vishṇu now came down upon earth and entered into the womb of the pious Aditi "with his four arms and his great eyes like the lotus, bearing the shell, the club, the lotus, and the disk, and wearing a yellow garment. He was black and comely; the radiance of his countenance was enhanced by glittering ear-rings in the shape of a fish; on his breast he wore the jewel *śrītatsa,* and he had bracelets on his arms and wrists, a brilliant aigrette, a girdle, and elegant anklets at his feet; he wore as an adornment his beautiful garland of wild flowers, round which hummed a swarm of bees; round his neck hung the *kaustubha* jewel; his brightness dispelled the gloom in the abode of the chief of beings." But scarcely was he born when he changed himself into a diminutive Brahman, "like an actor changing his make-up," and sought out the *asura* Bali, who was at that time engaged in cele-

FIGURE 91
Śiva in the pose of the *vīṇādhara* (lute-holder) "*dakshiṇāmūrti.*" South Indian bronze, fifteenth century.
— *Musée Guimet. Photo, Gauthier*

FIGURE 92

Śiva in the pose of the *vīṇādhara* "*dakshiṇāmūrti.*" Back view.
South Indian bronze, fifteenth century.
— *Musée Guimet. Photo, Gauthier*

brating the sacrifice *aśvamēdha* (horse-sacrifice), which was to secure the victory of the Titans. On seeing the dwarf attired in the Brahman costume, " with the girdle made of grass, the Brahmanical cord, the antelope-skin, and his hair falling in locks," Bali welcomed him unsuspectingly. After uttering a panegyric upon him in accordance with all the rules of Sanscrit poetry, the dwarf begged of him as a signal favour as much of the earth as could be covered in three footsteps, and Bali granted it, with a laugh.

FIGURE 93

Śiva in the pose of the *bhikshāṭanamūrti* (the beggar). Bronze from Pandananallūr.
— *Photo, Archæological Survey of India*

" All at once," continues the *Bhāgavata Purāṇa*, " the dwarf's diminutive form increased miraculously in stature. With one step he covered the earth, filling the atmosphere with his body and touching the four cardinal points with his arms; with the second step he invaded the sky; and with the third not an atom was left for him to occupy.[1] Within the body of this being with his illimitable faculties, Bali saw the whole of the universe, including all things material and spiritual. In his feet Bali

[1] This incarnation of Vishṇu is called *Trivikrama*, that of the god who took the "three strides."

saw the earth: the twilight was in the garments of this god with the mighty footsteps, the seven oceans were in his belly, and the garland of the constellations was upon his breast. In his two breasts were justice and truth, and in his soul was the moon. On his bosom was Śrī (Lakshmī), with a lotus in her hand, and the songs of the *Sāman* (chanting priest) were in his throat, together with all other sounds. In his arms were the immortals, of whom Indra is the chief, in his ears were the cardinal points, in his head were the heavens, in his hair were the clouds, in his nostrils the wind, in his eyes the sun, and in his mouth the fire. In his eyelids were the day and the night, in his brow was wrath, and in his lower lip desire. In his shadow was death, in his smile illusion, in his intelligence Brahmā and the whole of the gods, and, lastly, in the vital organs of his body were the whole number of beings both animate and inanimate."

FIGURE 94
Naṭarāja. Fifteenth century.
— *C. T. Loo collection. Archives of the Musée Guimet*

When they thus saw the "whole of the universe in the Universal Soul," the *asuras* felt themselves to be vanquished, and Bali, their leader, allowed himself to be loaded with chains.[1]

Somewhat similar is the *Matsya avatāra,* or incarnation of Vishṇu

[1] See Gopinatha Rao, op. cit., Vol. I, Pt. i, 161–81, with Pl. XLIX (Trivikrama from Māvalipuram), L (from Bādāmī), LI (from Ellora); and Krishna Sastri, op. cit., pp. 31–3.

FIGURE 95

Naṭarāja. South Indian, fourteenth–fifteenth centuries.
— *Collection of Count Philipon. Photo, Gauthier*

in the form of a fish. One day, while performing his ablutions, the sage Manu caught a tiny fish, which begged for its life. And, lo, the little fish began to grow, till it filled a whole lake and then the sea. It next warned Manu of the approaching flood and ordered him, as Jehovah did Noah, to place on board of an ark representatives of all living species. When the flood came, Manu, by the aid of the great serpent Vāsuki, moored his ark to a horn of the giant fish; and thus humanity was saved, and with it the whole animal world.[1]

The avatar of the boar (*varāha avatāra*) follows naturally upon that of the fish. Overwhelmed by the deluge, the earth (*Bhūmi-dēvī*) lay in the depths of the water, where the demons (*daityas*) held it captive. Then Vishṇu transformed himself into a gigantic wild boar: "Rushing across the heavens, with his tail raised, tossing his mane, all bristling with prickly hairs, trampling the clouds underfoot, and baring his white tusks, with flaming eyes," he plunged into the water, "following the trail of the earth by scent." At last he found it in the depths of the abyss, transfixed it with one of his tusks, and drew it up to the surface, not omitting to crush the hostile demons on his way. Hindu iconography frequently represents this episode, with the god in the shape of a giant with a boar's head, bearing in his arms the goddess of the earth, whom he had saved from the abyss.[2]

Next comes the avatar of the turtle (*kūrma avatāra*) and the churning of the seas (Fig. 154).[3] This is one of the most famous episodes in Hindu mythology and is often reproduced by the sculptors of India and Cambodia. After long warfare the gods (*dēvas*) and their enemies, the Asuras or Titans, came together one day on the advice of Vishṇu in order to obtain the ambrosia (*amṛita*) or drink conferring immortality, which was hidden in the sea of milk. The gods and the Asuras therefore went off together and uprooted Mount Mandara,

[1] Gopinatha Rao, op. cit., Vol. I, Pt. i, 126.
[2] Gopinatha Rao, op. cit., Vol. I, Pt. i, 128–45, with Pl. XXXVI (Māvalipuram) and XXXVII (Bādāmī); Krishna Sastri, op. cit., p. 22.
[3] Gopinatha Rao, op. cit., Vol. I, Pt. i, 126.

FIGURE 96
Naṭarāja. South Indian, fourteenth–fifteenth centuries.
— *Collection of Count Philipon. Photo, Gauthier*

FIGURE 97

Naṭarāja. Southern bronze, fourteenth–fifteenth centuries.

— *Madras Museum. Photo, Goloubew*

FIGURE 98

Statue known as Kṛishṇa dancing (in reality a Sambandha dancing). Southern bronze, fifteenth century.

— *C. T. Loo collection*

which Vishṇu, riding upon the back of the bird Garuḍa, sank in the depths of the ocean to serve as the dasher of the churn. The serpent Vāsuki was passed round this giant dasher to serve as a cord, and the churning began, the gods hauling at the tail of the serpent, and the Asuras at his head in rhythmical succession, each team in turn. In order to support Mount Mandara, which threatened to sink into the abyss, Vishṇu assumed the form of a giant tortoise and, placing himself beneath the mountain, held it up with his massive form. At the same time Vishṇu stood in the centre, under another form, between the two teams of gods and Asuras, and directed their mighty task. Suddenly a poison, the *hālāhala,* spurted forth from the seething waves and would have caused the very gods to perish had not Śiva swallowed it out of compassion for all creatures; and so virulent was the venom that the terrible god had a blue mark left for ever on his throat from the burning. Next a series of wonderful creatures rose from the ocean, one after the other: the white cow of Agnihotra, the horse Uchchaiḥśravas with his moon-coloured coat, Airāvata, the king of the white elephants, who was to bear Indra on his back, the ruby *kaustubha,* which was afterwards to adorn the breast of Vishṇu, the tree of plenty *pārijāta,* the source of good things, the Indian nymphs or *apsaras,* and then, wonder of wonders, the Indian Aphrodite, Śrī, or Lakshmī, who became the consort of Vishṇu: "Holding in her hand a wreath of lotus," says the *Bhāgavata Purāṇa,* "round which hummed the bees, she turned her gracious face, made lovely by the smile of modesty, and against whose cheeks sparkled beautiful ear-rings; her two breasts, perfectly matched and close together, were covered with powdered sandalwood and saffron; her belly was so slight that it was scarcely seen; her every step was accompanied by the tuneful jingle of the anklets which adorned her feet, and her whole body was like a golden liana" (cf. Fig. 71 and 101). Last of all, there rose from the tossing waves a

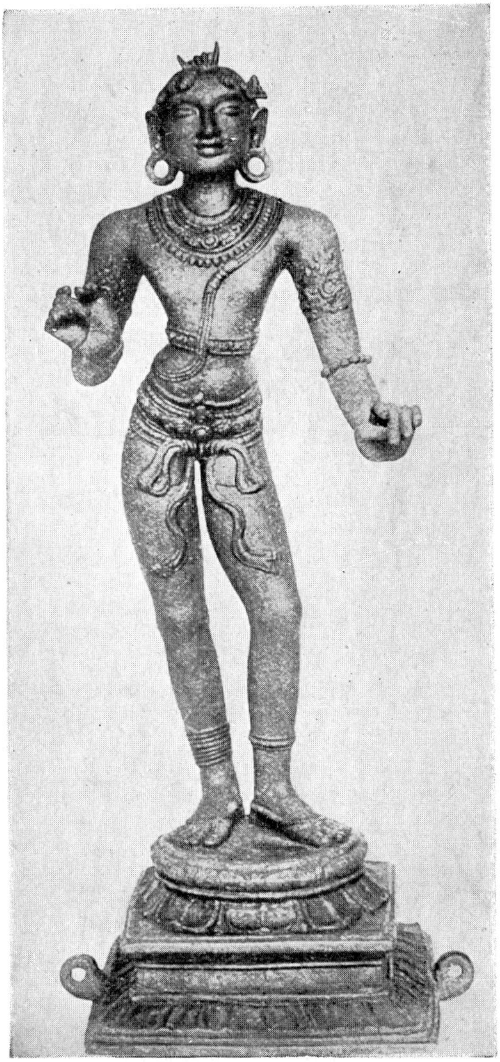

FIGURE 99

Sundara mūrti Svāmi.
— *Colombo Museum. Photo, Archæological Survey of Ceylon*

black youth bearing a vase filled with the draught of immortality, the divine ambrosia (*amṛita*).[1]

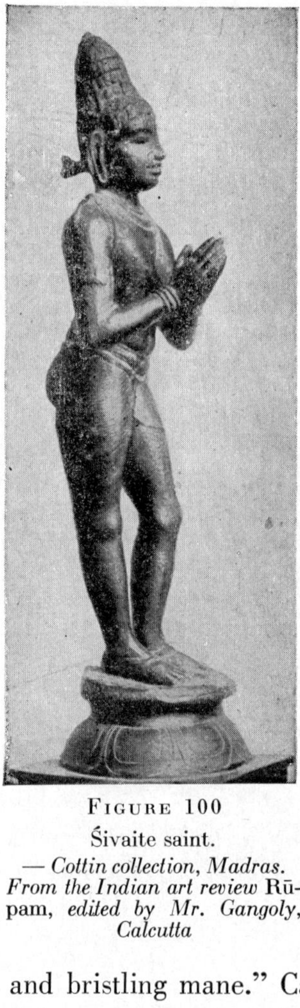

FIGURE 100
Śivaite saint.
— *Cottin collection, Madras. From the Indian art review* Rūpam, *edited by Mr. Gangoly, Calcutta*

At this moment, however, occurred an event which almost frustrated the sublime discovery. The Asuras, or Titans, seized the vase and snatched it from the gods. But Vishṇu changed himself into a woman, a courtesan of dazzling beauty, who ensnared the will of the Asuras by her charms, took the ambrosia from them, and distributed it to the gods. And, a fresh struggle having broken out between the Asuras and the Dēvas, the latter, fortified by the ambrosia, carried off a complete victory.

One of the avatars of Vishṇu which are most often represented is that of the man lion (*narasiṃha*). Puffed up with pride, the *asura* Hiraṇyakaśipu was once insulting the name of Vishṇu, crying: " If he is everywhere, as people claim, why is he not in this column? " — and the Titan smote one of the columns of his palace with all the might of his fist. At that very moment a terrible roar broke from it, and a fearsome beast bounded forth. It was " the god, in the form of a man and a lion, with eyes as red as gold heated in the fire, and a countenance whose size was increased by a thick and bristling mane." Casting himself upon the *asura,* the lion god " threw him backwards over his thigh and tore with his claws, as

[1] For a good representation of this scene on the "bas-reliefs" of Bādāmī (sixth century), see R. D. Banerji: *Basreliefs of Badami,* Memoirs of the Archæological Survey of India, No. 25 (1928), Pl. XXII.

easily as in sport, that skin which the lightning itself could not pierce" (Fig. 80).[1]

The chief human incarnations of Vishṇu are those of Kṛishṇa and Rāma.

In reality Kṛishṇa was originally a separate god, or, rather, a popular hero raised to the rank of a demigod, until, in the pietistic religion of mediæval Bengal, he became the one universal god. Those learned in Indian lore even distinguish several Kṛishṇas, afterwards fused by the popular religion into a single divinity, who was given out to be the principal avatar of Vishṇu. The story of the god which we will now briefly relate is based upon this process of syncretism as it appears in the *Bhāgavata Purāṇa*.

FIGURE 101
Lakshmī. Southern bronze, seventeenth century.
— *Musée Guimet. Archives of the Museum*

Kṛishṇa "the Black," the most personal and anthropomorphic deity of the Indian pantheon, was born, then, at Mathurā on the Yamunā (*Jumna*), of the royal house of the Yādavas. Scarcely had his mother Dēvakī borne him, when his uncle, King Kaṃsa, having been turned against him by an

[1] See Gopinatha Rao, op. cit., Vol. I, Pt. i, 145–60 and Pl. XLIII, the splendid Kēvala *narasiṃha* from Bādāmī.

FIGURE 102
Kṛishṇa Govinda. *Chār*-wood carving. Southern India, seventeenth century.
— *Musée Guimet. Archives of the Museum*

oracle, sent to seek him in order to put him to death. The child was saved by being hidden, with his brother Bala-Rāma, in the house of the shepherd Nanda, so that he who was later to be the universal god spent his youth among the herds; hence the name " cowherd " (*gopāla*) which it attached to him during this phase of his existence (cf. Fig. 98, 102, 161, 229, 230, 231).[1] The *Bhāgavata Purāṇa,* followed by the whole Krishnaite literature, relates his loves with the milkmaids (*gopīs*), at the same time intimating that we should regard his fleshly union with them as symbolic of the theme of the mystical union of the faithful soul with its god.

The divine cowherd appears in the guise of a beautiful youth, " with a peacock's feather on his head, and a cassia-flower (*karṇi-*

[1] Cf. Coomaraswamy: *Portfolio of Indian Art*, Museum of Fine Arts, Boston, Pl. LXXVI, painting of the Rajput school of Kangrā, early eighteenth century, Kṛishṇa disguised as a milkmaid, milking a white cow.

kāra) at his ears, clad in a robe as yellow as gold, and adorned with garlands" (cf. Fig. 232). "He entered the forest, which trembled beneath his tread, and filled the holes of his flute with the ambrosia of his lips. On hearing the sounds of his flute, which enchant the souls of all creatures, every woman in the park was talking about him. The peacocks danced intoxicated with joy," and the gazelles ran up and presented to the celestial musician "the offering of their affectionate glances"; when he started to walk, they followed his footsteps and lost all thought of their shady retreats; "the cows pricked up their ears as though to drink from a cup the ambrosia which distils from the lips of Kṛishṇa in the strains of his flute"; their calves, "still holding in their mouths a sip of the milk that ran from the udder of their mother," listened as though under a spell; all the beasts, ravished by the celestial harmony, thronged to the spot, "still holding between their teeth the mouthful that they were chewing"; some listened in

FIGURE 103
Bodhisattva of Vihāra Sāri.
—*From a cast in the Trocadéro.*
(*See also Kinsbergen:* Photographien naar Oudheden van Java)

astonishment, attentive and with closed eyes; others, " motionless and with tears in their eyes," cast a caressing glance at the divine cowherd (see Fig. 102 and 229).[1]

Together with the *gopīs,* the amorous milkmaids, Kṛishṇa started dancing the *rāsa,* the voluptuous pastoral dance: " he seized them and clasped them in his arms, passing his hand over their hands, through the curls of their hair, over their knees, their waist and breasts, leaving upon them the marks of his nails in play, sporting with them, glancing at them and smiling to them, at once inflaming and satisfying their desires." Suddenly, flouting their passion, he disappeared from their view; distraught and like madwomen, they sought him from grove to grove. At last he reappeared and the dance of the *rāsa* began once again: by virtue of his mysterious power, the beloved one is present everywhere; while the milkmaids danced, each one of them thought that she could feel him at her side and possessed him for herself alone.

The *Gīta Govinda* of Jayadēva, a Bengali poet between the twelfth and the thirteenth centuries, has sung this classic episode of Hindu literature in still more burning verses: " His body, blue in hue, is powdered with sandalwood, his tunic is yellow, his garland is made of woodland flowers; his mischievous wiles set swaying the jewels of the pendants that adorn his cheeks; he delights to smile." He is surrounded by the flock of milkmaids: " One of the shepherdesses, with rich, full, heavy breasts, clinging passionately to Kṛishṇa, sings the melody of rapturous love. Another, all too simple, swoons with ecstasy before the face of the god, whose wiles cause his eyes to swim and overflow with love. Another, with full hips, approaches close to his cheek and whispers some nothing into the base of his ear, and kisses her beloved; his downy neck quivers, it is the chosen spot. Another, with her hand longing for caresses, draws him towards her by his tunic, upon the brink of the Yamunā, in the reed hut to which

[1] Cf. O. C. Gangoly: *Masterpieces of Rajput Painting* (Calcutta, 1927), Pl. XIV.

FIGURE 104

Buddha in the *dharmachakra mudrā*. Bōrōbudur.
— *From Kinsbergen:* Photographien naar Oudheden van Java.
By permission of Messrs. Phogel

he has retired. Another young beauty, intoxicated with pleasure by the pastoral dance, was sung by Kṛishṇa upon his flute, and the palm of her hand beating the measure mingles the tinkling of her rows of bracelets with the harmonious sounds. One he embraces, another he kisses, and he cajoles another who entices him; he looks upon the smile of a third and runs after a fourth. Thus does he sport with the troop of innocent maidens upon pleasure bent. By the seduction he exerts over all things he causes their bliss; the feast of love distils from his tender limbs, as dark as a lotus wreath. The lovely wantons kiss him limb by limb, all over, everywhere." In strains of passionate tenderness the poem next rehearses the appeals of Rādhā, the favourite of the divine cowherd, her distress when he hides himself from her sight in sport, and her exuberant joy so soon as she finds him again. . . .[1]

Indian art delights to represent Kṛishṇa *gopāla,* during this phase of his life, in the form of a beautiful youth playing the flute as he keeps the flocks of his adopted father, Nanda: like the Greek Orpheus, the divine cowherd charms by his songs heifers and *gopīs* alike (Fig. 102).[2]

But the whole of Kṛishṇa's existence is not spent in the arms of the milkmaids. In the *Mahābhārata* we shall see what a commanding part he plays in battle, as the charioteer and counsellor of the hero Arjuna. He is not only an Apollo, but a Hercules, and while still quite young, proved his strength by lifting Mount Govardhana and holding it up for seven nights, in order to shelter the flocks of Nanda against the hurricanes sent by the jealousy of Indra. He slew the black serpent Kāliya, which infested the lake of the Yumanā: the fight between the divine infant and the serpent, which enwinds him

[1] Cf. Coomaraswamy: *Portfolio of Fine Art,* Museum of Fine Arts, Boston, Pl. LXXIV, an illustration to the *Gīta Govinda* of the Rajput school of Kangrā (Kṛishṇa returning to Rādhā).

[2] Cf. Coomaraswamy: *Catalogue of the Indian Collections in the Museum of Fine Arts, Boston,* Pt. V, "Rajput Painting," Pl. XVIII, LXVI, LXX, LXXI, LXXII, LXXIII, LXXIV, LXXV, LXXVIII–LXXXII, LXXXIV, LXXXV.

with its coils, but which he crushes in sport, recalls the similar story of which Hercules is the hero in Greek mythology. Finally, still wrapped in this living adornment, he begins to dance an ineffable dance and forces the reptile to dance it with him. In like fashion he slays the demon Arishṭa, who has assumed the form of a giant buffalo, and the monstrous horse Kēśin, which feeds upon human flesh.

After these youthful exploits Kṛishṇa returned to Mathurā, his native place, and vanquished a raging elephant in single combat in the arena, as well as all the other adversaries opposed to him by his uncle, the tyrant Kaṃsa, from whom he ended by delivering the city. Kṛishṇa was unable, however, to maintain his position at Mathurā for long; assailed by the superior forces of the Yavanas (that is, the Greeks), he abandoned the city and went and built an inaccessible citadel on the shores of the ocean at Dvārakā in Gujerat. The exploits of the divine hero find a continuation in his marriage with Rukmiṇī and his victory over the *asura* Bāṇa, who enjoyed the protection of the other great popular god, Śiva in person. After this victory the *Bhāgavata Purāṇa* shows us Śiva doing homage to Kṛishṇa, or, rather, recognizing him as the Universal Soul — that is, as identical with himself.

The other great incarnation of Vishṇu is Rāma. Here we are no longer dealing with a demigod, but with a truly human hero, the legends about whom form the subject of the epic of the *Rāmāyaṇa*, attributed to the poet Vālmīki.

Rāma is the son of Deśaratha, king of Ayodhyā (or what is now Oudh), and Kausalyā, the first of his wives. At the age of sixteen he marries the beautiful Sītā, daughter of the King of Mithilā, for he alone has succeeded in stretching the wonderful bow of Śiva, and Sītā is the prize in this contest. The young hero likewise bends the bow of Vishṇu, which becomes his own and secures his victory over all enemies.

We have just seen how Kṛishṇa appears to us as the hero of a strangely tender mysticism — and even of a somewhat wantonly erotic cult. In contrast to him, Rāma is the champion of duty, and throughout his whole career his character continues to be deeply moral: he is the very type of chivalrous honour. Struck by his good qualities, his father Daśaratha resolved to place him upon the throne. But the old King's second wife, Kaikēyī, took advantage of his weakness to make him give the crown to her own son Bhārata, sending Rāma into exile for fourteen years. Rāma submitted to this order and, followed by the faithful Sītā, who refused to abandon him, set out for the wild forests of central India: " There the wild beasts disport themselves without fear, and abandon themselves to their loves without restraint, but at the sight of man they are seized with fury. The miry pools of the forest, with their crocodiles, are always impassable, even for the elephants inflamed with love. Their paths, where the wild cock crows, are blocked with twining plants and thorns. At night men sleep upon the ground, on couches of dead leaves, their bodies worn out by weariness. Day and night they must be content with the fruits that have fallen from the trees; they must endure hunger to the point of exhaustion. They must wear the braid of hair and don the girdle of bark " (of the Brahman ascetics).

After performing various stages of their journey Rāma, his brother Lakshmaṇa, and the faithful Sītā took up their quarters in a hermitage on the banks of the Godāvarī, in the Deccan. Here the three exiles endured the attacks of a number of Rākshasas, or demons, which they beat off one after the other. Rāvaṇa, the king of the Rākshasas, who reigned over the island of Laṅkā (Ceylon), undertook to avenge his people by carrying off Sītā, for whom he had conceived a criminal passion. Mounting his flying chariot, drawn by flesh-eating asses, he alighted near the hermitage on the Godāvarī. In order to draw Rāma away from his beloved, Rāvaṇa's lieutenant, Mārīcha, changed himself into a gazelle and appeared before the hero: " It was a large gazelle, a lovely gazelle, of changing hues.

FIGURE 105

Javanese head of Buddha in the Leiden Museum.
— By permission of Messrs. Van Oest

Jewels sparkled at the tips of its horns, its head was dappled with black and white; its mouth was like a red lotus and a blue lotus, its ears like a water-lily tinged with azure; its neck was somewhat long, its belly shone like the pearl and its shell, its flanks were as brilliant as the *madhūka*-flower. The emerald blazed upon its hoofs, its legs were delicate, its stature perfect, and all the hues of the rainbow were poured out upon its croupe." Sītā passed by, gathering flowers. She saw the marvellous gazelle, longed for it, and asked Rāma to capture it for her. Rāma rushed off in pursuit, but the gazelle drew him far away from the hermitage, and Rāvaṇa, who had been watching for this moment, took advantage of it to carry off Sītā, in spite of the resistance of Jaṭāyus, the king of the vultures; he bore her off to Laṅkā, where he imprisoned her in his palace until she should consent to marry him.

On their return to the hermitage Rāma and Lakshmaṇa were in despair and started off in search of Sītā. They found an ally in Sugrīva, king of the monkeys, who had been driven from his throne by his brother Vālin. Rāma helped Sugrīva to slay Vālin and recover his throne, and the grateful Sugrīva sent out the whole tribe of the monkeys to find Sītā. Hanumat, the simian hero, crossed the sea at a single mighty bound and reached the island of Laṅkā, where he found Sītā; after endless adventures — one of which is that he is captured for a time and has burning cotton tied to his tail — he returned from over the sea, bringing Rāma news of his beloved.

On hearing the news the army of the monkeys, led by Rāma, built a bridge over the sea and invaded the isle of Laṅkā. The whole of the sixth canto of the *Rāmāyaṇa* is taken up by the battles of Rāma, Lakshmaṇa, and Hanumat against Rāvaṇa and his demons. In the end Rāvaṇa was vanquished by Rāma in person, and the victor caused Sītā to be brought to him, whereupon she arrived, her soul overflowing with joy. But the hero's heart was torn by a doubt: "Though thou art at my side," he cried, "thou dost hurt me as a

FIGURE 106
Bōrōbudur.
— *Photo, Goloubew*

lamp hurts a sensitive eye. . . . What man could take back and cherish a woman who has lived in the house of another? How should I take thee back, I who am proud of my noble family, once thou hast been pressed to the bosom of Rāvaṇa and he has looked upon thee with his depraved eye?" When she heard these words, the eyes of Sītā, who had defended herself so fiercely against the encroachments of Rāvaṇa, filled with tears. Wounded to the quick, she caused a pyre to be built, and cast herself into the flames. "But Rāma listened sullenly to the cries of sorrow that rose from the crowd; he remained for a long time pensive, and, in spite of his fortitude, his face was bathed in tears." But the god Agni appeared in the midst of the flames, drew forth Sītā, and restored her to her husband; upon which Rāma, accompanied by his faultless lover, returned to Ayodhyā, where he at last received consecration as king.[1]

Besides Vishnuism the great popular religion of the Hindus is Śivaism.[2] Śiva, who plays the part of the destroyer in the Hindu *Trimūrti,* or triad, proves to be an essentially composite divinity. He is connected with the Rudra of the Vedas, the god of the forests and the whirlwinds, known, as early as the time of the Vedas, by the euphemistic epithet of Śiva, the "kindly." In the same spirit he is also called Bhava, "the god of prosperity"; but he is also Kāla, or Time, the destroyer, and Bhairava, the god of terror. To his votaries, as the sum of all these varied aspects, he is, above all, Mahādēva, the "great god," the one and only cosmic god, of whom the other divinities are merely the emanation.

We see how multifarious were the forms ultimately assumed by the ancient god of the whirlwind. Representing, as he did, the untamed forces of nature, it was quite in order that in the world of

[1] See W. Stutterheim: *Rāma-Legenden und Rāma-Reliefs in Indonesien* (Munich, 1924–5); Ananda Coomaraswamy: *Catalogue of the Indian Collections in the Museum of Fine Arts, Boston,* Pt. V, "Rajput Painting," Pl. X–XV and XXXVI–XXXVII.

[2] Cf. Jouveau-Dubreuil: *Archéologie du sud de l'Inde,* II, "*Iconographie,*" pp. 9–59 (Śivaite iconography).

Figure 107

Bōrōbudur. Descent of the bodhisattva from the heaven of the Tushita (satisfied or beatified ones).
— *Photo, Goloubew*

Hindu philosophy he should symbolize the powers of destruction which are at the basis of cosmic evolution, death being the very law of existence, as a condition of life, or, better still, as the eternal generator of life. In this superior wisdom, transcending both good and evil, both kindness and cruelty, both being and not-being — a wisdom, in fact, of a Nietzschean order — lies the whole of Śivaism. This conception is curiously illustrated by the iconography of Śiva, who appears at times as a naked ascetic, whose actions, in the eyes of

FIGURE 108
Bōrōbudur. The bodhisattva victorious in the archery contest.
— *Photo, Goloubew*

the frivolous, are those of a madman. His body is smeared with ashes; his long hair, with its tangled locks, is knotted carelessly on top of his head. He haunts charnel-houses and cemeteries, dances ecstatic dances without apparent reason, or indulges in inconceivable austerities in hermitages in the Himalayas. But at the same time his religion tolerated the most lewd practices, and the symbol under which he was worshipped was to be no other than the *liṅga,* or phallic emblem, Śiva being even represented and worshipped under this primitive form of the *liṅga,* sometimes conventionalized and sometimes quite realistic, and standing upright in the *yoni*. There is a profound symbolism in this, whose philosophic import we should be careful not to misinterpret; for it shows us the god of destruction as one and the same with the creative principle, the act of death as the source of generative power.[1]

The dread ascetic has, as a rule, four arms, the two upper ones bearing the tambourine (*ḍhakkā*) and the hind (*mṛiga*), while the lower ones represent the gesture of giving (*varada hasta*), and the

FIGURE 109
Bōrōbudur. Dance in the episode of Sudhana.
— *Photo, Goloubew*

gesture of absence of fear (*abhaya hasta*). In addition to his two human eyes, he has an eye in the middle of the forehead. His sole garment is a tiger-skin, and he wears a live serpent round his neck as a collar. On his high Brahmanical topknot he wears the crescent moon, a skull, the fifth head of Brahmā, and the siren of the Gaṅgā.

Each of these attributes is connected with some episode in the life of Śiva. The image of Gaṅgā, or the goddess of the Ganges, recalls the descent of the sacred river. In former days, indeed, it flowed only in heaven. King Bhagīratha subjected himself to incredible austerities

[1] The Śiva-pūjā often express a sense of great piety, devotionalism, and mystic tenderness. See Coomaraswamy: *Les Miniatures orientales de la collection Goloubew (Oriental miniatures of the Goloubew Collection), Museum of Fine Arts, Boston, Ars Asiatica,* XIII (1929), Pl. LXXXV.

in order that the sacred water might come down and purify the earth; but since, by descending in a mass, it would have caused a new flood, Śiva in his mercy consented to receive the waters on his head; for a thousand years they swirled among the braids of his

FIGURE 110
Bōrōbudur. The bodhisattva asking his father's permission to depart.
— *Photo, Goloubew*

hair, before gushing forth in seven springs from the slopes of the Himalayas. One of the most powerful of the rock-carvings at Māvalipuram represents this descent of the beneficent waters in the guise of a cascade of male and female serpent divinities (*nāgas* and *nāgīs*) amid the homage of prostrate creation (Fig. 62).

Thus this fierce god, this deity of destruction, is capable of acts of stupendous self-sacrifice. During the churning of the sea, in order to save both gods and living creatures, he consented to drink the poison cast up by the sea, or by the serpent Vāsuki, and he preserved the mark of the scorching indelibly imprinted upon his throat — whence the epithet Nīlakaṇṭha, or " blue throat," which is applied to him.

FIGURE 111
Bōrōbudur. The bodhisattva cuts off his hair.
— *Photo, Goloubew*

The fifth head of Brahmā which adorns Śiva's head-dress is an allusion to an act of quite an unexpected nature as coming from the deity of the *liṅga* and redounds entirely to his credit, though the form which it assumed was somewhat violent: in a fit of virtuous indignation at an act of incest contemplated by Brahmā, Śiva cut off one of the culprit's five heads, after which he was seized with remorse — for Brahmā is the father of the gods — and was overcome by madness. This madness went so far as to make him commit various strange actions, such as the seduction of the wives of the anchorites in the forest of Tāragam — though, to be sure, the anchorites were heretics! In their fury they hurled at him a flaming ax and a huge antelope, whereupon he seized both of these and took them as the attributes of two of his arms. Next, by the magic of the sacrificial flame, the

FIGURE 112
Bōrōbudur. The bodhisattva washes his garments.
— *Photo, Goloubew*

heretics created a savage tiger, which rushed upon the god. But, " with a gentle smile, he seized it and, with the nail of his little finger, ripped off its skin and wrapped himself in it as in a silken stuff." Lastly the heretics raised up a monstrous serpent, but Śiva seized that too and knotted it round his neck as a necklace. As for the demon which Śiva tramples underfoot as he dances the *tāṇḍava,* it is either one of the *asuras* of Tripura, the city of the Titans destroyed by him in the course of the eternal struggle between the gods and the *asuras,* or else the malevolent dwarf Muyalaka, stirred up against him by the heretical monks, whose back he broke with the tip of his toe.

Hindu iconographers have classified the principal aspects of Śiva which correspond to the various forms of his many-sided activity as follows: *anugrahamūrti,* or beneficent aspects of the god,[1] and *saṃhāramūrti,* or destructive aspects[2] — as, for example, Śiva Vīrabhadra or Śiva Bhairava, the "god of terror," a naked ascetic who

FIGURE 113
Bōrōbudur. Suppliants.
— *Photo, Goloubew*

haunts funeral pyres, accompanied by vultures;[3] *bhikshaṭanamūrti,* or the aspect of the mendicant ascetic, who is also naked (Fig. 93);[4] *nṛittamūrti,* or his aspects as *Naṭarāja,* the "king of the dance" (Fig. 94–97);[5] *mahēśamūrti,* or the three-headed form which enables

[1] See Gopinatha Rao: *Elements of Hindu Iconography,* Vol. II, Pt. i, 205–20, Pl. XLIX–LV.

[2] See ibid., Vol. II, Pt. i, 145–94, Pl. XXX–XLVII.

[3] See ibid., Vol. II, Pt. i, 77–188, Pl. XLI–XLIV; Krishna Sastri: *South Indian Images of Gods and Goddesses,* pp. 151–9.

[4] See Gopinatha Rao, op. cit., Vol. II, Pt. i, 306–9, with the splendid plates LXXXVII and LXXXIX.

[5] See ibid., Vol. II, Pt. i, 223–70, Pl. LVI–LXIX; Banerji, op. cit., Pl. II, a.

him to display three of these aspects at once (Fig. 81–83).[1] Among these manifestations, we should not forget that of the *liṅga*, the incarnation of Śiva in his most elemental form, expressive of his potentialities and latent powers, just as the *Naṭarāja* symbolizes the god in his highest activities.

FIGURE 114
Bōrōbudur. The offering of Sujātā.
— *Photo, Goloubew*

Thus Śiva became the pantheist god *par excellence* (cf. Fig. 83). It is this aspect of him which is celebrated in one of the finest poems of the *Harivaṃśa:* " I worship thee, Father of this universe, which thou dost traverse by invisible ways, great mystic tree with the shining branches, terrible deity with the myriad eyes and the thousand armours. Thee do I implore, which art of divers aspects, now per-

[1] See Gopinatha Rao, op. cit., Vol. II, Pt. ii, 379, Pl. CXVI, CXVII.

fect and just, now false and unjust. Protect me, thou the only god, with thine escort of wild beasts, thou who art also the pleasure of the senses, the past and the future, imperceptible atom which dost

FIGURE 115
Bōrōbudur. The bodhisattva receives the handful of grass for the Buddha to sit upon.
— *Photo, Goloubew*

abide in the heart of the disintegrated elements, one and only substance of organic bodies, owing thy birth to none save thyself, O Universal Essence! "

There is a Tamil poem which expresses this cosmic character of Śiva even more powerfully: " The ages," it runs, " during which many millions of the gods of heaven shall follow one after the other, each of them living out the appointed period of his life, the time during which many Brahmās shall die, the time after which Vishṇu shall cease to be, these ages are scarce as one moment for Śiva. When the time shall be fulfilled at which the sea, the earth, the air, the fire, and the wind shall be annihilated, many millions of Vishṇus

FIGURE 116
Bōrōbudur. The Assault of Mārā and the Temptation, right-hand side.
— *Photo, Goloubew*

shall perish, and many millions of Brahmās shall die also: then shall Śiva collect together all the heads of these gods, of these heads he shall make himself a necklace, and he shall dance upon one foot a dance that none can imitate, in which this necklace shall clash against his eight shoulders; and he shall sing mysterious tunes such as none other can sing, and he shall taste of pleasures that none other has known."

Let us pause a moment over this symbol of the Naṭarāja, one of the most deeply charged with philosophical thought that Indian wisdom has handed down to us (Fig. 94–97). With regard to the origin of the dance of the *tāṇḍava,* we can no doubt descry in the pre-Aryan past of the Deccan the wild leapings of some half-demoniac divinity amid the cemeteries by night, around the dismal flames of

FIGURE 117
Bōrōbudur. The Assault of Mārā and the Temptation, left-hand side.
— *Photo, Goloubew*

the funeral pyres. But it was not long before Indian speculation read a deeper meaning into this primitive theme. Henceforth the dance of the god became the very process of the creation, preservation, and destruction of the universe, or rather, to adhere to the Indian terminology, of the "five activities (*pañchakṛitya*)": production, preservation, destruction, incarnation, and deliverance. The scene of this dance, symbolized in the representations of it in art by the flame-fringed aureole (*tiruvāśi*) which surrounds it, is the cosmos as a whole. "Our lord," says a sacred text, "is the dancer, who, like the heat latent in wood for kindling fire, diffuses his power through both spirit and matter, and causes them each in turn to dance." One of the poems of Kabīr, translated by Rabindranath Tagore, expresses the same idea: "Dance, my heart, dance today for joy. Songs of love fill both day and night with music, and the world doth hearken to their melodies. Mad with joy, life and death dance to the rhythm of this music. The mountains and the ocean and the earth do dance. Amid bursts of laughter and sobbing, humanity doth dance!"

In these words we penetrate to the profound significance of this symbolism. On turning from Buddhist poetry and morality, so pure and gentle that the heart at once goes out to them, we are perhaps a little taken aback by this Hindu polytheism with its confused, innumerable throng of contradictory forms. But in the philosophy of Śivaism its apparent fancifulness falls into some order and takes on a metaphysical significance which is, in its way, as noble and elevated as that of Buddhism itself, and perhaps even richer. It is a grand and profound doctrine, which will remind us of certain aspects of the theories of Nietzsche, for it, too, transcends both good and evil, being higher than both and going beyond optimism and pessimism alike: it contains a pessimism that is in some sort heroic — for the god dances on corpses among charnel-houses; but it contains an optimism as well, a pitiless and inhuman optimism — or superhuman, if we prefer so to call it; for out of all this destruction is born and perpetuated a fearful joy, the joy of matter eternally renewed.

In what magnificent language do the Śivaite hymns sing of this state of mind: "The staff of a mendicant monk, an ax, an antelope-skin, ashes, serpents, and a death's-head — such, dispenser of all favours, are thy sole garment, thy furniture and thine only adornment. The gods have as their portion, one this form of wealth, and

FIGURE 118

Bōrōbudur. Sudhana at the fountain.

— *Photo, Goloubew*

one that, which thy majesty rejects with disdain. For the illusion of the objects of sense cannot deceive the being whose whole joy lies in contemplating his own soul. When thou dost dance for the preservation of the world, the earth, smitten by thy feet, trembles as though on the point of destruction, the sky reels, the army of the planets is swept away by the movement of thine arms, and the firmament, touched by thy head-dress, is ready to crumble to dust: so full of seeming contradictions is thy power, though ever at harmony with itself. Thy gardens are the cemeteries, the vampires form thy court, the ashes of funeral pyres are thy sandalwood, a chaplet of human skulls thy garland of flowers; thy mood is sinister, and no less so is thy name. None the less art thou the supreme felicity of those who call upon thy name, O dispenser of favours! Thou art the sun, thou art the moon, thou art the wind, thou art the water, thou art the heaven and the earth, thou art the universal soul, thou art at once the all and its every part. Glory be unto thee, which art both the atom and the cosmos, O god whom we dearly love. Glory be unto thee, which art the All. Glory be unto thee which art *more than the all and dost include the all!*" [1]

We see the process by which this doctrine, though in so many respects unmoral and inhuman, resolves itself in the end into a mystical quietism. The Śivaite saints of the early Middle Ages, such as Tirujñāna Sambandha Svāmi, Appār Svāmi, and Sundara mūrti Svāmi, who flourished between the seventh and the ninth centuries, often sound a note in their hymns which reminds us of Catholic mysticism. The delightful Dravidian bronzes which perpetuate the likeness of these child saints (Fig. 99 and 100) are an intimation to us that, in the unity of the human mind, the most diametrically opposed principles are mutually dependent, and that, without denying his own nature, the god of terror was capable of giving rise to a cult of abnegation, charity, and tenderness.

[1] See A. Coomaraswamy: *The Dance of Shiva* (New York, 1918; London, 1925).

Figure 119
Above, the bath of the bodhisattva. Below, Landing of Hiru.
— *Photo, Goloubew*

In this cosmic deity, in fact, all contradictions become reconciled. We have seen that he had as his essential symbol the *liṅga,* or phallic organ. But at the same time this god of the generative forces "consumed love" — and the way in which this happened forms one of the most charming legends in Hindu mythology. At the prayer of the goddess Pārvatī, Kāma, the god of love, had tried to disturb the heart of Śiva during his solitary meditations. Without word or gesture the divine ascetic turned upon him the terrible glance of the eye set in the midst of his forehead. "Love did not perish, for he is immortal. But, consumed as though by a flash of lightning, he has been since then the god without a body (*anaṅga*)."

In the end, however, the terrible ascetic yielded to the desires of Pārvatī, the goddess of the mountains, who is also known as Durgā, "the Inaccessible," Kālī, "the Black," or simply Dēvī, "the Goddess" (Fig. 73, 163, 233, 235). The consummation of their union made the whole world tremble. And, as a matter of fact, this earth-goddess is no more nor less than the *śakti,* or Energy of Śiva, projected outside himself and personified under a feminine form, to be all the more surely united to him afterwards in this sexual union (Fig. 76). She is therefore represented as in every way resembling him. "Durgā," says the *Harivaṃśa,* " is both wisdom and pleasure, both darkness and light. The elder sister of Yama, the god of death, she is covered with a garment of black silk. She appears under a thousand graceful or splendid forms. At times her glance is horrible, at times it is all sweetness. . . . Her favourite resort is in the Vindhya mountains. Her joy is in battle. Now she appears all covered with rags, now resplendent in magnificent garments. She is the night and the twilight. She walks with dishevelled hair. She is death, which delights to rend and devour the bleeding, palpitating flesh, and she is also the resplendence of the stars, the dutifulness of young girls, and the happiness of wives."

These very varied aspects of the generative and destructive Energy

FIGURE 120

Bōrōbudur. *Jātaka* 504. Bhallāṭīya.

— *Photo, Goloubew*

find a rendering in the works of art.[1] On a number of reliefs at Ellora and Elephanta we shall see the goddess as lover and wife, full of tenderness and modest emotion (Fig. 75). One of these reliefs at Ellora, in particular, shows us Pārvatī in a mythological scene connected with the *Rāmāyaṇa*: Śiva and Pārvatī are enthroned upon Mount Kailās (Kailāsa), the Himalayan Olympus, which serves as their residence, while the *rākshasa* Rāvaṇa, the demon monster of the *Rāmāyaṇa*, starts shaking the mountain in order to obtain the intervention of Śiva against Rāma. The terrified Pārvatī clings to her spouse with a gesture full of womanly spontaneity and freshness, while Śiva holds the mountain steady and crushes the Titan with his toe (Fig. 77 and 160).[2]

Side by side with these representations of the goddess, full of a delicate and touching humanity, in which she is no more than a loving woman, there are others of a very different character. In these Durgā is the queen of battles, or, rather, of slaughter: we see her mounted on a lion in the character of Mahishamardinī,[3] or "slayer of Mahisha," the *asura* or buffalo demon, whom she is piercing with her trident. As Kālī she appears as an old woman, with tongue lolling out and threatening fangs, dressed, like her consort, in a tiger-skin and a necklace of skulls; around her are grouped yet other Śivaite goddesses, the *Sapta mātṛika*, or Seven Mothers, symbols, like her, of life and death, of radiant beauty and hideous ugliness (Fig. 88 and 89). Even under this terrible aspect she is the object of an ardent mystical devotion on the part of the "Śaktist" sects, as the worshippers of the female Energy are called: "Because thou dost love the funeral pyres," runs one of their hymns, "I have made a pyre of my heart, that thou mayest come, O gloomy goddess,

[1] See Gopinatha Rao, op. cit., Vol. I, Pt. ii, 327–400.

[2] See ibid., Vol. II, Pt. i, 217, Pl. LIII. In Rajput paintings we have delightful representations of the love of Śiva and Pārvatī. See Gangoly: *Masterpieces of Rajput Painting*, Pl. XXX, XXXII, XXXIII.

[3] Or *Mahishāsura-marddani.* See Gopinatha Rao, op. cit., Vol. I, Pt. ii, 345, Pl. CIII–CV; and Krishna Sastri, op. cit., pp. 207–11.

and dance in it thine eternal dance. Enter into me, enter into me, dancing thy rhythmic dance, that I may gaze upon thee with closed eyes."

In the popular modern art of southern India Śiva and Pārvatī appear under a less clearly defined aspect, as a pair of divinities riding on the back of the bull Nandi (Fig. 234) or accompanied by this animal, which arose out of the churning of the sea, after which

FIGURE 121
Arrival at Nandana, as in the Buddhist poem of the *Maitrakanyaka Avadānaśataka*, no. 36.
— *Photo, Goloubew*

it was used by Śiva to ride upon. Sometimes Śiva and Pārvatī are escorted by their son Ganesh (Gaṇēśa) or Gaṇapati (Gaṇādhipati), the god with an elephant's head (Fig. 233 and 162).[1] Ganesh, with his head and trunk and one tusk (the other having been broken in a mythological adventure) and his cunning little eyes and round belly, is accompanied by his crony the rat, as sly as himself, who, in case of need, carries him on its back; he has as his attributes the goad (*aṅkush* or *aṅkuśa*) and the rosary (*akshamālā*) and is one of the most popular figures in India. Uniting in himself, as he does, the

[1] See Gopinatha Rao, op. cit., Vol. I, Pt. i, 36–67; Krishna Sastri, op. cit., pp. 169–76; and the delightful Ganesh at Calcutta reproduced by Percy Brown: "The Art Section of the Indian Museum of Calcutta," in *Indian Art and Letters*, 1930, I, Pl. II.

nature of the two most intelligent creatures in creation — man and the elephant — it was natural that he should have become the god of men of letters. We may add that he is remarkably fond of good cheer — which is hardly likely to make him unpopular with the wits. And, finally, to put the finishing touch to his prepossessing

FIGURE 122
Bōrōbudur. Rudrāyaṇa asking for information about the Buddha.
— *Photo, Goloubew*

character, he is able, in case of need, to combine the greatest kindliness — for there is no deity more benevolent — with a remarkable steadfastness in battle.

The second son of Śiva and Pārvatī is Skanda,[1] the god of war, sometimes represented with six heads and riding upon a peacock.

Finally, Hindu syncretism has created some composite divinities,

[1] Or Kumara, or Subrahmaṇya. See Gopinatha Rao, op. cit., Vol. II, Pt. ii, 415· and Krishna Sastri, op. cit., p. 177.

such as Hari-Hara, a combination of Vishṇu (Hari) and Śiva (Hara).[1] The statues of this god, which are particularly frequent in pre-Angkorean Cambodia, are divided down the middle by an imaginary vertical line, the part to the right of which represents Śiva, with his hair knotted on top of his head like an ascetic, and the half-eye in his forehead, while the part to the left represents Vishṇu, with his high royal head-dress or tiara (Fig. 131, 132, 148). Still more composite, but less frequent, is the representation of the *Trimūrti,* or Hindu triad, having as its principal figure Śiva, with Brahmā and Vishṇu issuing from his body to the right and left — an interesting combination, for it reminds us that the gods of the Hindu religion can in the last analysis be resolved into one another, and that all this polytheism is simply the poetical expression of a grandiose monism.[2]

To complete this rapid sketch of Hindu beliefs, something must be said about the epic legends. We have referred to those of Rāma; but there remains the other mass of epic poetry, the *Mahābhārata,* which is likewise an integral part of the Hindu faith. The original subject of the poem is the account of the struggle between the two clans established in the region of Delhi, which are, moreover, closely related to each other: the Pāṇḍavas and the Kauravas, descended respectively from two brothers, Pāṇḍu and Dhṛitarāshṭra. The heroes of the primitive poem are the five sons of Pāṇḍu: Yudhishṭhira, Bhīma, Arjuna, Nakula, and Sahadēva. Their birth was miraculous, for Kuntī, the mother of the first three, and Madrī, the mother of the last two, really conceived them through the agency of the gods. Thus Arjuna, the "Brilliant," who is in some respects the principal figure of the epic, is the son of Indra. The throne is in the possession of the Kauravas, the chief of whom, Dhṛitarāshṭra, has the seat of his rule at Hastināpura in the Dooab. But this king's eldest son,

[1] See Gopinatha Rao, op. cit., Vol. II, Pt. i, 332; and a beautiful sixth-century Hari-Hara at Bādāmī, in Banerji, op. cit., Pl. III, b.

[2] See Gopinatha Rao, op. cit., Vol. II, Pt. ii, 382–401.

Figure 123

Bōrōbudur. Group of musicians.

— *Photo, Goloubew*

Duryodhana, conceives a hatred for his cousins the Pāṇḍavas and causes them to be exiled. The five brothers accordingly retire into the woods — a frequent theme of Hindu legend — taking with them their common wife, the beautiful Draupadī, daughter of the King of the Pañcālas; they next settle in the region of Indraprastha (Delhi), but,

FIGURE 124
Bōrōbudur. Forest scene.
— *Photo, Goloubew*

having gambled away their new kingdom to their Kaurava cousins, they once more depart into exile into the forest.

The Pāṇḍavas, however, have a supernatural protector, the hero Kṛishṇa, the leader of the Yadavas, a demigod disguised as a man, who acts as adviser to Arjuna. Encouraged by him, they claim back their kingdom from their cousins, and when the latter refuse to give it up, the great war begins. It occupies cantos VI to X of the epic, together with the bloody battle of the Kurukshētra, which is split up into as many episodes and single combats as a battle in the Iliad.

In the end the Pāṇḍavas are victorious and their leader, Yudhishṭhira, ascends the throne. But the triumph of the heroes does not constitute the end of the epic, which has a melancholy finish, for in it we witness the death of Kṛishṇa as a human being and see how his subjects, the Yadavas, exterminate one another as the result of a curse sent from heaven, while he himself dies, like Achilles, of a

FIGURE 125
Bōrōbudur. Ship.
— *Photo, Goloubew*

wound in the heel and ascends into heaven. The five Pāṇḍavas in turn, feeling the approach of old age, abandon the throne and start out for the east, like pilgrims in search of the infinite, towards the Himalayas, among which is hidden the Indian Olympus, the fabulous Mēru. They climb upwards through forests and glaciers. In vain do four of them succumb by the wayside, together with Draupadī. Yudhishṭhira, the sole survivor, at last reaches heaven, where he is welcomed by Indra and restored to his own people.

But this plot is only the pretext for poetical digressions. Embedded in the vast poem are a number of separate poems, which are so many masterpieces. The most remarkable, perhaps, in its classic perfection

FIGURE 126
Avalokitēśvara. Javanese bronze, ninth–tenth centuries.
— *Musée Guimet. Archives of the Museum*

is the legend of Nala and Damayantī, which is interpolated into the third canto of the epic. This is yet another story of princes exiled in the forest, like those of Rāma and Sītā or of Viśvantara and Madrī.

The great-souled Nala, " a tiger among men, the hero with the flawless body," who reigns on the banks of the Nerbudda, is the ideal type of the Indian rajah, handsome, elegant, valiant, amorous, and chiv-

FIGURE 127
Prajñāpāramitā (Buddha as the Supreme Wisdom).
— *Leiden Museum. Photo, Van Oest*

alrous. He has won the heart of Damayantī of the long eyes and lovely hips, daughter of the King of Vidarbha (Berar). So mighty is his love that the gods themselves who had come to sue for the hand of the young girl withdrew to make way for him. But once united with his beloved, Nala, like the Pāṇḍava heroes mentioned above, yields to his passion for gambling, and dices away his kingdom. He goes into exile in the forest, followed by the faithful Damayantī, who refuses to leave him. Unlike Rāma, he allows himself to be led astray by the Evil One, and, afraid to let the young woman share the miseries of his outcast life, he takes advantage of her sleep to abandon her in the heart of the jungle. Terrified and unable to find her husband, Damayantī plunges alone into the impassable forests, among the wild plants, the rocks, and the haunts of wild beasts. At last she is saved by a caravan, and after various adventures reaches the city of Chēdi, where the Queen, who is related to her family, welcomes her and treats her with honour, after which she sends her back to her father, the King of Vidarbha. As for Nala, after abandoning his wife he has the good fortune to

FIGURE 128
Pre-Angkorean statue, seventh century.
— *Musée Guimet. Photo, Gauthier*

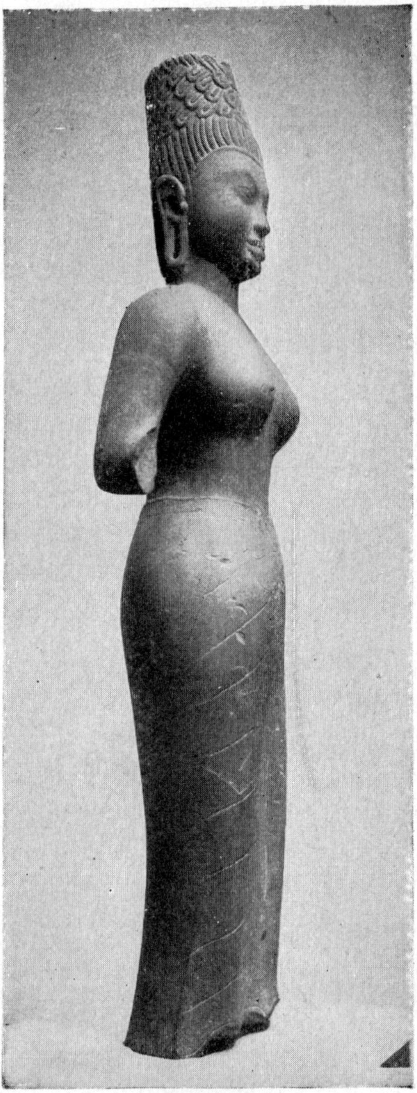

FIGURE 129
Pre-Angkorean statue.
— *Musée Guimet. Photo, Gauthier*

save the life of a serpent-king, who, in his gratitude, endows him with magic power. Now, the King of Vidarbha, believing his daughter to be a widow, thinks of marrying her to somebody else. But, thanks to the powers which he received from the serpent deities, Nala arrives in time, disposes of all his rivals, makes himself known, and recovers his beloved. "On seeing her husband as he had been in the past, Damayantī uttered a loud cry. And King Nala, as resplendent as ever, embraced Damayantī and his two children and was received by them with joy. Then the fair one with the long eyes, laying the head of Nala on her bosom, began to sob. After which, clasping in his arms his wife, with her limbs marred with dust, and her pure smile, the tiger among men remained for a long time plunged in sadness." And the poem ends with the happiness of the husband and wife: "Having recovered her husband, Damayantī rejoiced like the earth which welcomes the rain when the corn has begun to sprout. Even so, when her weariness was once dispelled, her whole being bloomed with joy at attaining the summit of her desires, and she shone like the night when illuminated by the moon."[1]

Another poem included in the *Mahābhārata*, though quite different in its inspiration, is the "*Bhagavad gītā*," or "Song of the Blessed One." This is a philosophical poem — possessing, moreover, brilliantly poetical qualities — in which Kṛishṇa, while fighting at the side of the hero Arjuna, rouses him to do his duty in the approaching battle. At the moment of giving the order to attack, the great-souled Arjuna, seized with a compassion which is quite Buddhist in character, hesitated as he thought of the thousands of victims who were about to perish. It was now that Kṛishṇa developed to him the pure Hindu doctrine of a serene cosmic indifference as

[1] Cf. Ananda Coomaraswamy: *Catalogue of the Indian Collections in the Museum of Fine Arts, Boston*, Pt. V, "Rajput Painting," Pl. XL–LIV.

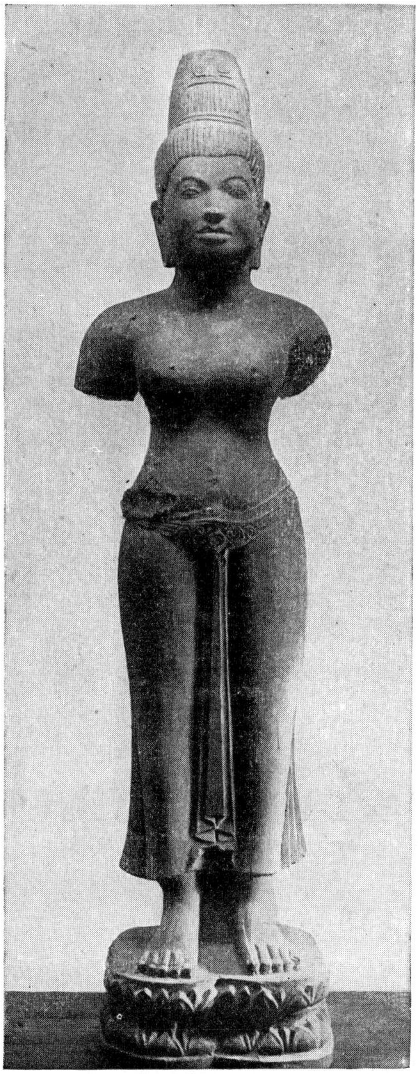

FIGURE 130
Pre-Angkorean statue, from a cast in the Trocadéro.
— *Photo, Gauthier*

FIGURE 131
Hari-Hara in the Museum of Phnom Pēnh, from the cast in the Trocadéro.
— *Archives of the Musée Guimet*

opposed to the pity of Buddha: "Thou dost feel pity where pity has no place. Wise men feel no pity either for what dies or for what lives. There was never a time when I and thou were not in existence, and all these princes, too. Nor will the day ever come in future when all of us shall not exist. . . . There is no existence for nothingness, there is no destruction for that which is. Know that the very tissue of this universe is the Imperishable; it lies in no man's power to destroy it. Bodies come to an end, but the soul which is clothed in them is eternal, indestructible, and infinite. Fight then, O Bhārata! It is as much a mistake to believe that one man kills as that the other is killed. There is never any birth, nor any death. Nobody has begun, and nobody will cease to be. Having no beginning and no end, the one and only Soul is not smitten when the body is struck. . . . That which is born is sure to die, and that which is dead is sure to be born. Faced with the inevitable, pity has no longer any place. The origin of things escapes us; the object of our perceptions in the course of their career, they elude us once more in their end. Of what use are lamentations? Consider that pleasure or pain, wealth or poverty, victory or defeat, are of equal worth. Prepare, then, for the combat! . . . Give thought to nothing but the act, never to its fruits, and let not thyself be seduced by inaction. For him who achieves inward detachment, neither good nor evil exists any longer here below." We see that here, too, as in Śivaism, Hinduism attains to a Nietzschean serenity, superior to humanity. It consists in a love of action for action's sake, in the shape of a complete acquiescence, joyful and voluntary, in the universal movement (dance). "O world," wrote Marcus Aurelius, "all that thou dost bring me is good unto me." But the acquiescence of the Stoic philosopher had something resigned, disillusioned, and negative about it. That of Hinduism, fierce and even cruel as it may appear in its applications, seems to us infinitely more sane and virile from the philosophical point of view.

HINDU ART

DURING THE MIDDLE AGES HINDUISM SERVED AS THE INSPIRATION OF a powerful artistic movement in the sphere both of architecture and of sculpture.[1]

Mediæval Hindu architecture includes three great schools: that of the Mahratta territory, with which we may associate that of the Carnatic during the Pallava period; the school of Orissa; and, thirdly, the school of the Carnatic in the Tamil period proper, after the tenth century.

The style of the Mahratta territory is usually designated by the name of the two powerful local dynasties, the Chālukyas (550–757) and the Rāshṭrakūṭas (757–973), which reigned during the early

[1] Cf. Prasanna Kumar Acharya: *Dictionary of Hindu Architecture*, Oxford University Press, 1927; A. Coomaraswamy: "Indian Architectural Terms," *Journal of the American Oriental Society*, Vol. XLVIII, No. 2, pp. 250–75.

Middle Ages in what is now the Bombay Presidency.[1] The principal monuments of this art are, for the Chālukya period, the temples of Aihoḷe, dating from about 600, the Mālegitti Śivālaya and three other temples at Bādāmī, dating from about 625, the temple of Virūpāksha at Paṭṭakadal, dating from about 740, and the earliest grottoes of Ellora — for instance, the Cave of the Avatars, Rāvaṇa-kā-Khai, Dhumar Leṇā, and the Rāmēśvara, dating from the seventh century. To the next period, that of the Rāshṭrakūṭas, belong the temple of the Kailāsa at Ellora, dating from about 757 to 783, and the Śivaite sanctuary at Elephanta, dating from about 850 to 900. We may well associate with this style the temples in the Carnatic belonging to the period of the Pallavas, who ruled over the Madras Presidency from about 400 to 750.[2] The principal Pallava monuments, such as the temples of Mahābalipuram, Māvalipuram, or Māmallapuram, dating from the seventh century, and of Kāñchī, dating from the eighth century, are, moreover, plainly contemporary with those enumerated above (Fig. 57, 58).

All these Pallava or Chālukya temples (or those, at least, which are open to the sky) can be distinguished from the temples of Orissa at a glance by the absence of the bulbous *śikhara*. On the other hand, they still have the *maṇḍapas*, or porticoes crowned with a kind of corniced pyramid, surmounted in Pallava architecture by the little pinnacled pavilions called "*pañcharam*." Moreover, several of the temples at Māvalipuram, the *rāthas*, have this peculiarity: that they are monolithic; that is, they are really sculptured rocks. Similarly, the most important of the Chālukya and Rāshṭrakūṭa temples in the Mahratta territories, such as the Kailāsa at Ellora and the temples of Elephanta, are excavated in the rock; but whereas the *rāthas* of

[1] Cf. H. Cousens: *The Architectural Antiquities of Western India* (London, The India Society, 1927); H. Cousens: *The Chālukyan Architecture of the Kanarese Districts*, Archæological Survey of India, Vol. XLII (1926).

[2] See A. H. Longhurst: *Pallava Architecture*, Memoirs of the Archæological Survey of India, No. 17, Pt. I (1924); No. 33, Pt. II (Māmalla period) (1928); No. 40, Pt. III (1930); Richard C. Temple: "A Visit to Seven Pagodas," *Indian Antiquary*, 1929.

FIGURE 132
Hari-Hara of Mahā Rosei.
— *Musée Guimet*

Māvalipuram, formed of rocks rising from the ground, remain open to the sky, the rock temples of the Mahratta territories, hewn and excavated in the depths of the rock on a mountain side, give the impression of subterranean temples " swallowed up whole as the result of some cataclysm " (Goloubew). Hence their quite peculiar character (Fig. 59, 60). All the same, if we study the longitudinal section of the Kailāsa, as drawn by Burgess, we shall be convinced that these peristyles and *maṇḍapas,* these pyramidal towers with stepped cornices and *pañcharam* — in short, the whole general conception of the monument — is the same as that of the Pallava temples at Māvalipuram, merely adapted here to the necessities of subterranean excavation. It is, moreover, this principle of sculpture in the live rock that has resulted, on the one hand, in the rocks hewn into animal forms by the masters of Māvalipuram, and, on the other hand, in the animals of the Kailāsa at Ellora, which are also monolithic — for instance, the elephants at the entrance and those of the stupendous " battle of the elephants " which seems to support the base of the temple (Fig. 72).

The school of Orissa is characterized by its curvilinear and bulbous towers, known as *śikharas,*[1] with strongly marked ribs, which seem to spring heavenwards as with a spontaneous motion and are crowned by a protruding cushion, or *āmalaka,* usually surmounted by a light, vase-shaped ornament, or *kalasa.*[2] Besides the *śikhara,* these buildings are distinguished by their porches, or *maṇḍapas,* with pyramidal roofs, formed by a number of stepped cornices. This simple, vigorous, and powerfully synthetic style is chiefly represented in the province of Orissa between the eighth and twelfth

[1] See Gurudas Sarkar: "Notes on the History of Śikhara Temples," in *Rūpam,* April 1922; Ramaprasad Chanda: "Beginnings of the Śikhara," *Rūpam,* January 1924; Gangoly: *Indian Architecture,* Calcutta, Rūpam, Pl. XXXII–XLII.

[2] See Mano Mohan Ganguly: *Orissa and her Remains—Ancient and Medieval (District Puri),* Calcutta and London, 1912. The sculpture of Orissa is very interesting as forming a transition between the Gupta or Pāla art of Bengal and the Dravidian art of the Deccan. See Ramaprasad Chanda: *Bhanja Dynasty of Mayurbhanj and their Ancient Capital, Khiching,* Archæological Survey of India, 1923–5; and Fig. 85 of the present work.

FIGURE 133
Statue at Phnom Kulēn.
— *Photo, Goloubew*

FIGURE 134
Statue at Phnom Kulēn.
— *Photo, Goloubew*

centuries. The chief buildings in this style are those of Bhuvaneśvar and Purī: the temple of Paraśurāmēśvara, dating from about 750, that of Muktēśvara, dating from about 950, and that of the Liṅgarāja, dating from about the year 1000; next come the temples of the Rājrānī and of Jagannātha-Purī, dating from about 1150, and that

FIGURE 135
Angkor-Vat.
— *Photo, École française d'Extrême Orient*

of Megheśvara, of about 1200; and, lastly, the temples of Koṇārak, dating, like those of Sūrya and Liṅgarāja, from the thirteenth century (Fig. 56). In the same style are the temples of Khajurāho, in the Bundelkhand, and notably that of Kaṇḍārya Mahādēva, dating from about the year 1000.[1]

The third architectural group is that of the so-called Dravidian temples — that is, those built in the Carnatic after the fall of the

[1] See *Archæological Survey of India, Report, 1922-3*, Pl. XXXIV-XXXVI.

Pallava, under the Tamil dynasties of the tenth to the seventeenth centuries. The chief of these monuments are the great *vimānas* of Tanjore, built about the year 1000 by the Choḷa dynasty, and the temples of the modern Carnatic, such as the *maṇḍapa* of Śrīraṅgam, Vellore, belonging to the sixteenth century, and Madura, dating

FIGURE 136
Brahmā of Battambang, first style.
— *Musée Guimet; Fustier donation*

from the seventeenth century.[1] Another school is that of the region of Mysore, with the temples of Haḷebīd (Mysore) built under the local dynasty of the Hoyśalas, between the twelfth and thirteenth centuries, and the unfortunately ruined temples of Vijayanagar (Hampi), such as the Viṭhoba, dating from the sixteenth century.[2] These Dravidian temples, especially those of the Carnatic,

[1] See Jagadisa Ayyar: *South Indian Shrines* (Madras, 1920).

[2] See A. H. Longhurst: *Hampi Ruins, described and illustrated* (Madras Government Press, 1917); A Sewell: *A Forgotten Empire, Vijayanagar* (London, 1900).

usually consist, firstly, of gates surmounted by a tower, or *gopura,* which give access to the temple and are the characteristic feature of this architecture; secondly, of the *maṇḍapa,* a porch or columned hall preceding the sanctuary, which we have already noted in the temples of Orissa and the Chālukya or Pallava temples; and, thirdly, of the sanctuary properly so called, or *vimāna,* which is likewise surmounted by a tower in the shape of a truncated pyramid with several storeys. Both the *vimānas* and the *gopuras* are seen here as heavy masses of stone which take the same form of a truncated pyramid, overloaded and entirely covered with carvings; but here the sculpture is no longer of any value in itself, but only as a motive of ornamentation. This ornamentation, which almost suggests goldsmiths' work executed in stone, becomes more and more elaborate, from the *vimāna* of Tanjore, in the eleventh century (Fig. 61) to the great temple of Madura, in the seventeenth century. Nor is it any less profuse in the interior in the *maṇḍapas,* as is shown by the famous cavalcade of Śrīraṅgam. To quote W. Cohn, we have here a sort of "Hindu baroque"; but, thanks to the exuberance of its inspiration, the inexhaustible fantasy and prodigious variety of the sculptural motives, it none the less produces a powerfully decorative effect.[1]

For the sake of clearness, we have enumerated these various schools on geographical and static principles, paying no attention to the links of evolution which connect them. Yet these links none the less exist. The two earliest in date of these Indian schools of architecture — that of the Mahratta territory and that of the Pallavas — serve as the starting-point of the other two. The *śikhara* of Orissa is, indeed, no more than an upward extension, with a more soaring curvilinear outline, of the pyramid with rounded tiers that charac-

[1] See Jouveau-Dubreuil, *Archéologie du sud de l'Inde,* Vol. I, *Architecture,* Annales du Musée Guimet, Bibliothèque d'Études, Vol. XXVI (1914). For the "Hindu baroque" of Madura, Tanjore, Śrīraṅgam, Kumbhakonam, Tiruvarnāmalai, Chidambaram, etc., see the photographs by H. von Glasenapp: *Heilige Stätten Indiens* (Munich, 1928), Pl. 135–171.

FIGURE 137

Vishṇu in his avatar as a horse(?). First Angkorean style.
— *Musée Guimet. Archives of the Museum*

terizes the Mahratta style, as seen in the temple of Mālegitti Śivālaya at Bādāmī, or of that belonging to the Pallava style, as seen in the temple on the shore at Māvalipuram, the intermediate stage being provided by the temples of Khajurāho. Again, the truncated pyramid of the *Choḷa* or Tamil school is another resultant of the same elements: starting from the stepped pyramid with rounded tiers, as seen on the *maṇḍapa* of Sūrya Deul, at Koṇārak, or on the Muktesvara at Kāñchī, the slope of the pyramid has only to be made continuous by increasing the number of tiers and reducing the width of the step by which they are separated, to give us the *maṇḍapas* and *gopuras* of Tanjore and Madura. The intermediate stage is, moreover, provided by the temples of the Hoyśala school of Mysore, referred to above: the temple of Somnāthpur, dating from 1248, and the temple of Nuggehalli, at Mysore, dating from 1249.[1]

Jain architecture, though akin to that of Orissa, is a style by itself. It was evolved in the sanctuaries of Jainism, and notably at Mount Abū in Rajputana, in the Vimala Shā and Tējahpāla, dating from 1032 and 1232, at Girnār in Kathiawar, whose temples date from 1230 and 1278, and at Pālitāna in Gujerat, where they date from the ninth century. The essential features of a Jain monastery of the best period are: a porch consisting of four colonnades forming a cross which meet in an octagonal building supporting a curvilinear dome copied from the *śikharas* of Orissa, but hollow inside and more slender and soaring; next comes the sanctuary, preceded by its vestibule, and also surmounted by a curvilinear tower. Round these principal *śikharas* are grouped all those that crown the various secondary edifices. This profusion of pillars, kiosks, towers, domes, pinnacles, and spires, added to the quality of the material and the infinite variety of the decoration — at Mount Abū they are of white

[1] See Vincent Smith: "Architecture and Sculpture in Mysore, Hoysala Style," in *Indian Antiquary*, Vol. XLIV (1915); R. Narasimhachar: *Architecture and Sculpture in Mysore*, Vol. I, *The Kesava Temple at Somanathapur* (Bangalore, 1917); Vol. III, *The Lakshmidevi Temple at Dodda-Gaddavalli* (1919).

Figure 138

Buddhist head. Second Angkorean style.
— *Musée Guimet. Archives of the Museum*

marble, deeply hollowed out and, as it were, chased like goldsmiths' work — succeeds in producing an impression of elegance and lightness worthy of Arab art.[1] It is not at all surprising that the earliest Indo-Moslem architects drew so much of their inspiration from Jain models (Fig. 168–169).

The sculpture associated with the Hindu architecture of the early Middle Ages is quite as interesting as the buildings themselves. Like them, indeed, it is directly connected with the Buddhist art of the preceding age. This continuity is particularly noticeable in the group of temples at Mahābalipuram, Māvalipuram, or Māmallapuram, near Madras, in the Carnatic.[2]

The sculpture of Māvalipuram is the highest achievement of the art of the Pallavas, a people which, as we have seen, held sway over the Deccan from about 400 to 750. But, far from representing foreign invaders, as some have believed, the Pallavas merely carried on in this part of the eastern Deccan the traditions of the kings of Andhra, among whose vassals they had doubtless been numbered in past days. Thus a connexion is established between Māvalipuram, the Pallava capital, and Amarāvatī, the former capital of the Andhras. We may, moreover, consider that the art of Amarāvatī, as certain reliefs from Nāgārjunikoṇḍa in the Musée Guimet bear witness, lasted till well on into the fifth century — that is, down to the beginning of the Pallava period. This influence of the art of Amarāvatī on the development of Pallava sculpture seems to us incontrovertible. It doubtless explains why the inspiration of the works at Māvalipuram is less severe, more human, and more touching than in the other Śivaite or Vishnuite sanctuaries.

[1] Cf. D. R. Bhandarkar: "Some Temples on Mount Abu," *Rūpam*, July 1920.

[2] See Rodin, Ananda Coomaraswamy, Havell, and Goloubew: *Sculptures śivaites*, Collection *Ars Asiatica*, No. III (Paris, Van Oest, 1921), Pl. XXVIII–XLVII; A. H. Longhurst: *Pallava Architecture*, Memoirs of the Archæological Survey of India, No. 33, Pt. ii (1928), Pl. XXI, XXV, XXVIII–XXXIII; A. Coomaraswamy: "Two Pallava Marble Pillars," *Bulletin of the Museum of Fine Arts, Boston*, No. 167 (June 1930).

FIGURE 139

Buddhist head. Khmer art, eleventh–twelfth centuries.
— *Musée Guimet. Archives of the Museum*

The principal relief at Māvalipuram is the great rock-carving known as the Arjuna-ratha, which, according to an earlier view, which has been revived by some critics, represents the "penance of Arjuna"; but has recently been identified by V. Goloubew, whose view we adopt, as the "descent of the Gaṅgā" (Gaṅgāvataraṇa). We know what scene of mythology is referred to in this episode: it is the descent from heaven to earth of the sacred river, the Ganges, as described in the legend related in Book IX of the *Bhāgavata Purāṇa.* This enormous sculpture in high relief, measuring nearly thirty yards in length and twenty-three feet in height and entirely covering one face of the cliff, groups a whole world of animals, ascetics, genii, and gods round the cascade in which sports a band of male and female serpent deities (*nāgas* and *nāgīs*), symbolic of the sacred waters (Fig. 62). What we have before us here is a vast picture, a regular fresco in stone. This relief is a masterpiece of classic art in the breadth of its composition, the sincerity of the impulse which draws all creatures together round the beneficent waters, and its deep, fresh love of nature.

Nor is the value of the various details any less great. In particular we may draw attention to the ascetic prostrating himself on the left of the cascade (Fig. 63): this amazingly realistic figure with its synthetic, rugged, and direct workmanship, at once restless and simple, has all the quality of a Rodin. Again, what joy is expressed in these pairs of gods or genii, whose supple, elongated nude figures dance in the air in the style of Amarāvatī and Aihoḷe (Fig. 64, 65)! For such details are excellent evidence in proof of the theory advanced by us above, to the effect that Amarāvatī finds a direct continuation at Māvalipuram, except that in the latter place there is greater power than at Amarāvatī. The serpent-king (*nāga*) and the female divinity (*nāgī*), that "sweet and perturbing water-nymph (*douce et troublante ondine*)," as she has been called, who symbolize the sacred waters, are both splendid pieces of sculpture (Fig. 65).

FIGURE 140

Buddhist head. Khmer art.

— *Musée Guimet. Archives of the Museum*

Māvalipuram can also show a vigorous and broad treatment of animals which is directly derived from the canons fixed by the Gupta artists. Perhaps we may even say that here the Indian art of representing animals, of which we saw the beginnings at Sārnāth and Sāñchī, reaches its height. What majesty there is in the group of elephants in adoration before the descent of the waters, to the right of the cascade, where they seem to be presiding in the name of the animal kingdom over the august mystery (Fig. 64)! [1] What life there is in the "ascetic cat" standing on its hind legs a little farther on (Fig. 66)! And what supreme elegance in the pair of deer which look on at the scene from the mouth of a cave opposite, on the left-hand side, with the lifelike action of the stag scratching his nose with his hind foot (Fig. 67)! Moreover, the cliff of the Gaṅgā is not the only one which has masterpieces to show. There is another rock-carving which has preserved for us an admirable and intensely life-like pastoral scene of the milking of a cow, which is licking her calf's back with a deft movement of the tongue (Fig. 68). More amazing still is the monolithic sculptured block showing a family of monkeys, with the male picking vermin off the female while she suckles her two little ones: here again we have a keenly observed scene, as humorous as it is realistic (Fig. 69).

Special mention should be made of the detailed groups in the reliefs at Māvalipuram which represent nude figures: the goddesses, dancing female genii, and water-nymphs in the Descent of the Gaṅgā, to which we referred above; the group of the Pallava king Mahendravarman and his wives,[2] and the group of Lakshmī and the elephants, surrounded by her women (Gaja-Lakshmī), in the cave of the *varāha avatāra* (avatar of the boar), the group of Pārvatī holding the little Skanda on her knees in the Dharmarāja-ratha, and the

[1] See the comparison with the splendid elephants in the relief of Isurumuniya, Aṇurādhapura, Ceylon, "so impressive in their quiet dignity and truth," by A. M. Hocart in *Ceylon Journal of Science*, Section G, *Archæology*, Vol. I, Pt. 3 (January 13, 1927), p. 96, and Pl. XLVIII.

[2] See *Annual Bibliography of Indian Archæology* for 1926 (Leiden, 1928), Pl. VII.

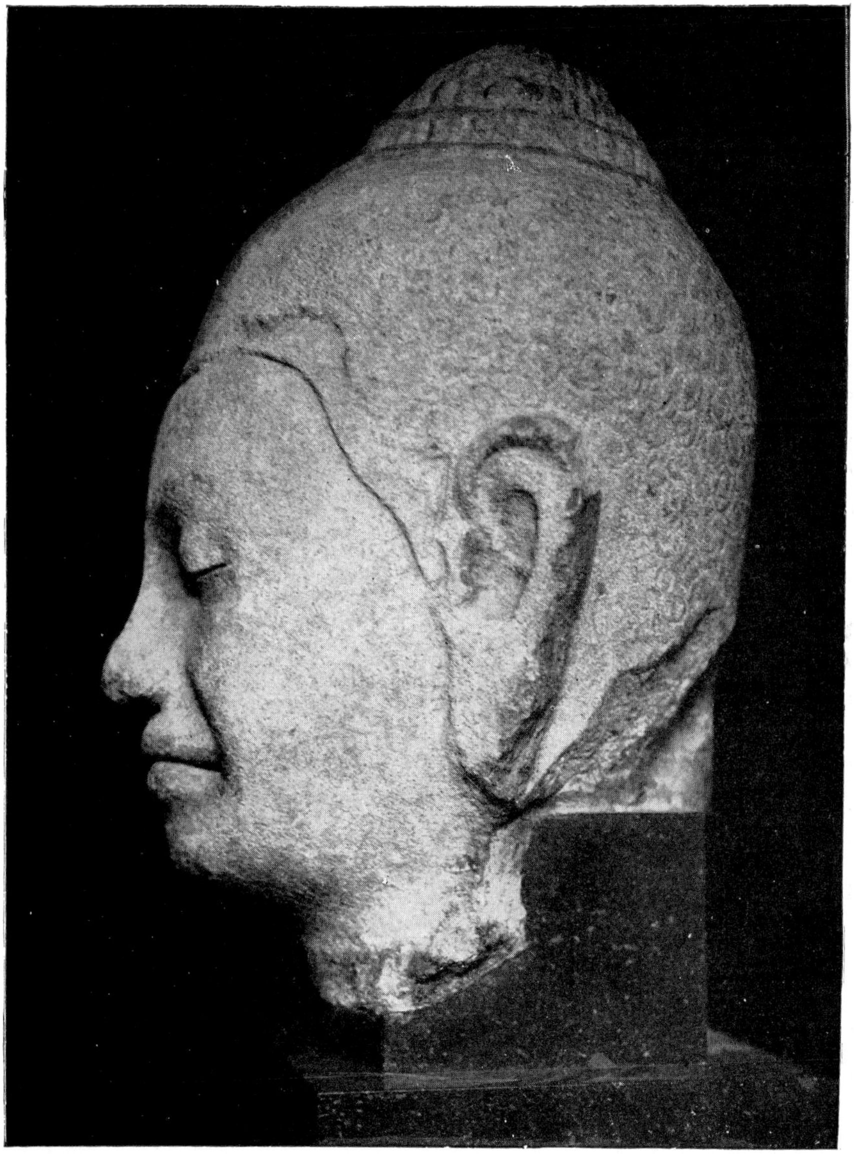

FIGURE 141

Buddhist head. Khmer art.

— *Musée Guimet. Archives of the Museum*

pairs of Pallava princes and princesses in the Arjuna-ratha. Never has the decorative value of the female figure been more successfully emphasized than in these elongated nude figures with their chaste grace, which are closely akin to those in the latest manner at Amarāvatī and to those of Ajaṇṭā (Fig. 70–71).[1]

And lastly, to consider them from the point of view of the *ensemble*, the descent of the Gaṅgā at Arjuna-ratha is not the only scene on a large scale at Māvalipuram of which we may admire the skilful composition and dramatic qualities. We may note the same sense of dramatic effect, the same sureness in the grouping of the figures, in several other reliefs — for instance, the battle of the goddess Durgā with the demon-buffalo Mahisha (Durgā-Mahishamardinī), the sleep of Vishṇu on the serpent Ananta in the Mahishamaṇḍapam, and the scene of Vishṇu in the form of a boar drawing the earth out of the water, in the cave of the *varāha avatāra.*[2]

The transition between the style of Māvalipuram and the Chālukya and Rāshṭrakūṭa style of Ellora and Elephanta is provided by the Chālukya reliefs of Bādāmī and Aihoḷe, in the district of Bijapur. The caves of Bādāmī date from the end of the sixth century (578) and the whole of the seventh. The reliefs in the first cave, which are Śivaite, and those of the third cave, which are Vishnuite, contain some splendid scenes: in the first cave, a dance of Śiva, with a freedom of movement which was possibly to show a falling off in the later Naṭarāja; and in the third cave a majestic and decorative king

[1] Also the delicious group of Gorardhanadhara Kṛishṇa reproduced by A. H. Longhurst: *Pallava Architecture*, Memoirs of the Archæological Survey of India, No. 33 (1928), Pl. XXVIII; and the Pallava King Paramesvara-varman I and his queen (*c.* A.D. 675) in Gangoly: "Another Panel from Arjuna's Ratha, Mahāvalipuram," in *Rūpam*, October 1926, p. 73; Krishna Sastri: *Two Statues of Pallava Kings*, Memoirs of the Archæological Survey of India, No. 26 (1926); Coomaraswamy: "A Pallava Relief, Durgā," *Bulletin of the Museum of Fine Arts, Boston*, XXV, No. 148 (April 1927), p. 23.

[2] For the Pallava school of painting see the delightful frescoes of Sittanavāsal, attributed to the time of Mahendravarman I (600–625), reproduced by Mr. Mehta: *Studies in Indian Painting*, pp. 1-14; and the article by M. Jouveau-Dubreuil in *Indian Antiquary*. Vol. LII, pp. 45–7.

lion (Narasiṃha), and half-nude pairs of gods of a wonderful and voluptuous elegance.[1] The temples of Aihoḷe belong to the same

FIGURE 142
Buddhist head.
— *Stoclet collection, Brussels. Photo, Stoclet. By courtesy of M. Stoclet*

Chālukya period (about 634), and their sculptures (a Brahmā, a Vishṇu, a Śiva, etc.) are of a tall, slender elegance directly derived from Amarāvatī (Fig. 40).[2]

[1] See R. D. Banerji, op. cit., Pl. II, XVIII, XIX, and XX.
[2] See H. Cousens: "The Ancient Temples of Aihoḷe," *Archæological Survey of India, Report, 1907–8*, pp. 189–209, Pl. LXXVI; H. Cousens: *Chālukyan Architecture of the*

The other Chālukya and Rāshṭrakūṭa temples in the Mahratta territory, and especially those of Ellora and Elephanta, also contain remarkably fine sculptures. The cult from which most of these works draw their inspiration is naturally the worship of Śiva, the fierce

FIGURE 143
Buddhist head. Khmer art.
— *Musée Guimet. Archives of the Museum*

deity symbolizing the cosmic force, Nature with her eternal process of creation and destruction. Hence stern faces and menacing figures abound at Ellora. Yet Gupta classicism is everywhere present. It is this classicism that marshalled those stupendous combats of elephants which run round the base of the temple and seem to support it

Kanarese Districts, Memoirs of the Archæological Survey of India, Vol. XLII (1926), Pl. XVI, XVII, XXI.

(Fig. 72). It also inspires the images of Śiva. The Śiva on the Kailāsa at Ellora, like that at Elephanta, is still a Gupta figure, in which the Buddhist aureole is replaced by the royal tiara, and which, instead of standing for pity and renunciation, symbolizes in its tumultuous

FIGURE 144
Khmer head.
— *Musée Guimet. Archives of the Museum*

grandeur the whole of life. The sentiment is different, but the æsthetic principle remains the same (Fig. 73, 75, 81, and also 86, 91).

Even when represented in the character of Bhairava, the god of terror — even in the dread dance of the Naṭarāja, the body of Śiva is as simple and pure in line and as smooth, chaste, and soft in its nudity as the corresponding figures at Mathurā and Sārnāth (see the Bhairava of Elephanta [1] and the Naṭarāja in the cave of Rāvaṇa-kā-Khai at Ellora, Fig. 74).[2] Moreover, when Śiva is called upon to represent, not the force of destruction, but the instinct of love which

FIGURE 145
Buddhist head. Khmer art.
— *Haase collection. Archives of the Musée Guimet*

is perpetually creating life, what supreme charm and tender radiance emanate from his whole being! In this connexion we need only mention the bas-relief of the nuptials of Śiva and Pārvatī at Elephanta [3]

[1] See Gopinatha Rao, op. cit., Vol. II, Pt. i, p. 192, Pl. XLVI (*Andhakāsuravadhamūrti*).

[2] Also Gopinatha Rao, op. cit., Vol. II, Pt. i, p. 262, Pl. LXIII.

[3] This group forms part of a scene of the *Gaṅgādharamūrti*. Cf. Gopinatha Rao, op.

(Fig. 75) and the scene of their kiss on the Kailāsa at Ellora (Fig. 76). The Naṭarāja and the Bhairava just mentioned were expressive of the exaltedly poetic participation of the soul in the principle of universal violence. The nuptials of Śiva now show us the other aspect of the same creed. The young King, leading by the hand, with a gesture of inexpressible pride, this maiden as modest as an Athenian virgin, is still the cosmic force which, but yesterday, was a pitiless outburst of unbridled joy in destruction, but now expresses itself in a love-song of infinite sweetness. As for the relief of the kiss, which in its Śivaite symbolism far transcends the divine idyll which it represents, it is in our opinion one of the most powerful works in the art of the whole world — a sort of oriental Rodin. We may add that, like Māvalipuram, the Kailāsa has some true pictures to show us: for instance, the relief showing Rāvaṇa shaking the mountain on which Śiva and Pārvatī are enthroned, in which the subterranean violence of the Titan, the serenity of the god as he crushes him with a gesture, and the womanly agitation of the goddess as she shrinks in terror against her spouse, all go to make up an *ensemble* admirable in its breadth (Fig. 77).

We may note how closely these Śivaite figures of Ellora and Elephanta approximate to the Buddhist art of earlier centuries when they represent the deity under his smiling aspect. The Śiva of the nuptials of Śiva and Pārvatī at Elephanta, the Śiva crushing Rāvaṇa at Ellora, at once recall the beautiful bodhisattva princes at Ajaṇṭā. They have the same supreme elegance, the same nobly elongated bodies, the same blend of strength and grace, and sometimes even the same costume (the high royal head-dress, etc.); while the female figures, in turn, such as those of Pārvatī, might be the sisters of the very Botticellian princesses who figured as the companions or

cit., Vol. II, Pt. i, p. 317, Pl. XC. For the same style see also the admirable group of Śiva and Pārvatī in the *Kalyāṇasundamūrti* scene at Elephanta, reproduced by Gopinatha Rao, op. cit., Vol. II, Pt. i, Pl. CIII, p. 346.

temptresses of the bodhisattva at Ajaṇṭā. Moreover, we should do well to pause before certain of these figures, and especially before two of the three figures in demi-relief between the columns of the entrance porch of the Kailāsa, representing the three river-deities, Gaṅgā,

FIGURE 146
Buddha of Preakhan.
— *Musée Guimet. Archives of the Museum*

Yamunā, and Sarasvatī (Fig. 78, 79).[1] In such works as these, with their noble beauty of rhythm, worthy of Athens or Florence, Indian sculpture perhaps reaches its apogee. At any rate, occupying as they do a middle position between the *yakshiṇī* of Bhārhut and Sāñchī,

[1] Cf. *Archæological Survey of India, Report, 1924–5*, Pl. XXXII, the two exquisite reliefs of Gaṅgā and Yamunā, from the foot of the right and left door-jambs, Dah Parbatiya, District of Darrang.

FIGURE 147

Converted *yaksha*.

— *Musée Guimet. Archives of the Museum*

with their heavy, intoxicating sensuality, and the eighteenth-century statues of Lakshmī, rigidly confined within the rules of an artistic canon which has degenerated into the commonplace, the two river-goddesses of Ellora offer an ideal of feminine beauty which we shall

FIGURE 148
Hari-Hara.
— *Musée Guimet. Archives of the Museum*

find again at Bōrōbudur, and which, though free from any Greek influence, almost succeeds in rediscovering our own classic ideal by its own exalted qualities.

The masterpiece of this sculpture is perhaps the giant figure of Śiva in the form known as the *Mahēśamūrti* at Elephanta — that is, the three-headed bust representing the three aspects of the god (Fig.

Figure 149
Śivaite head.
— *Musée Guimet. Archives of the Museum*

81).[1] There has been much discussion about the iconographic significance of this statue. In the view of a number of archæologists, the central head, "with its calm and majestic expression," represents either Śiva in the role of creator (Brahmā), or Śiva as the preserver

FIGURE 150
Śivaite head.
— *Musée Guimet. Archives of the Museum*

(Vishṇu); the head on the left, "with its menacing brows and half-open lips, and the fang showing at the corner of the mouth," would represent Śiva as the destroyer, the god of terror (Bhairava); and, lastly, the gentler and more smiling third head, on the right, would

[1] See Rodin, A. Coomaraswamy, Havell, and Goloubew: *Sculptures śivaites*, Collection *Ars Asiatica*, III (Paris, Van Oest, 1921), Pl. XV–XXVI.

represent Pārvatī, as the *śakti* of Śiva. But these interpretations, which would explain this three-headed figure at Elephanta as a sort of *Trimūrti* (triad), are now generally abandoned, and it looks as though we have here a *Mahēśamūrti*—which is the opinion of Mr.

FIGURE 151
Head of a *dēvatā* (deity).
— *Musée Guimet. Archives of the Museum*

Coomaraswamy. However this may be, the three countenances of the one being are here harmonized without a trace of effort: there are few material representations of the divine principle at once as powerful and as well-balanced as this in the art of the whole world. Nay, more, here we have undoubtedly the grandest representation of the pantheist God ever made by the hand of man (Fig. 83). In a magnificently poetic outburst Rodin has celebrated " this full, pouting mouth, rich in sensuous expressions, these lips like a lake of pleasure, fringed by the noble, palpitating nostrils." Indeed, never have the exuberant vigour of life, the tumult of universal joy expressing itself in ordered harmony, the pride of a power superior to any other, and

FIGURE 152
Buddha seated on the serpent.
—*Museum of Phnom Pĕnh. Photo, École française d'Extrême Orient*

the secret exaltation of the divinity immanent in all things found such serene expression. In its Olympian majesty, the *Mahĕśamūrti* of Elephanta is worthy of comparison with the Zeus of Mylasa or the Asklepios of Melos.[1]

The Śivaite school of Bādāmī, Ellora, and Elephanta lies at the origin of that Dravidian sculpture, in stone or in bronze, which is

[1] For the Hindu school of painting of Mahārāshṭra, see D. V. Thompson: "Notes on some Early Hindu Paintings at Ellora," *Rūpam*, April 1926, p. 45, with coloured plates.

FIGURE 153

Buddha seated on the serpent.

— *Musée Guimet. Archives of the Museum*

likewise, as a rule, connected with the cult of Śiva and flourished in the south — especially in the Carnatic — from the palmy days of the Tamil Empire of the Choḷas at Tanjore in the eleventh and twelfth centuries till the period of the empire of Vijayanagar in the fourteenth, fifteenth, and sixteenth centuries, when it was at its height. This sculpture has left us a quantity of masterpieces, many of which have fortunately found their way into the museums of Europe and America. We here reproduce a few specimens either from the C. T. Loo collection, or from that of the Comte René Philipon, or else from the Museé Guimet. First of all, we have a series of seated figures representing Śiva, Brahmā, and the Seven Mothers of Śivaism, the *Sapta māṭrikā*,[1] great stone statues from the Deccan, dating from the fifteenth century and once in the possession of Monsieur Loo (Fig. 86–89). Then we have a Śiva, from the Musée Guimet, in the pose known as the *jñāna* "*dakshiṇāmūrti*" (image of wisdom); in this highly important work the god is represented as the master of wisdom, seated under a banyan-tree on a rock in the Himalayas, in the pose known as the *vīrāsana,* with the left leg crossed and resting on the right knee, and one of the hands making the gesture of reassurance (Fig. 90).[2] In these pure and harmonious bodies, with their slender, elegant torsos, redeemed from all weak over-refinement by their breadth of shoulder and virile power of build, in the caressing softness of the lines and the supple and happy pose of the limbs, we see a continuation of the whole tradition of Ajaṇṭā, Ellora, and Elephanta. These statues of Śiva, Brahmā, and the Mothers might have been taken from the finest of the Rāshṭrakūṭa reliefs, from the nuptials of Śiva and Pārvatī to the river-goddesses of the Kailāsa. As yet we find none of the exaggerations and commonplaces of the "Hindu baroque" into which the art of the south was to

[1] Cf. the *māṭrikā* panels at Ellora and in the Lucknow Museum in Hirananda Sastri: *The Origin and Cult of Tārā,* Memoirs of the Archæological Survey of India, No. 20 (1925), Pl. I.

[2] Cf. Krishna Sastri, op. cit., Fig. 54 (Āvūr); Gopinatha Rao, op. cit., Vol. II, Pt. i, 281–3.

degenerate from the seventeenth century onwards. Here we still have an art that is classic in the full sense of the word, both because it remains faithful to the " grandeur of taste " of native Gupta classicism, and also because it has reached such a height of perfection that, even

FIGURE 154

Angkor-Vat. The churning of the sea. From a cast in the Indo-Chinese Museum in the Trocadéro.
— *Photo, Giraudon*

for the non-specialist public, it takes its place on the highest level of universal æsthetics. We almost incline to regard these southern sculptures in full relief of the Vijayanagar period as the noblest specimens of Indian art. At any rate, they possess a virile elegance and plastic balance superior to anything which had been seen up to that time.

This elegance is displayed above all in the bronzes. There are a few Dravidian bronzes recently acquired by collections in Paris which may be reckoned among the masterpieces of this school, and all friends of Indian art must congratulate themselves upon seeing the Western public thus placed in a position to comprehend the uni-

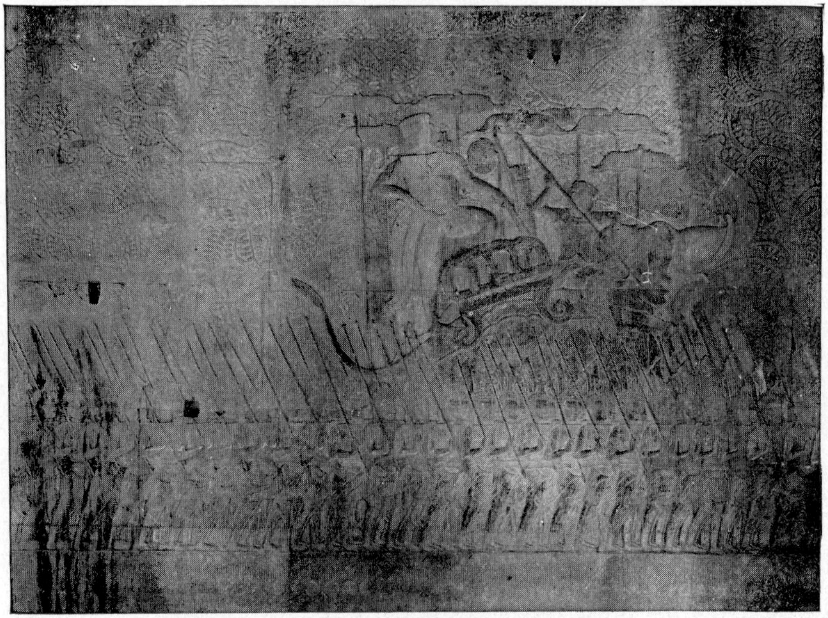

FIGURE 155
Angkor-Vat. The army on the march. Relief in the Trocadéro.
— *Archives of the Musée Guimet*

versal value of this art from such well-chosen examples. One of these bronzes, about thirty-two inches high and dating from the fifteenth century, has been presented to the Musée Guimet. It represents with supreme elegance and slender rhythmic grace Śiva as protector of art and letters — literally "Śiva with the lute," or *Vīṇādhara "dakshiṇāmūrti,"* a sort of Indian Antinous with the pure grace of an Apollo, to which the pronounced sway of the body at the hips and the high Śivaite head-dress add a further charm.[1] Besides the swaying attitude of the *ābhaṅga*, we may note in particular the softness of the torso, the exquisite curve of the lower part of the back, the delicate gesture of the first of the right hands, with thumb and forefinger joined in the *kaṭaka hasta* (flower gesture), the flawless modelling of the

FIGURE 156
Angkor-Vat. The army on the march. From cast in the Indo-Chinese Museum of the Trocadéro.
— *Photo, Giraudon*

limbs, with the bend in the left leg, which is advanced in the pose known to Indian theorists as the *ālīḍha*, unconsciously repeating one of the most felicitous poses of Greek statuary (Fig. 91–92).

Quite different in character are three bronzes recently added to the René Philipon and C. T. Loo collections and to that of the Musée

[1] See Gopinatha Rao, op. cit., Vol. II, Pt. i, 289–92, Pl. LXXX (Museum of Madras) and LXXXI (Vaḍaraṅgam).

Guimet, which we also reproduce, together with a similar figure from the Madras Museum (Fig. 94, 95, 96, 97).[1] These, too, are Dravidian works of the fourteenth and fifteenth centuries, and again represent Śiva, but not this time as the Apollo-like youth whom we were admiring just now; he is now the embodiment of a more powerful and Dionysian harmony — that of the Naṭarāja, the dread dancer of the cosmic dance, the symbol of a superhuman poetic exaltation in which, as we have seen, India has expressed her heroic and almost Nietz-

FIGURE 157
Angkor-Vat. Decorative scenes.
— *Photo, École française d'Extrême Orient*

schean acceptance of universal joy, pain, and force. Whether he be surrounded or not by the flaming aureole of the *tiruvāsi* (*prabhā maṇḍala*) — the circle of the world which he both fills and oversteps — the king of the dance is all rhythm and exaltation. The tambourine which he sounds with one of his right hands draws all creatures into this rhythmic motion, and they dance in his company. The conventionalized locks of flying hair and the blown scarfs tell of the speed of this universal movement, which crystallizes matter and reduces it to powder in turn. One of his left hands holds the fire which animates and devours the worlds in this cosmic whirl. One of the

[1] Cf. Rodin, Coomaraswamy, Havell, and Goloubew: *Sculptures śivaites*, Collection *Ars Asiatica*, III, Pl. I–XII.

god's feet is crushing a Titan, for "this dance is danced upon the bodies of the dead," yet one of the right hands is making the gesture of reassurance (*abhaya mudrā*), so true it is that, seen from the cosmic point of view, and *sub specie æternitatis,* the very cruelty of this universal determinism is kindly, as the generative principle of the future. And, indeed, on more than one of our bronzes the king of the dance wears a broad smile (Fig. 97). He smiles at death and at life, at pain and at joy, alike, or rather, if we may be allowed so to express it, his smile is both death and life, both joy and pain, and this Nietzschean smile at universal suffering seems to us to possess very nearly the same æsthetic value as the *misereor super turbas* of the Christian and the Buddhist. From this lofty point of view, in fact, all things fall into their place, finding their explanation and logical compulsion. Here art is the faithful interpreter of the philosophical concept. The plastic beauty of rhythm is no more than the expression of an ideal rhythm. The very multiplicity of arms, puzzling as it may seem at first sight, is subject in turn to an inward law, each pair remaining a model of elegance in itself, so that the whole being of the Naṭarāja thrills with a magnificent harmony in his terrible joy. And as though to stress the point that the dance of the divine actor is indeed a sport (*līlā*) — the sport of life and death, the sport of creation and destruction, at once infinite and purposeless — the first of the left hands hangs limply from the arm in the careless gesture of the *gaja hasta* (hand as the elephant's trunk). And lastly, as we look at the back view of the statue, are not the steadiness of these shoulders which uphold the world, and the majesty of this Jove-like torso, as it were a symbol of the stability and immutability of substance, while the gyration of the legs in its dizzy speed would seem to symbolize the vortex of phenomena.

Thus the very India that just now, in Buddhist art, offered us the most soothing doctrine of gentleness, Franciscan pity, and tenderness now presents, in its Śivaite art, the most inspiring lessons of rigour, serenity, and superhuman asceticism. For ever blessed be the sacred land to which humanity is indebted for such enrichment!

After rising to this pitch of austerity it is quite refreshing to descend to a lower level, where other bronzes from the south, in the Musée Guimet, show us a more human dance — that of the infant

FIGURE 158
Angkor-Vat. *Dēvatā* (deity).
— *Photo, École française d'Extrême Orient*

Kṛishṇa, the divine cowherd, the beloved of the milkmaids, whose cult mingles a spiritual quietism with idyllic scenes at once carnal and tender.[1] He is a charming figure, in which Hindu art is seen to triumph in a subject somewhat analogous to that of the Greek Eros, not to speak of our own *sacro bambino* — who is, however, less wanton. Even in Śivaism we find figures which are quite similar, such

[1] See Krishna Sastri, op. cit., Fig. 25 (butter-dance of Bāla-Kṛishṇa); Gopinatha Rao, op. cit., Vol. I, Pt. i, LX (*Navanīta nṛittamūrti* in the Madras Museum); Coomaraswamy: *Portfolio of Indian Art*, Museum of Fine Arts, Boston, Pl. LVII (a very charming figure).

as the Sambandha in the Loo collection (Fig. 98). Still more pleasing are the bronzes of the infant Kṛishṇa dancing the serpent-dance (Kāliya-Kṛishṇa).[1] And, since we have mentioned these Krishnaite reliefs, whose heart-felt piety is in such strong contrast with the

FIGURE 159
Angkor-Vat. *Dēvatā.*
— *Photo, École française d'Extrême Orient*

superhuman intellectualism of the Śivaite philosophers, we will also reproduce a wood-carving from the Carnatic, dating from the seventeenth century and presented by Monsieur Jouveau-Dubreuil to the Musée Guimet, which represents Kṛishṇa the cowherd, the Indian

[1] See Krishna Sastri, op. cit., Fig. 26 (Madras Museum); Gopinatha Rao, op. cit., Vol. I, Pt. i, LXIV, 213.

Orpheus (Gāna-Gopāla, or Vēṇu-Gopāla), charming the heifers of his herd with his flute. Here we are obviously not dealing with a work of very high art, as we were just now; but we may none the less take a pleasure in the elegance of this blooming scene (Fig. 102).[1]

These are but a few examples out of thousands of southern Indian art during the period of the Choḷa kingdom and afterwards of the Vijayanagar Empire. But the sanctuaries and museums of India contain hundreds of others, the chief types of which should be mentioned; for a whole iconographical classification has grown up for the Śivaite and Vishnuite sculpture, as it did formerly for Buddhist sculpture. To take only the ritual gestures, it is necessary here to note a few that are characteristic of Śivaite works. These *hasta* (hand-gestures), as they are called by Indian art-critics, are often most elegant and noble and have lent an added richness to the already existing wealth of the old Buddhist *mudrā*. Thus to the *mudrā* analysed above we may add the *lamba hasta* (pendent hand) or *lola hasta* (hand moving to and fro) — the hand drooping negligently, or half-raised at the end of an arm half-outstretched, a gesture which in the most beautiful of the Śivaite statues assumes quite a flower-like grace; the *gaja hasta,* in which the arm is extended across the breast with the hand drooping — one of the left hands, that is, of the Naṭarāja. The literal meaning of the phrase is " the gesture of the elephant," for it is imitated from the soft flexibility of an elephant's trunk when swaying half-outstretched in the air. Next comes the *tripatāka hasta,* or gesture of the three fingers, so called because the divinity (Śiva) holds the shell, the ax, or the hind between the raised thumb and forefinger, while the ring-finger is bent and the little finger again outstretched — a gesture, as we can see, so dexterous as to be almost precious. It is also known as *kartarī mukha,* or the " scissors gesture." There is also the *nidrita hasta* — literally, " the sleeping hand " — the gesture of the hand lying at rest on some

[1] See Gopinatha Rao, op. cit., Vol. I, Pt. i, 207; Krishna Sastri, op. cit., p. 44.

FIGURE 160

Banteai Srei. Śiva and Pārvatī on the Kailās with Rāvaṇa shaking it.
— Photo, Goloubew. By permission of Messrs. Van Oest

object, with the palm open. In the Naṭarāja the hand shaking the little drum ought at the same time to make the gesture of the *ḍamaru hasta,* and the hand holding the fire that of the *ardha chandra hasta* (half-moon). A particularly elegant gesture is that of the hand of Śiva which holds the bowl, the palm being thrown backwards, while the *kapāla* (bowl or skull) is held between the middle and ring fingers, the forefinger and little finger being delicately crooked as though to avoid touching it. Equally refined are the gestures of the *kaṭiga* (hip), with the left arm hanging down and the hand resting very lightly upon the hip, and the gestures of the *kaṭaka hasta* [1] — that is, the holding of an attribute, chiefly a flower, in the hand (Fig. 93). Lastly we have the *sūchī hasta,* with the "pointing" finger, a gesture indicative of drawing attention or of surprise, and the *jñāna mudrā* (wisdom gesture), with the palm turned towards the breast, and the thumb and forefinger touching.

Among the accepted poses we shall also find the seated posture known as *sukhāsana* (posture of ease), with the right leg on the ground, the left leg being folded, a posture accompanied by the gesture known as the *abhaya* (fearless) *mudrā;* the *utkaṭika,* or attitude of "divine wrath," with the right leg in the same position as above, the left being propped against the chair to assist the sitter in rising; the pose of Kṛishṇa as the cowherd (*gopāla*), with the hip thrust out sideways so as to throw the weight of the body upon the left leg, while the right leg is slightly bent and crossed in front of it; not to speak of some twenty or more attitudes which Indian theorists have classified and described at great length. Equally careful is their classification of the various head-dresses. Thus Śiva's braided curls (*jaṭā*) are knotted in a graceful pyramid surmounted, as occasion demands, by the skull, the serpent, and the crescent, in order to form the *jaṭā mukuṭa,* or "diadem of braided hair." In the pose known as the *bhikshāṭanamūrti* these curls are spread out like a halo — the *jaṭā*

[1] Or *siṃhakarna* (lion's ear).

FIGURE 161

Banteai Srei. Door with scene of Kṛishṇa in high relief.
— Photo, Goloubew. By permission of Messrs. Van Oest

maṇḍala — and in the Naṭarāja they are crowned with a fan of peacock's feathers. Often, too, the god's hair is braided into a high truncated cone in the form of a tiara, and called the *kirīṭa mukuṭa.*

FIGURE 162
Ganesh. Cham style.
— *Museum of Tourane. Photo, Parmentier. By permission of Messrs. Van Oest*

In the case of the god of terror, this head-dress is sometimes crowned by a tongue of flame.[1]

The various iconographic types are determined at a glance by the

[1] For the representation of these postures, gestures, etc., see Krishna Sastri, op. cit., Pl. I–IV, pp. 269–72; Gopinatha Rao, op. cit., Vol. I, Pt. i, Pl. I–IX, pp. 1–32 (explanation of terms).

FIGURE 163

Pārvatī.

— *Museum of the École française d'Extrême Orient at Tourane. Photo, Parmentier-Goloubew*

ritual attitudes. The types of Śiva, in particular, very rapidly became stereotyped, both in art and in religious tradition. We have already had occasion to describe certain of these in connexion with the photographs reproduced: for instance, the Naṭarāja (Fig. 94–97), the Śiva in the pose of the *vīṇādhara* (lute-holder) "*dakshiṇāmūrti*" (Fig. 91, 92), the Śiva in the attitude of *jñāna* (endued with wisdom) "*dakshiṇāmūrti*" (Fig. 90), etc. But there are many other accepted types besides these. In the first place, the "*dakshiṇāmūrti,*" or representations of Śiva as a sage — whether as god of meditation or of art and letters — include, in addition to the *vīṇādhara* and *jñāna mūrti,* two other forms: the *vyākhyāmūrti* (pose of speech),[1] which is, however, almost identical with the *jñāna,* and the *yogamūrti* (mystic pose), which represents the god meditating in the attitude of the yogi, with the legs crossed in the *padmāsana* attitude.[2] Next comes the *bhikshāṭanamūrti,* or representation of Śiva in the guise of a naked beggar with four arms, the upper right hand holding a little drum, the lower right hand drooping in the *lamba hasta,* one of the left hands holding the alms-bowl made out of a skull, and the upper left hand making the gesture of the *kaṭaka hasta,* as though holding a flower (Fig. 93). Certain of these statues — for instance, those of Pandananallur and Tiruvenkadu, reproduced by Gopinatha Rao [3] — are nude figures of rare delicacy, worthy of the best Greco-Roman work. The Śiva in the attitude known as the *kālasaṃhāramūrti* (or *kālaharamūrti*), in which he is conceived as the conqueror of Time — a little figure which he crushes beneath his foot — is usually represented with the bust turned slightly towards the left, the weight of the body being thrown on to the right leg, which is brought across to the opposite side, while the left leg is gracefully bent so as to crush the figure of Time; the upper right hand holds the ax, the

1 Or *vyākhyāna dakshiṇāmūrti.* See Gopinatha Rao, op. cit., Vol. II, Pt. i, pp. 274–84 (with numerous plates).

2 See Gopinatha Rao, op. cit., Vol. II, Pt. i, pp. 284–9, Pl. LXXVI–LXXVIII.

3 See Gopinatha Rao, op. cit., Vol. II, Pt. i, pp. 306–9, Pl. LXXXVI–XC.

FIGURE 164

Dancing-girl attired in jewels. Cham style. Seventh century.
— *Tourane Museum*

upper left hand the hind, the lower right arm makes the gesture of surprise (*sūchī mūdra*), and the lower left arm is in the attitude of *āliṅgana mudrā*, clasping the *śakti* of the god.[1] When the bronze is the work of a master, as in the Bṛihadīśvara temple at Tanjore, the bend of the body in the *ābhaṅga* attitude is again equal in elegance to the most noble Greek poses. A frequently occurring pair is that of the *Umāsahita mūrti* or *Sukhāsana mūrti*, representing Śiva and Umā seated in the attitude of dalliance, or *lalitāsana*.[2] The bronzes representing this scene often possess a strange charm: the goddess, with her left leg hanging down and the right leg bent and slightly raised, is propping herself up on her couch with her extended left arm, while the right hand is in the *kaṭaka mudrā*, gesture of holding a flower or of argumentation. When Skanda, son of Śiva and Umā, is represented between his parents, the same group is called *Somaskanda*.[3] There is one rather special type that is not lacking in attraction — that of the hermaphrodite Śiva (*ardhanārī* or half-woman) — that is, Śiva and his consort united in one body, the right-hand side of the body being of the male sex, and the left-hand side of the female sex.[4]

One of the most pleasing types in the iconography of Vishnuism is the Kodaṇḍa Rāma or Rāma with the bow (the bow, however, is not shown), in which the right arm is raised at a right angle in the gesture of the archer, or *dhaṇurdhāri hasta*, while the left arm is lowered in the *lamba* or *lambita hasta* (pendent hand). When combined with the elegant curve of the *ābhaṅga*, this double gesture, expressive at once of the strength of the archer and of the vibra-

1 See Krishna Sastri, op. cit., p. 142, Fig. 88–89; O. C. Gangoly: *South Indian Bronzes*, p. 26, Pl. I.

2 See Gopinatha Rao, op. cit., Vol. II, Pt. i, p. 130, Pl. XXI; and Krishna Sastri, op. cit., p. 110, Fig. 69.

3 See Krishna Sastri, op. cit., p. 107, Fig. 67, 68; Gopinatha Rao, op. cit., Vol. II, Pt. i, Pl. XXII.

4 See Gopinatha Rao, op. cit., Vol. II, Pt. i, 321-32, Pl. XCV–XCVIII; Krishna Sastri, op. cit., p. 120, Fig. 76–80.

FIGURE 165

Śiva. Cham style.
— *Museum of the École française d'Extrême Orient at Tourane. Photo, Parmentier-Goloubew*

FIGURE 166

Śiva. Cham style.
— *Museum of the École française d'Extrême Orient at Tourane. Photo, Parmentier-Goloubew*

tion of the invisible bow, produces a rare impression of pride and nobility.[1]

FIGURE 167
Cham monster.
— *Museum of the École française d'Extrême Orient at Tourane. Photo, Parmentier-Goloubew*

Side by side with the statues of divinities, a place of their own must be assigned to the southern bronzes representing Śivaite saints.[2] We reproduce here one of the masterpieces of this style, the portrait of

[1] See K. N. Sitaram: "Kodaṇḍa Rāma," in *Rūpam*, October 1921; Gangoly: *South Indian Bronzes*, Pl. XII, XIII; and Gopinatha Rao, op. cit., Vol. I, Pt. i, LV.

[2] See Gopinatha Rao, op. cit., Vol. II, Pt. ii, pp. 473–92, with delightful pictures, Pl. CXXXIV, CXXXVII; O. C. Gangoly: *South Indian Bronzes*, Pl. XIV–XX; A. Coomaraswamy: *Bronzes from Ceylon*, Memoirs of the Colombo Museum, Ceylon (1914).

FIGURE 168
Jain Temple at Delhi.
— *Photo, Johnston and Hoffmann*

the famous saint Sundara mūrti Svāmi, nearly twenty inches high, in the Colombo Museum (Fig. 99). This saint, who wrote so many pious hymns — a sort of Dravidian St. Louis Gonzaga — who died at the age of eighteen at the height of his mystical inspiration, is represented as a beautiful youth with broad shoulders, a slender waist, and long thighs, with his right hand raised in the *kaṭaka hasta*, as though holding a flower, and the left arm drooping softly, with the hand in a delicate gesture of instruction or argument. The poise of the body, with the weight thrown on the bent left leg, has a remarkable beauty of rhythm. In spite of a certain preciosity of gesture and attitude, the statuette remains charming in its simplicity and candour — in fact, it is inspired by a moving sincerity. As Mr. W. Cohn observes, though this statue belongs to a worship so remote from our own, such human tenderness and piety emanate from it that it none the less speaks to our hearts. The face seems to be smiling at some ecstatic vision, and the lips to open as though to chant some hymn.

Almost as charming, and full of an equal fervour and a like simplicity, is another statuette in the Colombo Museum, representing the Śivaite saint Appār Svāmi, with his hands joined in the *añjali hasta* (gesture of supplication). There is also in the Colombo Museum a Tirujñāna Saṃbandha Svāmi, the child saint, one of the most delightful nude figures of a child that we know.[1] These two works seem to belong to the thirteenth century. The Madras Museum, for its part, possesses several bronzes of Śivaite saints that display a simplicity, a nervous elegance, and a softness worthy of the best bronzes of the Italian Renaissance. Or, rather, we may say that among the Italian sculptors who worked in bronze, there was no Fra Angelico; while there are certain of these statuettes that remind us of a Donatello with the soul of that Dominican friar (Fig. 99–100).[2] But here we are evidently in another clime, as is plainly shown by a delicious statu-

[1] O. C. Gangoly: *South Indian Bronzes*, Pl. XVII–XVIII.

[2] See Gangoly: *South Indian Bronzes*, Pl. XIV–XV; Gangoly: "A Statuette of a Shaiva Devotee" (with four illustrations), in *Rūpam*, July 1927.

FIGURE 169

Great Mosque at Ajmere.
— *Photo, Johnston and Hoffmann*

ette of the monkey-king Hanumat, about thirty inches high, now in the South Kensington Museum, which will best enable us to understand this art which has been so under-estimated.[1] What is more, there is no irony in it, none of the slightly mocking spirit of the

FIGURE 170
Mosque of the Quṭb, Delhi.
— *Photo, Johnston and Hoffmann*

Japanese sculptors. This little child monkey, with its marvellous elegance, embodies in a humble bronze all the kindliness of the friend of Rāma, all the self-sacrifice of the saviour of Sītā, all that brotherly feeling for animals which was a part of Hindu pantheism.

And, lastly, the Dravidian bronzists have left us actual portraits,

[1] Cf. Coomaraswamy: *Arts and Crafts of India and Ceylon*, Pl. 5, No. 49.

such as those of Kṛishṇa Dēva Rāja (1509–29), king of Vijayanagar, with his two wives beside him — works characterized by the same elegant simplicity.[1]

FIGURE 171
The Quṭb Minār.
— *Photo, Johnston and Hoffmann*

We shall still find masterpieces among the bronzes of the south even well on in the seventeenth century. For instance, we ought not to ignore the Lakshmī of the Musée Guimet, in which she is represented

[1] See Coomaraswamy: *History of Indian and Indonesian Art*, Fig. 245, Pl. LXXVI; and Coomaraswamy: "*Südindische Bronze*" (a queen, *c.* 1100), in Washington Freer Gallery, *Pantheon*, July 1930, p. 338.

in the ritual attitude of the goddess, with the right forearm raised and the right hand in the gesture of holding a flower (*kaṭaka hasta*), while the left arm hangs down by the side of the thigh, and the left hand droops negligently in the gentle gesture of the *lola hasta* (Fig. 101).[1]

FIGURE 172
Gate of 'Alā al-Dīn, Delhi.
— *Photo, Johnston and Hoffmann*

In accordance with Indian canons of art, the bust turns decidedly towards the right, while the hip is thrust out in such a way that the body rests upon the left leg, the right leg remaining slightly bent. This principle of " counterpoise " is also emphasized by the excessive

[1] Cf. the charming "Devī as Umā. Copper. .590 m., southern India. Fourteenth to fifteenth century. Gift of Sir William Beardsell" in the Museum of Fine Arts, Boston (A. Coomaraswamy: *Portfolio of Indian Art*, Pl. LII).

slenderness of the waist, contrasting with the fullness of the breasts and hips. The work has real elegance; the elongated limbs, the softness of the abdomen, the very exaggeration of the characteristics of Indian female beauty, and the sideward thrust of the hip, so pronounced as almost to appear dislocated, cannot fail to exert an immediate fascination. Yet it must be admitted that, in such works as this, art is on the way towards degenerating into conventional devices. Evidently the artist has automatically applied canons a thousand times repeated.[1] We have only to note the rows of Lakshmīs in the neighbouring cases, exactly similar in nature, but lacking in the same elegance, to be sure that immediately afterwards we shall come to what W. Cohn calls the commonplaces of Hindu Baroque.

None the less, we may note that, in spite of this process of decadence, the achievements of the animal-sculptors were well maintained for a long time to come. Thus the buildings of Haḷebīd in Mysore, such as the temple of Hoyśalēśvara, dating from the twelfth century, and the temples of Vijayanagar, or the temple of the Hazāra Rāmasvāmi (or "Thousand Rāmas"), can still show processions of elephants in the great naturalistic tradition of Sāñchī and Māvalipuram in the reliefs on their bases, as ornate as a piece of lace-work.

At the other end of India, in Bengal, Buddhist art, which had been driven out of the south by the triumph of Śivaism, held its own for a longer period, under the Pāla and Sēna dynasties — which flourished from 750 to 1060 and from 1060 to 1202 respectively — and afterwards in Nepal. But it developed in a direction analogous with that followed by Śivaite art. Here, again, the origin of this art is to be sought in the melting softness and simplicity of Gupta art: but the Gupta canon is progressing by imperceptible degrees towards a more elongated elegance and poses of a greater preciosity — a more pronounced sideward sway of the hip, more drooping attitudes, more

[1] For iconography of Lakshmī, see Krishna Sastri: *South Indian Gods*, p. 187.

sophisticated *mudrās*, a highly curious blend of great flexibility with a more hieratic character, a profusion of decorative motives and personal adornments, a taste for complicated ornamentation, for a setting of pointed arches, flames, and points, the whole effect producing an impression as of a sort of Indian flamboyant style. To state the case more precisely, all these Bengali bodhisattvas, dating from the tenth to the twelfth centuries, form a real transitional stage between Gupta art on the one hand and the statues of Nepal and Tibet on the other, the latter being, moreover, directly derived from them.[1] We shall examine these at greater length in discussing their influence upon central Asia in the fourth volume of the present series.[2]

[1] See J. C. French: *The Art of the Pal Empire of Bengal* (Oxford University Press, 1928); A. Coomaraswamy, *Portfolio of Indian Art,* Museum of Fine Arts, Boston, Pl. XXIV (Padmapāṇi in *lalitāsana*, .152 m., late Pāla or Sēna period, twelfth century) and Pl. XXVII (group of Śiva and Umā, .160 m., tenth to eleventh century); Coomaraswamy: "An Illustrated Nepalese MS.," *Bulletin of the Museum of Fine Arts, Boston,* XIX, No. 114 (August 1921), pp. 47–9.

[2] The whole of this question of Bengali, Pāla, and Sēna art is reviewed again in detail in Vol. IV of the present work, Ch. ii (Fig. 166 *et seq.*), in which I have attempted to define the Pāla æsthetic canon and show how it lingered on in Nepalese and Tibetan art. I would therefore refer the reader to Vol. IV for the later history of Buddhist art—both sculpture and painting—in north-eastern India.

CHAPTER II

Farther India and the Malay Archipelago

JAVANESE ART: INDIAN INFLUENCE AND THE MALAY REVIVAL

THERE IS AN OBSTINATE PREJUDICE THANKS TO WHICH INDIA IS constantly represented as having lived, as it were, hermetically sealed up in its age-old civilization, apart from the rest of Asia. Nothing could be more exaggerated. We have seen how Iranian and Greek influences exerted an influence over Indian art for many centuries. Though the cultural originality of India ultimately absorbed the Greek influences, in our opinion these Indo-Iranian affinities never ceased to make themselves felt, from the days of the earliest Āryas down through the Sāsāno-Gupta period to the time of Akbar. But it is above all in connexion with the expansion of India that the idea of her isolation has to be combated. In the next volume of this work we shall see that, during the first eight centuries of our era, so far as religion and art are concerned, central Asia was a sort of Indian colony. It is true that the political supremacy over central Asia continued to be Tokharian, Chinese, Turkish, or Tibetan. On the other hand, India left her impress upon the Malay Peninsula and Archipelago and Indo-China in politics too.

It is too often forgotten that in the early Middle Ages there existed a " Greater India," a vast Indian empire. Though politically it was as loosely organized as the Hellenic empire of Greater Greece had been in earlier days, morally this Indian empire was equally homogeneous. In the ninth century of our era Ceylon and Pegu, Cambodia, Champa (or what is now southern Annam), Sumatra, and Java were as intimately connected with India as Cyprus, Cyrene, Sicily, and Marseilles had once been with Greece. Angkor, the Cham kingdom of the Quang-nam, and the Sumatro-Javanese Empire of Śrīvijaya were as closely bound up with the Buddhist land of Magadha and the Hindu empire of the Pallavas in the Carnatic as Syracuse or Corcyra, Naucratis or Sinope, could have been with Corinth or Miletus. A man coming from the Ganges or the Deccan felt as much at home there as in his own native land. In those days the Indian Ocean really deserved its name: it was an Indian sea in precisely the same sense as the Mediterranean had been a Greek sea during the fifth century B.C. No land illustrates the truth of this better than Java.[1]

In quite early days — no doubt, about the beginning of our era — the island of Java underwent the influence of Indian colonists, or, rather, " civilizers," who introduced with them the Hindu cults of Śivaism and Vishnuism, as well as Buddhism. Sumatra was also Indianized under more or less similar conditions. It was, moreover, in Sumatra that the first great Indo-Malay state came into being, that of Śrīvijaya (the modern Palembang), which in the eighth century brought under its hegemony a large part of the Malay Archipelago, including the western and central part of Java.[2] The kings of Śrīvijaya, who belonged to the powerful dynasty of the Śailendras, professed Buddhism. They erected a whole series of great Buddhist

[1] Cf. Karl With, *Java* (1922); N. J. Krom: *Hindoe-Javaansche Geschiedenis* (The Hague, 1926); P. Vogel: "The Relation between the Art of India and Java," in *The Influences of Indian Art* (London, India Society, 1925).

[2] Indian influence reached even Borneo, as is proved by the fine Buddha recently found at Kota-Bangoen and reproduced in the *Annual Bibliography of Indian Archæology, 1926* (Leiden, 1928), Pl. XI.

FIGURE 173

Tomb of ‘Alā al-Dīn, Delhi.

— *Photo, Johnston and Hoffmann*

sanctuaries in central Java, such as Kalasan (in 778) and Bōrōbudur.[1] In the middle of the ninth century central Java recovered its independence under local princes, who built the sanctuaries of Prambanan — which now belonged to the Śivaite cult. Next, from the tenth century onwards, the political centre of Java shifted to the eastern part of the island, where several dynasties reigned one after the other. The most important of these eastern dynasties reigned at Jaṅgala and at Kediri in the eleventh and twelfth centuries, afterwards at Singhasāri in the thirteenth century, and finally at Majapahit, in the fourteenth century.

Indo-Javanese art seems to make its appearance about the end of the seventh or the beginning of the eighth century of our era, with the group of buildings on the plateau of Dieng, in the centre of the island, including the temples of Chaṇḍi Puntadēva and Chaṇḍi Bīma, which are Śivaite sanctuaries due to local princes who had formerly been under the hegemony of the kings of Śrīvijaya.[2] The affinity between the statues from this group of temples — now in the Museum of Batavia and reproduced in Krom's albums — and the Indian Gupta art of the school of Mathurā is obvious at a glance. Yet, as early as these first works, we find an art which is already specifically Javanese, though still falling within the sphere of Indian æsthetic influence. The material alone, which is andesite, a grey volcanic trachyte, whose microlithic texture has a granulated feel to the touch, forced the Javanese sculptors to adopt a stronger style of workmanship than was necessary in the Indian sandstones. The impression of strength produced by Javanese art, and the value arising from its balance of masses, are caused in part by these material conditions.

[1] There is, on the contrary, a new hypothesis according to which the Empire of Śrīvijaya was "West Java," and Sumatra was only a dependency of it (see the works of Stutterheim).

[2] See N. J. Krom: *Inleiding tot de Hindoe-Javaansche Kunst* (The Hague, 1920); M. P. Verneuil: *L'Art à Java. Les Temples de la période classique indo-javanaise* (Paris, Van Oest, 1927).

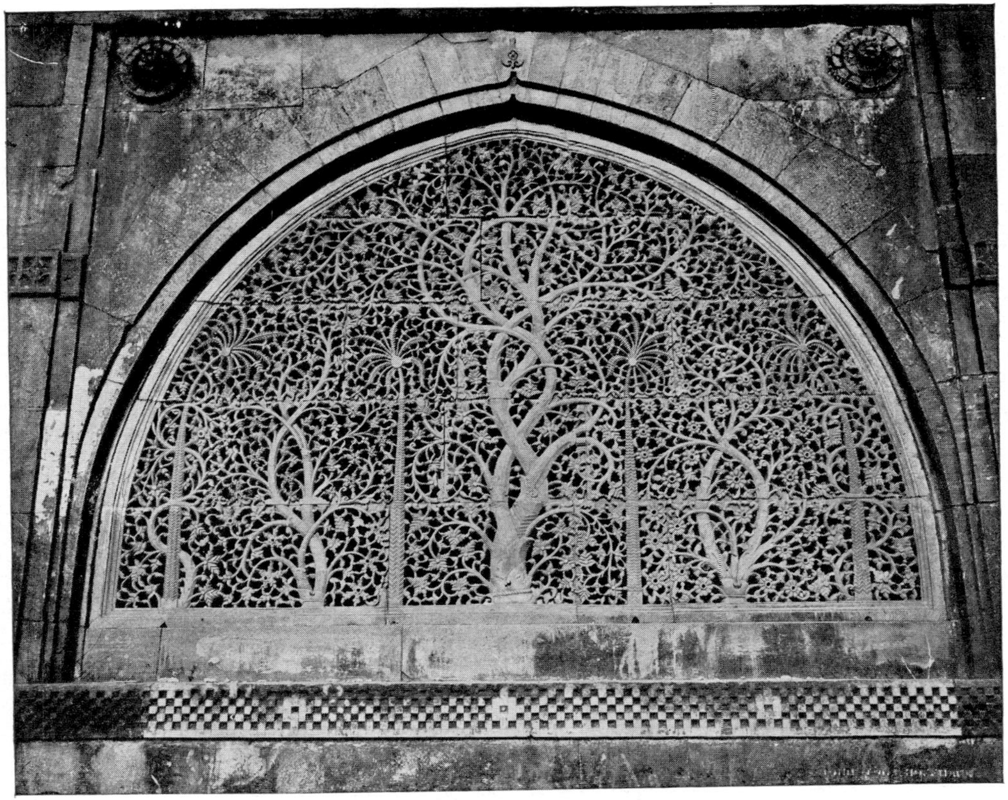

FIGURE 174

Window in the Sīdī Sayyid Mosque, Ahmedabad, *c.* 1500.
— *Photo, Johnston and Hoffmann*

The statues from Dieng — which represent the Brahmanic gods Śiva, Pārvatī, Ganesh, and Brahmā — are in general treated with a simplicity of form which, though still perhaps a little rugged, already reveals a command of material which was to remain the heritage of Javanese art. Some of the details are specifically native: for instance, the creatures chosen to bear the gods upon their backs are here no longer animals, but men with animals' heads, the ox Nandi being replaced by a man with a bull's head.

From the architectural point of view, these temples at Dieng have as a rule "the appearance of cubical constructions with strongly marked lines." The temple is "a simple square cella, one side of which is preceded by a broad porch or peristyle, while the other three sides are divided by pilasters into longitudinal bands filled with projecting niches or sculptured panels." The form of the roof varies; thus, at Puntadēva we find a sort of receding second storey, while at Bīma the building is surmounted by a pyramidal structure formed of a series of stepped tiers. The first of these forms seems to bear some resemblance to certain Pallava temples at Māvalipuram, and most of all to the pre-Angkorean Khmer architecture of Cambodia, of which we shall speak later; whereas the Bīma type has more resemblance to the *śikhara* of Orissa.

Between about 730 and 860, the period of Sumatran domination and of the Empire of Śrīvijaya, we reach the culminating point of Indo-Javanese art. The Sumatran dynasty of the Śailendra, which was a Buddhist one, covered the central regions of Java with fine buildings such as Chaṇḍi Kalasan, Chaṇḍi Mendut, and Bōrōbudur.

The Kalasan, which dates from 778, belongs to the first Dieng type, but is differentiated from it by its "icosagonal" form — that is, by its projecting niches along the sides, which developed into chapels with entrances of their own, the plan thus forming a Greek cross. With the Kalasan should be associated the little neighbouring temple of

Vihāra Sāri, which contains some reliefs of the highest order — for instance, the standing bodhisattva with his hand on his hip, of which there is a cast at the Trocadéro — a charming little prince of inimitable grace (Fig. 103).

FIGURE 175
Mosque of Ibrāhīm, Bījāpur.
— *Photo, Johnston and Hoffmann*

Chaṇḍi Mendut offers no lateral temples, but merely a longitudinal projection at each side. It is a square structure, with a sobriety which reminds us of the Doric, at once elegant and compact, with two storeys, the upper one receding, in accordance with the Dieng type. Its distinctive feature is the importance and height of its base, with the fine decorated plinth which adorns it, thus heralding Bōrōbudur.

Bōrōbudur is not a temple, like the buildings mentioned above, but is in theory a *stūpa* — though a *stūpa* of a very special form, the base with its reliefs and the stepped upper storeys being inspired by the architecture of the temples of the same period. It was built, ac-

FIGURE 176
Palace of Akbar, Agra.
— *Photo, Johnston and Hoffmann*

cording to Krom, in the second half of the eighth century and is a sort of artificial mountain, or, rather, "a mountain turned to the uses of architecture and supplemented by masonry," and including, in ascending order, firstly the enormous platform forming its base, which is square in plan with redan-shaped projections; secondly a high terrace with five tiers or storeys on the same plan as the platform, each tier receding farther than the one below, and adorned on its façade with a series of niches, one above the other, containing an equal number of statues of Buddha. We may judge of the importance of these statues when we realize that the whole structure at Bōrō-budur contained no less than four hundred and thirty-six niches;

FIGURE 177
Tomb of Akbar, Sikandra.
— *Photo, Johnston and Hoffmann*

thirdly, below the fifth terrace is a circular platform with three stepped tiers, on the edge of which rise seventy-two bell-shaped *dāgabas* or *dāgobas* (small *stūpas*); and lastly, in the centre of the highest storey is the hemispherical dome of the *stūpa* proper.

This enormous mass is admirably marshalled. Order, proportion, and taste are, indeed, the virtues of Indo-Javanese art. The curious thing is that whereas Indian art displayed a tendency towards the monstrous, towards exaggeration and overloading, especially in the Deccan, Indo-Javanese art refers every detail to the laws of what is a truly classic canon. For instance, though the sculptured ornamentation at Bōrōbudur is so abundant, far from overloading the building,

FIGURE 178
Tomb of I'timād al-Daula, Agra.
— *Photo, Johnston and Hoffmann*

as too often happens in India, it remains definitely subordinate to the architectural scheme. The wonderful seated Buddhas in the niches of each storey form a really integral part of the whole; beneath the graceful flame of the *kīrti mukha* (grotesque mask) which crowns the niches, they are, as it were, the smiling soul of the building (Fig. 104).[1]

[1] Cf. Gangoly: "Note on Kīrti mukha," *Rūpam*, January 1920 (with thirty-five illustrations).

The sculpture at Mendut and Bōrōbudur is, however, of value for its own sake. Not only is it an immense advance upon that at Dieng, if regarded from the Javanese point of view only, but when viewed in connexion with Indian sculpture too, it includes perhaps the purest masterpieces of the Gupta ideal of art. We need only glance, first at the Buddhist statues at Sārnāth and Mathurā, belonging to the Gupta art of the fourth century (Fig. 41, 42), and then at the statues of the Buddhas in the niches at Bōrōbudur, seated in the attitude of the *padmāsana* and making the ritual gestures (that of giving, argument, the *dhyāna mudrā,* the gesture of reassurance, the Wheel of the Law, etc., Fig. 104): in them we find the same simplicity of line, the same tender and caressing modelling: the smooth, rounded shoulders, the soft, almost melting contours of the bust and limbs, and the smooth faces, too, with their serene and pure grace. This softness is all the more remarkable because the material here employed is a volcanic trachyte, full of holes and granulations, whose intractable roughness only enhances the triumph of the most delicate chisel ever wielded by a sculptor. The famous little head of Buddha in the Leiden Museum (Fig. 105), charming in its blend of youth and seriousness, shows with what virtuosity the artists of the school of Bōrōbudur succeeded, thanks to this very volcanic ruggedness itself, in rendering the full warmth of the skin, and the varied, complex, palpitating life of the flesh, as well as ever the brush of a Renoir could do (cf. Fig. 105 and 106).

But we have already admired these qualities in the statuary of Mathurā and Sārnāth. The peculiar feature of Bōrōbudur are the bas-reliefs, long frescoes in stone, so perfect in their grouping and so harmoniously balanced in their composition that on looking at them we are reminded of the doors of the Baptistery at Florence, and the pictorial quality of a Ghiberti's art.[1] We cannot attempt to describe even

[1] See N. J. Krom and Van Erp: *Archæologische Beschrijving van Barabudur* (The Hague, Nijhoff, 1920); N. J. Krom: *The Life of Buddha in the Stūpa of Barabudur* (The

a tenth part of these reliefs; we need only realize that at Bōrōbudur they form nearly two thousand scenes, sixteen hundred of which are in a fairly good state of preservation. We will only draw attention to a few of them, which we reproduce here from the fine photographs

FIGURE 179
Tomb of I'timād al-Daula, Agra.
— *Photo, Johnston and Hoffmann*

of our master Victor Goloubew. Here, for example, on the lower part of the first gallery, to the right-hand side of the southern front, we have the story of a famous *jātaka,* in which Prince Sudhana is casting his ring into the water-pot of one of the *kinnarīs* at the fountain, while the other *kinnarīs* are returning to the city carrying their full water-jars: in the modest beauty of their gestures and the fine

Hague, 1926); A. Foucher: "Buddhist Art in Java" (the *stūpa* and bas-reliefs of Bōrōbudur), in *The Beginnings of Buddhist Art* (London, 1917).

Figure 180

Tomb of I'timād al-Daula.

— Photo, Johnston and Hoffmann

rhythm of their gait this procession of women with water-jars recalls a band of Athenian maidens or some figures of Botticelli or Ghirlandajo (Fig. 118). Here, again, are two scenes of a suavity worthy of the predecessors of Raphael: first comes the bas-relief of the bath of the bodhisattva in the presence of the divinities, who prostrate themselves on the river-bank or hover in the air; the whole scene is animated by an exquisite feeling for nature, which inspires the caressing design of the waters, the realistic rendering of the floral life of the forest, and the group of the sheep and lamb (Fig. 119). Next we have the arrival of Hiru at Hiruka, in which, in accordance with the legend, he is shown distributing to the inhabitants of the place the wealth which escaped the destruction of Roruka; the finely rigged ship which has brought Hiru to the spot and now tosses on the sea near the shore, and the native village, with its inhabitants casting themselves at Hiru's feet, form scenes full of fine observation (Fig. 119). The same classical breadth of *ensemble*, the same wreathing grace of movement, are to be found in the offering of Sujātā (Fig. 114), in the temptation by the daughters of Mārā (Fig. 116), whose dance is so regular in its rhythm that it might have come out of one of our modern schools of dancing (Fig. 117), or in the representation of the dancing-girl, naked beneath her veils, dancing at the court of Druma (Fig. 109).

In all these scenes we find a certain number of general subjects or types from which the sculptors of Bōrōbudur have succeeded in drawing the most varied effects, for their imagination is equal to that of the painters of Ajaṇṭā. First we have a type of Buddha which in no way differs from the Buddha of Sārnāth (Fig. 41), descending from his pedestal and mingling with life. And the beauty of this body, with its smooth, chaste, soft nudity, is still further enhanced by the gestures, with the serene beauty of their rhythm, and by the poses, every one of which is of a high plastic value (Fig. 110, 111, 112, 114, 115). Next we have the figures in an attitude of adoration before the Blessed One, bodhisattvas, gods, noblemen, or women, from whom emanates such a brooding tenderness (Fig. 111, 113, 115). This sentiment may be particularly felt in the female figures surrounding the prince bodhisattva, which are all the more moving because in them the tender attachment of the wife is transformed into mystical adoration; and it infuses an ineffable dignity and fervour into their attitudes of trustful abandonment. The whole scene is quite Florentine in its sweetness. But the superhuman contemplativeness of the spot in no way detracts from the plastic beauty of these nude female figures, harmonious as antiques, or the infinite seductiveness of these poses, each of which is like a caress (Fig. 112, 114, 119, 121, 122). Equally superlative is the elegance of the genii, *kinnaras,* and *apsaras,* who hover in the air round the Buddha like Gothic angels (Fig. 119). And sometimes we find a pure antique, such as the figure of the female musician in Fig. 123, which reminds us of the verse coined by Victor Hugo:

"*Le pâtre sur sa flûte abaissant sa paupière.*"
(The shepherd o'er his flute lowers his drooping lid.)

On the other hand, animal and vegetable subjects are an unfailing source of fresh inspiration to the sculptors of Bōrōbudur, as they were to our Gothic sculptors. At Bōrōbudur, as in the reliefs in our cathedrals, animals are often treated with a realism which, while revealing direct observation, is ennobled by its ideal inspiration. We may, in particular, point out the striking truth to nature and the sureness of touch with which the type of the elephant has been reproduced in all its attitudes — true portraits, which go so far as to render the almost human intelligence expressed in the physiognomy of the Indian elephant (Fig. 109). In like fashion sheep, pigeons, and peacocks are treated with loving care and, as in past days at Sāñchī, with a remarkable sense of decorative effect (Fig. 115 and 124). Similarly, every species of tree is the object of patient and loving study, the stone being hollowed out into a lace-work until the carver has drawn the maximum of ornamental effect from the design of leaf and flower (Fig. 112, 116, 119, 121, 122). The same sense of ornamental effect, worthy of goldsmiths' work, the same

FIGURE 181
Dīwān-i 'Āmm, Delhi.
— *Photo, Johnston and Hoffmann*

splendour of decoration, are to be observed in the architectural motives, with their curiously flamboyant style.

Though quite Indian in inspiration, in some details this art asserts its specifically Javanese character. Thus it has been pointed out that the species of forest-trees represented here do not belong to the flora of India, but to that of Java. All the same, we are here dealing with works permeated with the Indian æsthetic ideal. Indian naturalism, which we saw in process of formation at Sāñchī and Ajaṇṭā, triumphs at Bōrōbudur in the same flower-like freshness of the female or youthful forms, and in the same realism of the animal forms. But here it seems to have become more ordered. After the naïve effusions of earlier days, at Bōrōbudur we rise to a graver ideal. To sum up

FIGURE 182
Dīwān-i 'Āmm, Delhi.
— *Photo, Johnston and Hoffmann*

our impressions in a single formula, at Bōrōbudur the naturalism of Ajaṇṭā has become a true classicism.

There are a certain number of sculptures in the museums of Java and Holland which are connected with the art of the Śailendra period — that is, to that of the Sumatran hegemony of Java. Quoting from Krom's album (*Ars Asiatica,* Vol. VIII), we may mention the statues of Vishṇu, Ganesh, and Bhatāra Guru, from the region of Mendut, now in the Museum of Batavia: " Their tall, slender forms, even that of the Ganesh, which is naturally heavy, and their fine ornamentation, without any overloading, are perfectly in harmony with those of the bodhisattvas of Mendut." We may note the majesty of bearing of the Bhatāra Guru and the fine Aryan type of head. In this connexion we may also note that, even under Buddhist princes such as the Śailendra, Brahmanical art remained in repute — the same being true in the reverse sense in the ages which followed. Equally elegant, or even more so, are the statue of Mañjuśrī from Plaosan, in the collection at Jogjakarta, and the statue of Avalokitēśvara in the attitude of the *padmāsana* and making the gesture of the *varada mudrā,* in the same collection.[1] In these two works we are approaching the end of the Śailendra period.

Towards the middle of the ninth century, as we said above, central Java shook off the Sumatran supremacy of the Śailendra kings and recovered its independence under native princes, who built the temples at Prambanan, which now belonged to the Hindu religion. The Lara Jonggrang group of buildings, at Prambanan, consists of eight temples standing on a very high platform, in the centre of which stands a great Śivaite temple, and next to it a temple of Vishṇu and a temple of Brahmā. The sculpture of this group of temples has less serenity than that of Bōrōbudur, but is more living and dramatic in its inspiration and more impetuous in its movement. Is this due to the influence of Śivaite and Vishnuite tendencies, or is it the effect of the Malay temperament? For the rest, it still lies within the sphere of the classic canons of Indian art. What could be more moving in its simplicity, for instance, than the relief in the temple of Vishṇu representing two nude figures of young suppliants, seated side by side, with their hands joined in an attitude of ineffable fervour? What could be more in harmony with Gupta ideals of art than the famous head in the Museum of Batavia (No. 32, measuring about fifteen inches), from one of the secondary temples at Lara Jonggrang,

[1] Cf. N. J. Krom: *L'Art javanais dans les musées de Hollande et de Java,* Collection *Ars Asiatica,* VIII (Paris, Van Oest, 1926), Pl. VIII–IX, XII.

FIGURE 183

Dīwān-i Khāṣṣ, Delhi.

— *Photo, Johnston and Hoffman*

representing a Śiva whose full, fresh countenance, serenely restful in its youthful charm, is in such contrast with the death's-head on his head-dress?

The great temple of Śiva at Lara Jonggrang is chiefly famous for its reliefs which narrate before our eyes the whole story of the *Rāmāyaṇa.*[1] Here we can do no more than refer our readers to the fine reproductions of them given by Herr Stutterheim (*Rāma Legenden und Rāma Reliefs in Indonesien*).[2] We need only mention a few particularly fine scenes from the principal series: that of Daśaratha saluting Viśvāmitra, with the noble, majestic figure of the old King; Rāma drawing the bow of Śiva and thus winning the hand of the fair Sītā — the first of the scenes in which we see the hero in the elegant attitude of an archer, together with a Sītā whose slender, undulating nude form reminds us of the daughters of Mārā at Bōrōbudur; the voluptuous group, full of fine psychological insight, of Queen Kaikēyī enticing King Daśaratha, and, immediately afterwards, the extraordinary dancing female figure, armed with the sword and shield, in the scene of the coronation of Bhārata, a figure full of frantic movement, which is already specifically Malay, in contrast with the Indo-classic rhythms of the dancing women at Bōrōbudur; the two panels, similar in movement, in which Rāma, in the guise of a charming prince of dazzling beauty, first shoots down the bird and the gazelle and then slays Vālin, the prince of the monkeys. In this connexion we may remark that in these three bas-reliefs Indian art has made a definitive contribution to the artistic types of the world, in the shape of this gesture of the divine archer, just as Greek art created the type of the discobolus (see Fig. 108). Moreover, the following scenes — the rape of Sītā, the battle between Vālin and Sugrīva — are full of an extraordinary movement and a dramatic intensity which are a novel thing in Indian art. But in spite of these characteristics,

[1] Cf. Alexander Zieseniss: *Die Rāma-Sage bei den Malaien, ihre Herkunft und Gestaltung* (Hamburg, 1928).

[2] And J. Kats: *The Rāmāyaṇa, as Sculptured in Reliefs in Javanese Temples* (Leiden).

FIGURE 184

Dīwān-i Khāṣṣ, Delhi.

— *Photo, Johnston and Hoffmann*

which reveal the Malay blood, Indian gentleness is still found in most of the representations of Rāma and Sītā. Here the heroine remains what she is in the text of the *Rāmāyaṇa,* an ideal of plastic beauty, feminine modesty, and conjugal tenderness. As for the Rāma of Lara Jonggrang, he is worthy to be compared to the Buddhas of

FIGURE 185
Dīwān-i Khāṣṣ, Delhi.
— *Photo, Johnston and Hoffmann*

Gupta art, especially in the idyllic scenes, in his attitudes of sadness or repose. In the chivalrous King and the bodhisattva Prince, in Rāma and the Buddha, the Indian æsthetic ideal has created two eternal types of moral and physical beauty, as flawless in body as all the most perfect achievements in this kind handed down to us by Greek art, and as noble in soul as the loftiest inventions of our Christian Middle Ages.

FIGURE 186

Zenana, Agra.

— *Photo, Johnston and Hoffmann*

A place apart should be assigned to the green bronzes of the Prambanan period, of which the Musée Guimet possesses an important series, bequeathed to it by Monsieur J. J. Meijer. These are small works, not more than about ten inches in height; but every one is a masterpiece. What purity and elegance there are in the standing Avalokitēśvara with the ten arms, which combines in itself the two characteristics of the finest Javanese style: simplicity of line and the decorative value of the rare ornamental motives (Fig. 126)! On the other hand, what amplitude there is in the neighbouring statue of Kuvēra, the god of wealth! To arrive at an estimate of the worth of these works, we have only to compare them to the analogous productions of the art of other parts of the East. For instance, the Avalokitēśvara of the Musée Guimet is treated in accordance with the accepted canons and is of the same rather cold and elongated type as the figures of the bodhisattva in Nepal or central Asia. Yet if this bronze is placed alongside of the Himalayan bronzes or the paintings at Tuen-huang, we feel what a difference there is between a living interpretation of a metaphysical theme and a purely abstract rendering of it. On the other hand, if we compare the Javanese statue of Kuvēra in the Musée Guimet with similar works of Indian or Chinese art, we find in the latter a heavy, corpulent grotesque, but in the former a figure whose traditional stout proportions in no way impair its grace and majesty. Perhaps it is in this very point that the Javanese sculptors give the full measure of their powers. When they work in stone, they are, after all, hampered by the intractability of the trachyte, and it is only in their bronzes that their skill reveals itself in all its softness. Not till now can we really appreciate the nobility of the shoulders, the exquisite quality of the torsos, the purity of the legs, the infinite charm of these nude figures from the tropics, which we are surprised to find displaying such classical qualities. If the Hellenic ideal is made up of moderation, plenitude, and taste as well as strength, these Javanese bronzes have all the merit of the Greek.[1]

It is interesting to note that the Indo-Sumatran art of Śrīvijaya made its influence felt in another direction, as far afield as the Malay

FIGURE 187
Mōtī Masjid or Mosque of the Pearl, Agra.
— *Photo, Johnston and Hoffmann*

Peninsula. The region of Vat Brah Dhātu, Jaiyā, in the Siamese portion of the peninsula, has yielded some bronzes of which Monsieur Coedès has published a study, and in particular a bodhisattva which,

[1] The Javanese bronzes in the Musée Guimet, J. J. Meijer collection, have been published by M. Hackin in *Chefs d'œuvre de la sculpture indienne et tibetaine au Musée Guimet* (Paris, Leroux, 1930); they may be compared with the delicious bronzes from Ceylon in the Museum of Fine Arts, Boston (Avalokitēśvara, Jambhala, and Mañjuśrī), reproduced in Coomaraswamy: *Portfolio of Indian Art*, Pl. XVI and XVII.

thanks to "the kindly serenity of the face, the noble carriage of the shoulders, and the magnificence of its ornaments," as well as the beauty of the torso, which is worthy of that of the Sārnāth Buddha, may be classed among the masterpieces of Gupta art in Indo-China (see Coedès: *Les Collections archéologiques du Musée National de Bangkok, Ars Asiatica,* XII [1928], Pl. XV–XVII).

The art of central Java survived in its original home in the sanctuaries of Vihāra Plaosan, dating from the beginning of the tenth century. But these temples remained unfinished, for the central part of Java, which had hitherto been the seat of Javanese civilization, was deserted about 920, either as the result of an act of vengeance on the part of Sumatra, or else owing to some geological cataclysm. From this time onwards the eastern part of Java became the centre of culture on the island.

In its beginnings the new Javanese art which now appeared — the art of eastern Java — still preserved a strongly Indian character. Moreover, it is possible to establish a continuity between Plaosan, the last stage of central Javanese art, and the earliest works in the east. On the one hand, we have the elegant and massive Maitrēya in the northern cloister at Plaosan, with his right leg in the European sitting posture, while the left is tucked up on the chair in the Oriental fashion, and the head and bust surrounded by a pointed glory in a flamboyant style; and, on the other hand, there is the portrait of the Javanese king Airlaṅga, who died in 1042, represented in the form of Vishṇu riding upon a *garuḍa* with a boar's head, a stone figure about fifty-seven inches high, from Belahan, in the east of the island, now in the museum at Mojokerto; here we find the same rather cold elegance, though still counteracted by a certain fullness of proportion, the same aristocratic serenity, the same pleasure to the eye afforded by the ornamentation of the throne and the richness of the jewels. A similar impression is produced by the statue of the Prajñāpāramitā, the Buddhist Holy Wisdom, from Siṅghasāri, now in the Leiden Museum, dating from the thirteenth century (Fig. 127). In our opinion, this last-named statue, in spite of its peculiarly Javanese charm, is so peculiarly representative of the metaphysics of the Mahāyāna that it can only be compared with

FIGURE 188
Mōtī Masjid.
— *Photo, Johnston and Hoffmann*

the "beautiful God of Amiens," who, Bible in hand, seems the very incarnation of Christian scholasticism. It has the same rather cold and wholly intellectual beauty, the same persistent classicism, the same elegant simplicity, and the same doctrinal assurance.

But Java had none the less begun to shake off Indian influences, as is proclaimed beyond a doubt by the group of buildings at

Panataran, dating from the fourteenth and fifteenth centuries. To convince ourselves of this we need only take Stutterheim's album [1] and compare the scenes from the *Rāmāyaṇa* at Prambanan with the same scenes at Panataran. At the latter place we definitely

FIGURE 189
Mōtī Masjid, interior.
— *Photo, Johnston and Hoffmann*

part company, not only with Indian art, but also with the Indian æsthetic ideal. Henceforward we shall be dealing with a purely indigenous Malay art, an " art of Wayang " — an Oceanian art.[2]

[1] *Rāma Legenden und Rāma Reliefs in Indonesien* (Munich, 1924–5).
[2] See *Cahiers d'art*, Paris, March–April 1929, "Oceanian Arts."

FIGURE 190
The Tāj Maḥall, Agra.
— *Photo, Johnston and Hoffmann*

The Indianized Empires of Indo-China: Angkor, Tourane, and Ayuthyā

Like Java, western and southern Indo-China to a large extent accepted Indian civilization. Not that there was any political colonization or conquest. The land remained under the power of the native races: the Khmers in Cambodia, who, together with the Mōn of southern Burmah, form a distinct race, akin to the Muṇḍa of India; and the Chams, a maritime race akin to the Malayo-Polynesians, in what is now southern Annam. But as early as the first centuries of our era both Khmers and Chams accepted Indian civilization. Indian or Indianized dynasties were set up among them, and they adopted Sanskrit as the sacred and court language, and Brahmanism and Buddhism as the national religions.[1] The kingdom of Champa, thus Indianized, first appears in history about the third century of our era, when it had as its chief centres the region of Tourane, in which was situated the first capital of the country, known in Sanskrit as Indrapura, the modern Tra-kiēu, and the region of Binh-dinh, in which was built the second capital, Vijaya (Cha-ban). In this historical setting the kings of Champa — all of whom bore Sanskrit names — carried on a struggle lasting for centuries, in the north against the Annamites, who were masters of Tonkin, and in the southwest against the Khmers, the hereditary enemies of the Cham people.[2]

In the Khmer territories of Cambodia, too, organized and Indianized states appeared about the third century of our era. One of these states, known to us only by the name given it by the Chinese — Fu-nan (Fou-nan) — had its centre in what is now Cochin-China. The other state, called by the Chinese "Chen-la" (Tchen-la), must have been situated farther to the north, in the direction of Laos. For

[1] See *Un Empire colonial français, l'Indochine*, ed. Georges Maspero, Vol. I: "*Le Pays et les habitants, l'histoire*" (Paris, Van Oest, 1929).

[2] See Georges Maspero: *Le Royaume de Champa* (Paris, Van Oest, 1928).

a long time the primacy was in the hands of Fu-nan; but in the second half of the sixth century Chen-la seized the hegemony and set up the historical empire of Cambodia. The centre of gravity of this empire does not, however, seem to have become fixed until the beginning of the ninth century, in the region of the Tonle-sap (Great

FIGURE 191
The Tāj Maḥall, Agra.
— *Photo, Johnston and Hoffmann*

Lake), where Angkor was afterwards to be built, and this city was not founded till quite the latter years of the ninth century, when it became the capital of the Khmer empire, which it was to remain for five and a half centuries. During the first half of this long period, from the tenth to the thirteenth centuries inclusive, the Khmer empire extended far beyond the frontiers of what is now the kingdom of

Cambodia — embracing, in fact, the whole of what is now Cochin-China, almost the whole of the modern Laos, and the whole southern part of what is now Siam — and repeatedly invaded the kingdom of Champa. The splendour of Angkor was in keeping with the majesty of this vast empire.[1]

Art in this Cambodian region begins with what is called the "pre-Angkorean" style, which lasted from about the sixth to the eighth century of our era, and even up to the beginning of the ninth. Chronologically, we do not think we are too much forestalling the identification of dates if we say that it corresponded with the end of the ancient "Fu-nan" and the beginnings of the "Chen-la" — that is, with the period of the two proto-Cambodian kingdoms which we have just mentioned. According to the surviving fragments of Sanskrit, Cambodian, and Chinese texts, Fu-nan and Chen-la purport to have been founded by Indian Brahmans married to native princesses or mythological beings, and these legends are symbolic of the close fusion of Indian and Khmer civilization, which was to give rise to that of the new state. As a matter of fact, Hindu influences — in the shape of that strictly Indian classicism which is known as Gupta art — are perhaps more noticeable here than in the Angkorean art of later ages. And yet the moment we find ourselves face to face with the works of this distant epoch, we feel that we are in the presence of an individual style, which, while not actually breaking with Indian æsthetic ideals, is developing them in the direction of new artistic conventions: the balance of masses alone would suffice to mark this difference.

In the region of Chau-doc, to the north of Cochin-China, and round about Prei-Krabas and Phnom Pēnh, the district which was the seat of the ancient Fu-nan and afterwards of "Chen-la of

[1] Cf. Commaille: *Guide aux ruines d'Angkor* (1912); Henri Marchal: *Guide archéologique aux temples d'Angkor* (Van Oest, 1928); H. Groslier: *Angkor* (Laurens, 1924).

the water," some archæologists belonging to the École française d'Extrême Orient, and especially Messrs. Henri Parmentier and George Groslier, have discovered the principal monuments of pre-Angkorean architecture, in the shape of isolated towers built of brick, which distinguishes them at a glance from the great temples of the Angkorean age.

FIGURE 192
The Tāj Maḥall, Agra, interior.
— *Photo, Johnston and Hoffmann*

The pre-Angkorean sculpture found in the same region is equally characteristic. As Monsieur Philippe Stern remarks, this sculpture can be recognized by its treatment of the garment — which is often indicated merely by means of incised lines — by the sideward thrust of the hip, which is still found here, to a very slight extent as compared with India, but, none the less, in a more marked degree than at Angkor; by the individual appearance of certain head-dresses, which are, as a rule, conical in form; and by the general use of the mitra, also conical in form, as the head-dress of deities. There are a few of these pre-Angkorean figures on exhibition at the Musée

FIGURE 193
Timur capturing Bayezid.
— *From Mehta:* Studies in Indian Painting (*1926*).
By courtesy of Mr. Mehta

Guimet, and some casts of other works appear among the collection at the Trocadéro (Fig. 128–130). We may note the large female statues, with a pronounced sideward thrust of the hip, and wearing the conical mitra. Another group consists of figures of Hari-Hara — that is, Vishṇu and Śiva united in a single being, which seems to have

FIGURE 194

Babur and Humayun. Mogul art, seventeenth century.
— *Vever collection. Photo, Pivot*

been one of the most popular deities in the Brahmanic pantheon of Cambodia. The Trocadéro possesses a cast of the Hari-Hara in the Museum of Phnom-Pēnh, of which the long lines of the nude form,

FIGURE 195
Humayun. Mogul art, seventeenth century.
— *Vever collection. Photo, Vever*

at once conventionalized and plastic, suggest " a Gupta style evolved by a brain of the Pharaonic age " (Fig. 131), and the style of which may be compared with a Vishṇu in the Bangkok Museum, published by Coedès in *Ars Asiatica,* XII, Pl. IX; while another Hari-Hara, from Mahā Rosei — this time an original, and, in our opinion, closer

FIGURE 196

Portrait of Akbar. Mogul art, seventeenth century.
— *Vever collection. Photo, Laniepce*

to the Gupta or Pallava style — greets visitors in the entrance hall of the Musée Guimet (Fig. 132).

We make no claim to advance any theory here about the pre-Angkorean art of Cambodia, for this would be, to say the least of it, premature. All we should like to do is to offer some of these works for the consideration of artists, in order to prepare the way for this vigorous and well-balanced art to take its legitimate place in the general history of æsthetic development. A comparison of the works themselves will settle better than all theories can do what survivals of Indian standards they reveal and how much there is in them that already foreshadows the more individualized art of the earliest Angkorean style, in addition to those factors which may, perhaps, betray the influence of Chinese T'ang sculpture — for, as Monsieur J. Hackin suggests, the fact that the balance of masses in these works is architectural rather than sculptural may be explained by Chinese influence.

The art of Angkor, according to a recent thesis on the subject by Monsieur Philippe Stern, head of the Indo-Chinese Museum at the Trocadéro, falls into two periods: the first Angkorean style, dating from the tenth century, and the second Angkorean style, dating from the eleventh and twelfth centuries. If we adopt the new chronological order proposed by Monsieur Stern, the first style would embrace the monuments at Roluoḥ, known as the Phimeanakas and the Baphuon; while the second style would embrace the temple of Angkor-Vat, dating from about the reign of Sūryavarman II (1112–52), and the temple of the Bayon, which, according to the latest hypothesis of Monsieur Coedès, may be dated about 1200, under the reign of Jayavarman VII (Fig. 135).[1] Theoretically, the temples of Cambodia

[1] Cf. *Le Temple d'Angkor-Vat* (*Mémoires archéologiques publiés par l'École française d'Extrême Orient*, Paris, Van Oest, 1929). For the new dating of the Bayon, see G. Coedès: "*Études cambodgiennes,*" *Bulletin de l'École française d'Extrême Orient,* Vol. XXVIII (1928), pp. 81–103.

FIGURE 197

Portrait of Jahangir.

— *Vever collection. Photo, Laniepce*

are surrounded by a wall of enclosure, each of whose four faces is broken by a gopura, consisting of a gate with a vestibule, surmounted by an ornamental tower in the form of a stepped pyramid. As for

FIGURE 193
Jahangir and his favourite.
— *Demotte collection. Photo, Laniepce*

the temples proper, sometimes, as at the Baphuon, the Bayon, and Angkor-Vat, they are built in a series of concentric galleries, one above the other, each resting on a platform the height of which doubles with every storey; in buildings of this type four *prasat* are built at the angles of the galleries on the upper storeys, each in the form of a stepped cone with slightly convex sides, dominated by a

FIGURE 199
Portrait of Shāh Jahan.
— *Louvre, Fonds Marteau. Photo, Pivot*

central tower of larger proportions; while sometimes the temples, with their galleries and courtyards, are built in one storey only. The various elements of which they are composed have obvious affinities with Hindu architecture. We find these gopuras in the Tamil temples of the Carnatic, too, while the *prasat* has some affinities with the

FIGURE 200
Portrait of Shāh Jahan.
— *Demotte collection. Photo, Laniepce*

śikhara of the temples of Orissa. Yet we are here dealing with an art which is distinctly Khmer, and the proof of this is to be found in the very clumsiness of the Cambodian architects, who only slowly improved their methods. At the outset, as Monsieur Philippe Stern observes, brick was almost exclusively used — for instance, at Roluoḥ, in the last quarter of the ninth century. In the Phimeanakas, which Monsieur Stern inclines to place quite towards the last years of the ninth century or the beginning of the tenth, brick is still combined with sandstone, which gradually comes into greater prominence and finally triumphs in the Bayon. From the period of the Bayon onwards the towers, which had hitherto been separate, are connected by galleries. The vaulted gallery supported upon two walls, which was unknown at Roluoḥ, had appeared, it is true, at the Phimeanakas, but still in a curiously tentative form, not rising much higher than two yards. The normal form of the vaulted gallery supported on pillars does not appear till the second style, at the Bayon, in the first half of the eleventh century, according to Monsieur Stern's chronology. Not till then did it acquire its ultimate form, when the Khmer temple also assumed its normal appearance. Here, then, we have a decidedly independent art, pursuing its slow development on the outskirts of Indian architecture, to use Monsieur Stern's expression.

There are two styles of sculpture corresponding to these two styles of Angkorean architecture, and these, too, have been defined by Monsieur Philippe Stern in his work *Le Bayon d'Angkor et l'évolution de l'art khmèr* (Paris, Geuthner, 1927). The Angkorean sculpture of the first style (tenth century) is characterized by heads with the eyebrows indicated by a straight, continuous ridge, a double line traced round the mouth and eyes, and another conventionalized sign with a point beneath the chin, representing the beard. This art is represented in the Musée Guimet by a number of heads and by a great statue of a seated Brahmā (Fig. 136), in all of which we may admire the solid and almost geometrical construction, for the sculpture of this school is treated in masses, in the architectural manner. As we see, this art is very remote from Gupta art and is specifically Khmer in character.

In the second Angkorean style of the eleventh and twelfth centuries, there is a complete change. The geometrical conventions of the first style — the continuous line of the brows, the marks outlining the mouth and eyes or indicating the beard — now disappear. Instead of these heads with their "conventionalized construction," we suddenly find ourselves in the presence of faces that are strangely gentle and living — so living, indeed, and so gentle that in this respect Khmer art at a single bound equals and surpasses all that Indian art has had to show us. As a matter of fact, taking it on the whole, Indian art tends to go beyond our comprehension and make us feel rather at a loss, the reason being that it was influenced by Buddhist humanism for too short a time: Sāñchī offers no representations of the faces of the Buddhist saints, while Gandhāra treats them in a commonplace way; Ajaṇṭā alone understood them and expressed them admirably; but almost immediately afterwards Buddhism gave way to Śivaism, about which all that can be said is that it represents — to say the least of it — a superhuman ideal. But in the second Angkorean manner of Cambodia, together with the Javanese art of Bōrōbudur, we find an art that is quite close to ourselves, infinitely idealistic, it is true, but also infinitely tender: here we have no effort at adaptation to make; even in the presence of the gods we feel, as in Greek art, the delightful sensation of a fullness of humanity, with which we are wholly in touch.

Over most of these statues of the second period hovers what has been called the "smile of Angkor." Few artists seem to us to have rendered this smiling countenance with half-closed eyes — which was unknown to the sculptors of the first period and was, no doubt, the expression of supreme Buddhist beatitude — with so much mystic feeling as those of Angkor. In the India of the Gupta period, and even at Ajaṇṭā, something material still lingered in it; but here it is really freed from all concern with the vicissitudes of life. Here indeed we have the unchanging, elusive smile which mysteriously reflects

FIGURE 201
Portrait of Shāh Jahan.
— *Vever collection. Photo, Laniepce*

the inward illumination of *nirvāṇa.* In the two Khmer galleries in the Musée Guimet the visitor will find a number of heads in which this expression of supreme wisdom finds its incarnate form. We reproduce a few of them here (Fig. 138–146). Such works as these give us a better insight into the soul of the great Oriental religion than any verbal teaching: he who understands them will have understood the whole of Buddhism. Nor should we imagine that this subject of the smiling Buddha becomes monotonous by repetition. On the contrary, though uniform in its inspiration, it assumes a different character with every type that it animates. Sometimes, when, for instance, it happens to shed its illumination upon some slender type revealing Indian influence, it remains absolutely immaterial and ethereal, so much so that the smile is the essential feature of the face (Fig. 138, 139);[1] at other times it acquires an even more poignant significance, when its great peace descends upon some mask-like native type with high cheek-bones and thick lips, breathing a deeply human quality (Fig. 140, 141). This contrast between the racial type and the gleam of supernatural illumination, this reflection of the divine light falling upon the dull matter, is perhaps the most moving thing to be found in our collections. It is even more curious to find this smile of Buddhist kindliness on what was originally a demon head, as happens in one of the finest Khmer figures in the Musée Guimet, representing a *yaksha* converted by Buddha, with protuberant eyes and fangs peeping out of the corners of the mouth, the whole face of this carnivorous monster being transformed and sanctified by the preaching of the Blessed One (Fig. 147).

But it should not be supposed that the " smile of Angkor " is confined to Buddhist heads alone. In the Musée Guimet we shall find it hovering over the face of a Hari-Hara and assuming a strangely enigmatic and mysterious significance in this elegant and juvenile figure (Fig. 148). In the same room we shall see it appearing on a

[1] See also *Bulletin of the Art Institute of Chicago,* Vol. XVIII, April 1924, frontispiece.

Figure 202

Portrait of Shāh Jahan.

— Demotte collection. Photo, Laniepce

Śivaite head, no doubt copied from some Indo-Khmer Brahman type, to whose face — still so pregnant with thought and so Aryan in type — it imparts an astonishing philosophic value (Fig. 149–150); and, lastly, we shall find the same expression on the face on a Brahmanic head of a *dēvatā* (deity), with a certain suggestion of the giant smiling heads which crown the Bayon and the gates of Angkor (Fig. 151).

On the other hand, the second Angkorean style has left us a few delightful nude figures, some more in the Gupta style, and others rather in the native style. Among the specimens belonging to the former category we may mention the Buddha in a state of meditation, in the attitudes of the *padmāsana* and the *dhyāna mudrā,* seated on the serpent Muchilinda, a figure about a yard in height, found by Commaille in 1913 at the door in the south façade of the Bayon, and now in the Museum of Phnom Pēnh: the purity of the Aryan profile (in spite of the lips, which are already rather thick), the calm and harmonious expression of the face, and the touchingly plastic quality of the bust, which seems to live and breathe — all these are traits in which the influence of the art so justly designated by Goloubew as "Indo-classic" is obvious (Fig. 152). On the other hand, the Buddha in the Musée Guimet (Fig. 153), seated in the same attitude on the serpent, while equally Gupta in character, already displays more of a native tendency in its face of the Mōn-Khmer type, as well as in the rather childlike softness of the bust and the simplified treatment of the hands. With these two works may be compared another very fine Buddha on the serpent, a sandstone statue of the twelfth century, about four feet high, found at Bimay, and now in the Bangkok Museum, reproduced by Monsieur Coedès in his *Collections du Musée de Bangkok* (*Ars Asiatica,* XII, Pl. XX, 1928).

And, finally, the Khmer artists produced admirable works in bronze. In strength and elegance the bronze statuettes reproduced by Monsieur Coedès in his fine work (*Bronzes Khmèrs; Ars Asi-*

FIGURE 203

Audience of Shāh Jahan.
— *Vever collection. Photo, Pivot*

atica, Vol. V) can vie with those of any Oriental people, with the exception of the Dravidians and Javanese: whether they be heads of Brahmans of an absolutely classic delicacy, with their faint half-smile beneath the indication of the beard; or exquisite female statuettes, which look as if they had stepped out of the bas-reliefs; or princes or warriors with the elegance of Egyptian work, but less hard in treatment; or torsos worthy of the Gupta period or of the antique; or little Buddhas in a state of meditation, like the great statues of Phnom Pēnh or the Musée Guimet on a small scale; or many-headed serpent deities and hundred-handed gods, which are splendidly decorative in effect — most of these tiny works are perfect little masterpieces.

But the Khmer sculpture *par excellence* is not in the round, but in bas-relief.

The development of Khmer bas-relief was as follows: starting with full, sculptural relief, it gradually developed into mere incision without any depth, like a mere tapestry-work in sandstone, such as we find at Angkor-Vat. When thus rid of the difficulties which must, in spite of all, have been offered to them by sculpture in the round, the artists of the Cambodian bas-reliefs recovered their full freedom of hand and set forth every aspect of the Khmer land and the Hindu heaven. At the Bayon at Angkor, as at Ellora, we find scenes from the lives of Śiva and Pārvatī (Śiva and Kāma, Śiva and Rāvaṇa); at the Baphuon and at Angkor-Vat, as at Prambanan, are scenes from the *Rāmāyaṇa;* while at Angkor-Vat we find battles from the *Mahābhārata,* the churning of the sea (Fig. 154), the exploits of Vishṇu and Kṛishṇa as related in the Purānas, etc. On the other hand, almost everywhere we find the king in his costume of state, the queens indulging in the pleasures of court life, the court in boats or in palankeens — notably on the southern façade of the Bayon and at Angkor-Vat — or a scene of a royal hunt from the backs of elephants, as on the grand terrace of the Phimeanakas; or again, at the Bayon

FIGURE 204
Shāh Jahan and his family.
— *Vever collection. Photo, Laniepce*

and on the façade of Angkor-Vat, the Khmer army marching through the forest, with the leaders riding on elephants, in chariots, or on horseback (Fig. 155, 156); besides battles by land or sea and the funeral of a king. Side by side with these historical scenes, there are

FIGURE 205
Aurungzeb.
— *Vever collection. Photo, Pivot*

also scenes of everyday life, as realistic as those of Egyptian art, showing a market, farming life, fishing, etc.

All these scenes are alive with an intensity of movement which links the scenes together and imparts to them a remarkable unity, as, for instance, in the churning of the sea from Angkor-Vat, in the ground-floor galleries of the Musée Guimet. At the same time the grouping of the figures and decorative motives is dictated by a just sense of proportion, a quality which is all the more precious here because the Khmer bas-reliefs are loaded with figures, and aim at finish of detail — both fish and trees, for example, being treated with a minuteness that is quite Assyrian. Since this sense of decorative effect is combined with narrative skill, these miles of friezes

FIGURE 206
Portrait of an emir of Bījāpur.
— *Musée Guimet. Photo, Pivot*

are marshalled with a truly classic faculty for composition. All these qualities, which are rather those of the painter than of the sculptor, together with the very low relief of the modelling, make the bas-reliefs of Angkor real frescoes in stone.

The latest Khmer reliefs of which we have any knowledge are those of Banteai Srei, of which Messrs. Finot, Parmentier, and Goloubew have recently published a study, *Le Temple d'Iśvarapura* (Paris,

Van Oest, 1926). Here we have a late type of art, dating from quite the early years of the fourteenth century and characterized by a remarkable softness of technique, combined, in the sculpture in full relief, with a curious revival of archaism; for instance, there is a statue of this period in the Musée Guimet which displays a suavity in the treatment of the nude that is quite characteristic of the "second style," while the head is quite geometrical in construction and has the beard indicated by a line, quite in the "first style." We here reproduce two of the bas-reliefs from Banteai Srei from photographs by Monsieur Goloubew: one a group, of great plastic merit, of Śiva on the Kailās, holding Pārvatī upon his knee, while Rāvaṇa is trying to shake the mountain (Fig. 160), and the other a scene of the young Kṛishṇa and his brother in the forest (Fig. 161) — a scene of a tender naturalism and pastoral grace which show a more intimate, tender, and sensuous inspiration than anything we have met with in Cambodia so far. At the same time the profusion and dazzling elegance of the decorative elements at Banteai Srei combine to produce what Monsieur Goloubew has called a "Khmer flamboyant style," which is a delight to the eye.

Moreover, these decorative qualities are to be found throughout the whole evolution of Khmer art. We need only mention a few of the sculptured motives used architecturally, such as the serpents rearing their seven heads, spread out in a fan, at the ends of the balustrades at Angkor. Never were motives of such decorative value produced even by India herself.

Cham art, which is not so well represented in our collections as Khmer art, is derived, like the latter, from Indian æsthetic standards, but is equally original.

The Cham temples are distinguished from the Khmer buildings by the fact that they always remained faithful to the use of brick, whereas in the Angkorean architecture of the second period brick

FIGURE 207

Portrait of Mullā Sa'd Allāh (d. 1650). School of Anupchatar.
— *Vever collection. Photo, Pivot*

was gradually ousted by sandstone. Moreover, instead of being connected by galleries, as in the second Angkorean style, these temples were always left as separate structures, even when grouped on the same site, as in the Śivaite sanctuaries of Mi-s'on, dating from the seventh century, the Buddhist monasteries of Dong-du'o'ng, dating from the ninth century, and Tra-kiēu or Indrapura, the ancient Cham capital. In short, we have here an architecture which never went beyond the stage of evolution of pre-Angkorean Khmer architecture — a fact which is perfectly explicable if we compare the dates of the two.

Cham sculpture is represented chiefly by the works in the museum at Tourane and has been popularized in Europe by the fine albums of Monsieur Henri Parmentier (*Sculptures chames du Musée de Tourane; Ars Asiatica,* Vol. IV) and Madame Jeanne Leuba. Many of its works are frankly Indian in appearance. We must, moreover, leave out of consideration the standing Buddha of Dong-du'o'ng, for it is merely a replica of a statue at Amarāvatī now in the Madras Museum (Fig. 33–34). But there are many other statues in the museum of Tourane which were certainly executed at Champa, and are still strongly influenced by the Indian manner; for example, the standing figure of Vishṇu, about forty inches high, from Da-nghi, dating from the sixth or eighth century, and the Avalokitēśvara of blackish sandstone from My-duc, are obviously Gupta in the smooth softness of the bust and torso, and the elegant simplicity of the long skirt in which the legs are sheathed, though in the treatment of the eyes, nose, and lips the faces already reveal a racial character which is Malayo-Polynesian. Although a little rigidly hieratical in its pose, too, the splendidly decorative figure in blue sandstone of Skanda on his peacock, about thirty-five inches in height, from Mi-s'on, dating from the seventh century, is still rather Gupta in style; while the powerful grey sandstone standing statue of Ganesh inhaling the fumes of an offering, about thirty-five inches in height, from Mi-s'on, dating from the seventh or eighth century, is directly inspired by Pallava India in the Tamil period. Sometimes, too, this art of Champa, with its Indian influences, attains a beauty never surpassed by the schools of the Ganges and the Deccan, without departing from

FIGURE 208
Portrait of a Mogul nobleman.
— *Musée Guimet. Photo, Pivot*

Indian æsthetic standards. This is especially true of the celebrated sandstone bust of Pārvatī, about fifteen inches in height, from Hu'o'ng-qua, which has a truly classic purity and nobility of profile (Fig. 163). It is true, above all, of the dancing female figures, about twenty-five inches in height, on the bas-reliefs from Tra-kiēu, in the

Tourane Museum, dating from the seventh century — the most exquisite of those visions of the dance in which the Khmer and Cham genius have added their mystery to the voluptuous suppleness of

FIGURE 209
Mogul portraits.
— *Musée Guimet. Photo, Pivot*

similar subjects in Hindu art: these little nude dancers, dressed in jewels alone, have all the flexibility and zest of the most delicate Indian nudes, yet with an added touch of exotic charm which suggests the whole of the Far East (Fig. 164).

From this time onward, indeed, Cham — that is to say, Malayo-Polynesian — racial influences diverted the Cham genius from the ideals of Gupta India and led it to evolve an artistic convention of its own. Thus we come to works of a deeply original stamp, often rugged

FIGURE 210
Mogul portraits.
— *Musée Guimet. Photo, Pivot*

and at times even a little barbarous, with a style full of abrupt contrasts and less elegantly correct than the Khmer works, but less cold, more vigorous, and, on the whole, broader. In this connexion we may mention the seated Śiva in the Javanese fashion in the Museum of Tourane, a brown sandstone figure, about thirty-four inches in height, from Dong-du'o'ng, dating from the ninth century (Fig. 165); another Śiva belonging to the same place and date, about forty-three inches high, and this time standing, which, for all its harsh ugliness, is a marvel of concentrated energy and sumptuous richness (Fig. 166); and, lastly, some sandstone busts of Śiva of the seventh and eighth centuries, about forty-eight inches in height, with the face full of imposing majesty and commanding nobility, while the triumphant breast and torso, with the marked sideward thrust of the hip, "have all the merit of the antique." [1] On the other hand, the Musée Guimet possesses a great pink sandstone statue of Śiva from Binh-dinh, whose face and nude bust have, in our opinion, a softness which is rather Sino-Annamite in character. It also contains a powerful relief, of a vigorous and barbaric character, representing a Brahman sacrifice; as well as several heads presented by Messrs. Bela Heine and Bouasse-Lebel, with the square faces, prominent cheekbones, and curious moustaches which are so characteristic of the Cham style.

Having once started out on this path, it was natural that the Cham genius should have given a fresh interpretation to the Brahman and Buddhist decorative motives: the serpent, the *makara* (crocodile), the Buddhist lion, etc. In fact, these specifically Indian subjects are here treated in accordance with an æsthetic ideal which by this time can scarcely be called Indian, in a spirit at once Malayo-Polynesian and Chinese. Adopting these motives, which at Angkor were still so classic, Cham originality turned them into a sort of conventionalized monster in a flamboyant style of astonishing decorative richness (Fig. 167).

In the course of the fourteenth century Champa was destroyed by the Annamites, who came down from what is now Tonkin, and the Khmer empire by the Siamese, who came down from the region of

[1] See Parmentier: *Les Sculptures chames au Musée de Tourane* (*Ars Asiatica*, IV), Pl. XXII.

FIGURE 211

Portrait of a *murshid* and his disciple.

— Louvre. Marteau bequest. Photo, Pivot

the upper Menam. The heritage of this Indo-Chinese art influenced by Indian standards now passed to Siam. In order to mark the continuity existing between Khmer and Siamese art we propose to treat the subject of Siamese art here in brief outline. For reasons of space, the study of Siamese art as a whole, with illustrations, will be reserved for the fourth volume of this work, dealing with the Far East (Vol. IV, Fig. 195–201).

In primitive times, before the coming of the Siamese, which dates only from the thirteenth century, the region which is now southern Siam was occupied by peoples of the Mōn race, akin to the Khmer and having as their centre the region of Lopburi, the ancient Dvāravatī. There are several Buddhist statues in the museums of Lopburi and Bangkok, dating from about the sixth century, which belong to this Mōn or "Dvāravatī" period. Monsieur Coedès, who has published a study of these works, with reproductions, in the *Transactions of the Siam Society* for 1925 and in *Ars Asiatica*, Vol. XII (1928),[1] points out their affinity with the pre-Angkorean art of Cambodia and, at the same time, their profoundly Indo-Gupta character.[2] In *Ars Asiatica*, Vol. XII, Pl. XII and XIII, he has also published reproductions of Brahman or Buddhist statues coming from the part of the Malay Peninsula that is now Siamese, which are no less remarkable for their Gupta qualities of simplicity, softness, and fullness of expression. These two sets of works prove that, about the sixth century of our era, a community of ideal and technique, in harmony with Gupta classicism, existed between the Indo-Mōn art of Dvāravatī, the art of the Malay Peninsula with its Indian influences, and the pre-Angkorean art of Fu-nan and "Chen-la of the water." It may even have been through the medium of these schools

[1] Coedès: *Les Collections archéologiques du Musée National de Bangkok* (Paris, Van Oest).

[2] Coedès: "Indian Influence upon Siamese Art," in *Indian Art and Letters*, 1930, I, pp. 18–42.

FIGURE 212

Gathering of dervishes.

— *Vever collection. Photo, Laniepce*

of pre-Siamese Siam that Indian influence came to give birth to the pre-Angkorean art of Cambodia.

During the eleventh and twelfth centuries, after this Indo-Mōn or Dvāravatī period, the land which was afterwards to be Siam fell under Khmer influences. At that time a local Khmer school flourished

FIGURE 213
Poet or dervish. School of Jahangir, Persian style.
— *Boston, Museum of Fine Arts. Formerly in the Goloubew collection. Photo, Goloubew*

at Lopburi. The Buddhas of this school, writes Monsieur Coedès, are characterized by the following features: beetling eyebrows, noses which are often longer and sharper than in the other schools of Khmer art, more prominent chins, hair which stops at the brow with a more pronounced roll than usual, and, lastly, a conical *ushṇīsha*. In his album of works from the Bangkok Museum Monsieur Coedès publishes a few fine specimens of this style, in particular a magnificent Buddha in meditation, seated in the "lotus" attitude, a sandstone figure nearly forty inches high, dating from the twelfth century.[1]

Siamese art, properly so called, starts in the thirteenth century with the school of Xieng-Sen. The Buddha in the Bangkok Museum belonging to this earliest school, reproductions of which have also been published by Monsieur Coedès, already display all the chief characteristics of Siamese sculpture: the oval face, the arched brows, the hooked nose, the mouth of moderate size — if anything, rather small — and the full chin.[2] They are distinguished from the other and later Siamese schools by the fact that, although the face is oval, it is still almost as short as the Khmer faces; and in particular by the shape of the *ushṇīsha,* which ends in a smooth ornament shaped like a lotus-bud.

Next comes a second Siamese school, that of Sukhodaya or Sokhotai, dating from the thirteenth and fourteenth centuries, which is distinguished from the last by the position of the legs in the attitude called the *padmāsana,* the shape of the *ushṇīsha,* which ends in a flame-shaped ornament, and the extremely elongated cast of countenance, which was afterwards to become general throughout the whole duration of Siamese art.

Siamese art reached its classic period in the school of Ayuthyā, which lasted from 1350 to 1767. In this, its definitive form, it is easy to see the differences which separate it from Khmer art. Instead of the square-cut faces of the Khmer style, we here find long, delicate, and often emaciated heads, with rounded eyebrows and a hooked nose — heads whose length is further accentuated by the flame-shaped *ushṇīsha,* which often tapers off into a sort of pinnacle. Instead of the heavily proportioned bodies which we find in the first Angkorean style, instead of the softly plastic bodies of the second style, we have here conventionalized forms reminiscent in their

[1] See *Ars Asiatica,* Vol. XII (1928), Pl. XXI. See also Vol. IV of the present work, Fig. 195.

[2] See Vol. IV of the present work, Fig. 195–201.

softness of the Gupta style — but of a much simplified Gupta style, emptied of much of its content. In this connexion it is interesting to compare a Gupta work of the fifth century, such as the copper Buddha from Sultānganj, now in the Birmingham Museum, with the original

FIGURE 214
Indo-Persian horseman, seventeenth century.
— *Demotte collection. Photo, Laniepce*

Siamese statuettes which have remained in the Indo-Chinese Museum at the Trocadéro. We shall at once note the points of resemblance — the smooth softness of the forms beneath the transparent stuff of the robe, with its side-lappets gracefully descending below the legs — and the points of difference — the aristocratic hardness of the

Siamese style. This Gupta background perceptible in the æsthetic standards of Siam comes, no doubt, partly from Ceylon and partly

FIGURE 215
Hunting the wild elephant.
— *Demotte collection. Photo, Laniepce*

from the Pala influences which filtered in from Magadha by way of Burma.

To sum up, in Siam we may watch the formation of an art which is obviously less original, personal, and individual than that of the

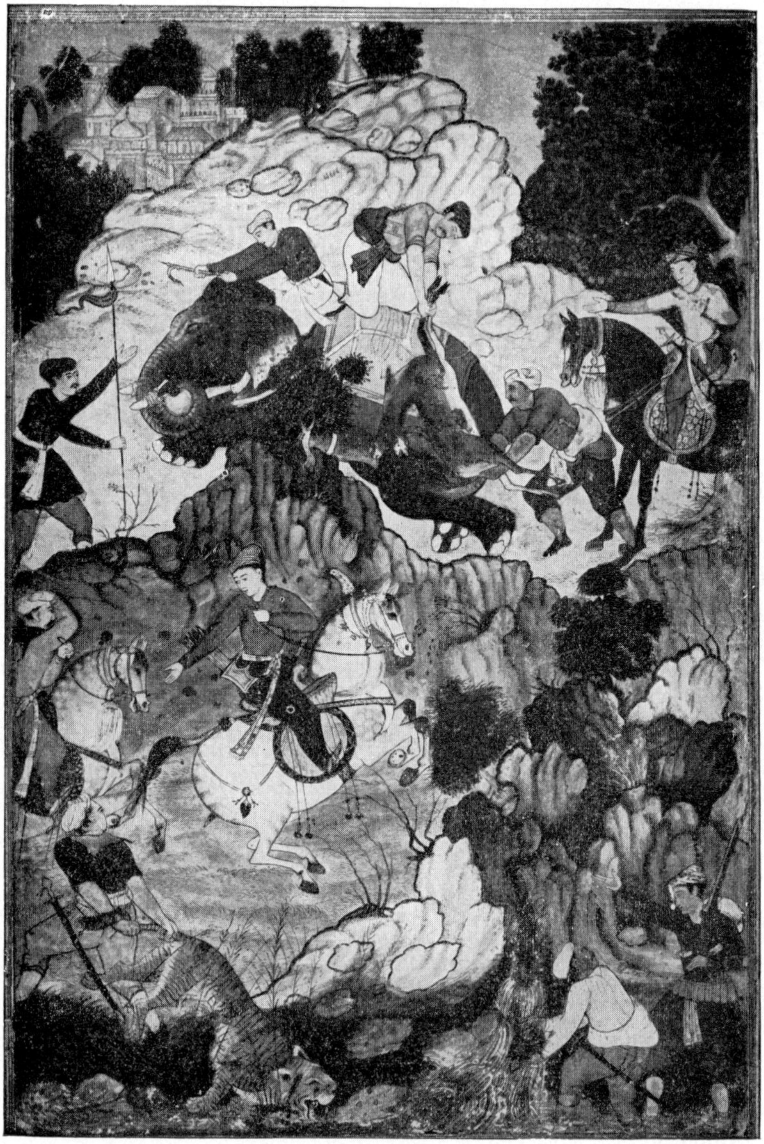

FIGURE 216

Hunting-scene.

— *Demotte collection. Photo, Laniepce*

Khmer schools — an art which is often rather hard, but singularly elegant and aristocratic. Nothing, moreover, could be more unjust than constantly to overwhelm it by a comparison with the works of the Khmer schools. Siamese art deserves to be loved for itself. It is a belated flower of Buddhist art, with a fragrance of its own, full of distinction and delicacy, a supremely civilized fragrance. There are certain statues in the Pila and Goury du Roslan collections which, in our opinion, may be numbered among the most charming productions of the sculpture of the Far East (see Vol. IV of the present work, Fig. 199).

CHAPTER III

Moslem India

INDO-MOSLEM CIVILIZATION UNDER THE EARLIEST TURCO-AFGHAN DYNASTIES

BETWEEN THE ELEVENTH AND THE EIGHTEENTH CENTURIES India was gradually conquered by the Muḥammadans who had come down from eastern Iran. At the beginning of the eleventh century the Turk Maḥmud of Ghazna subdued the Punjāb. In the early years of the thirteenth century the Afghan Muḥammad of Ghor and his lieutenants conquered the basin of the Ganges and founded a powerful sultanate at Delhi which held sway over the whole of Moslem India. At the beginning of the fourteenth century the sultans of Delhi even conquered part of the Deccan, as far as the outlying regions of Mysore and the Carnatic. But in the second half of this same fourteenth century they allowed their lieutenants, the Moslem governors of Bengal, Oudh, and the Deccan, to gain autonomy and finally independence. Thus Moslem India became split up into some ten local dynasties.

The period of the sultanate of Delhi, and of the local kingdoms which succeeded it, exerted a profound influence over Indian art. In fact, Islam created a new art in India, which combined in varying proportions, according to the region and the period, the ancient native traditions of art and the Arabo-Persian art imported by the new-comers.

Indo-Moslem architecture came into being in the thirteenth century under the sultans of Delhi, Quṭb al-Dīn Aibeg (1206–10), Iltutmish (1210–35), and 'Alā al-Dīn Khaljī (1295–1315).[1] To the age of the first two of these princes belongs the Great Mosque at Ajmere (*arhāī-din-ka-jhompra*), built about 1200 (Fig. 169), and the mosque Quṭb al-Islām at Delhi, with the minaret of the Quṭb Minār, built by Iltutmish (Fig. 170, 171). To 'Alā al-Dīn Khaljī is due the gate called by his name at Delhi, to the south of the Mosque of the Quṭb (Fig. 172–173).[2]

Even in these very earliest works the way in which the exigencies of the Moslem religion were adapted to the native resources of execution is clearly to be seen, (Fig. 168–169). The Mosque of Ajmere, as Fergusson remarks, is directly inspired in both plan and decoration by the Jain temple of the Vimala Shā at Mount Abū, also in Rajputana. The Quṭb al-Islām at Delhi was built on the actual site and out of the materials of Jain temples. Both here and at Ajmere all that has been done is to apply a sort of screen formed of eleven pointed arches to the front of the Jain building, with its cupolas arranged on an octagonal plan, and its forest of columns. As for the Quṭb Minār, a tower about eighty yards high in the form of a truncated cone, grooved and divided into five storeys by four circular balconies: though its form — that of a tapering minaret — is dictated by the exigencies of the Moslem religion, the treatment is undoubtedly the work of Hindu architects, with reminiscences both of the Gupta columns and of the mediæval *śikhara*. It is, above all, the decoration

[1] See E. B. Havell: *Indian Architecture, from the First Mohammedan Invasion to the Present Day* (London, Murray, 1927).

[2] See J. A. Page: *Guide to the Quṭb, Delhi* (Calcutta, 1927); J. A. Page: *Historical Memoir on the Quṭb*, Memoirs of the Archæological Survey of India, No. 22 (1926); J. F. Blakiston: *The Jami' Masjid at Badaun and Other Buildings in the United Provinces*, ibid., No. 19 (1926).

of these buildings — an infinitely complicated and delicate lace-work of stone — that directly recalls northern Hindu, and especially Jain, decoration, for which the Turco-Afghan conquerors seem to have had a particular predilection. As a matter of fact, by doing away with all representation of human or animal forms in Jain decoration, the Indo-Moslem architects found in its sprays of flowers, its wreaths, and its baskets the equivalent of their own arabesques and con-

FIGURE 217
Scene of country life. Indo-Mogul art.
— *Vever collection. Photo, Vever*

ventionalized foliage. By blending with it the magic of the Kufic script they achieved dazzling effects unknown even to Syro-Egyptian art (Fig. 174). A whole study might be devoted to distinguishing which motives of Indo-Moslem decoration are derived from Jain and Hindu sources and which can be traced to Egyptian and Persian ones. At any rate, a practised eye will soon recognize in this embroidery of sandstone or marble a twofold contribution — on the one hand that of Indian exuberance, with its subtropical vegetation and rampant jungle life; and on the other hand the finer, more austere, if over-refined efflorescence of the roses of Iran.[1]

[1] Cf. E. H. Hankin: *The Drawing of Geometric Patterns in Saracenic Art*, Memoirs of the Archæological Survey of India, No. 15 (Calcutta, 1925).

It was not long before Indo-Moslem architecture split up into several branches, like the first Indo-Moslem empire itself. We may distinguish, in particular, a Jaunpūr style connected with the ephemeral dynasty founded in that city between 1394 and 1476, the chief monuments of which are the mosques of Atala, dating from between 1401 and 1440, Lāl Darwāza, dating from about 1440 to 1459, and the Jāmi' Masjid, dating from between 1438 and 1478. The chief features of this Jaunpūr style are, to quote H. C. Fanshawe: "the high platforms upon which the buildings are constructed — the two-storeyed cloisters with their tiers of columns running round the great central courtyard one above the other, and the lofty gates in the form of propylæa, erected on the eastern side before a vaulted porch, and adorned with panels and cornices." There is also a Bengal style connected with the autonomous Moslem kingdom which flourished in that land from 1338 to 1537; this Bengal style, outstanding specimens of which are the monuments at Gaur, is characterized by curved roofs in the form of the segment of a torus cut by four vertical planes. There is also a style peculiar to Gujerat, where there was an independent Moslem kingdom from 1396 to 1572; the buildings here follow the Hindu and Jain types more closely than anywhere else, merely adding the indispensable Moslem elements of the dome and the pointed arch. The chief buildings belonging to this period are grouped round Ahmedābad, for instance the Mosque of Mahāfīz Khān, dating from the end of the fifteenth century, and the tomb of Abū Turāb, built a century later.[1] Lastly, the Moslem kingdoms of the Deccan — for instance, those of Bījāpur (1489–1686) and Golconda (1512–1687) — have also an architecture of their own. The buildings at Bījāpur, the Rawḍa of Ibrāhīm II 'Ādil Shāh (who died in 1626) and the Gūl Gumbaz or tomb of Muḥammad 'Ādil Shāh (who died in 1673), are characterized by a somewhat

[1] See J. Burgess: *Muhammedan Architecture of Ahmadabad*, Archæological Survey of Western India, Vols. VII and VIII (London, 1900, 1905); J. Burgess: *Muhammedan Architecture of Gūjarat*, ibid., Vol. VI (London, 1896).

"Occidental" style — that is, by a boldness and vigour indicative of distinctly Persian and Ottoman influences, a fact which is not at all surprising when we think of the origins of the dynasty (Fig. 175).[1] As for the Golconda style, it is characterized by its lofty windows, the plaster decoration on its minarets and its domes, narrow at the base and bulbous and swelling in shape, somewhat recalling the churches of Russia.

MOGUL INDIA

IN 1527 THE MUḤAMMADAN SULTANATE OF DELHI WAS CONQUERED by the Turkish prince Babur, a descendant of Tamerlane, the hero of Transoxiana. Having been driven out of his hereditary kingdom of Transoxiana, Babur sought his fortune in India, where he founded the kingdom known under the name of the Mogul (or Mughal) empire. His first five successors, Humayun (1530–56), Akbar (1556–1605), Jahanjir (Jehanghu) (1605–27), Shāh Jahan (1627–58), and Aurungzeb (1658–1707), added to the provinces subdued by Babur — the Punjāb, Dooab, and Oudh — almost the whole of India. For a time, it is true, Humayun was driven from his throne, and had to pass fifteen years in exile, either in Afghanistan or in Persia (1540–55). His son, the great Akbar, completed the subjugation of northern India and started upon the conquest of central India as far as the Godāvarī. Under Shāh Jahan and Aurungzeb the Deccan itself was annexed as far as the borders of the Carnatic.

Each of these princes appears before us under his own characteristic aspect.[2] Babur, the founder of the dynasty, is like the hero of a mediæval romance of chivalry. This knight-errant, who was heir

[1] See E. B. Havell: *Indian Architecture* (London, 1927), p. 191 ("Evolution of the Bījāpūr Style").

[2] See *Delhi Museum of Archæology, Loan Exhibition of Antiquities, Coronation Durbar,* 1911, Pl. XXX–LIX.

FIGURE 218

Solomon surrounded by angels, demons, and animals.
— Demotte collection. Photo, Laniepce

to the most magnificent tradition of valour that had ever existed in Asia — for was he not descended from both Jenghiz-Khan, the Con-

FIGURE 219
Conquest of India by Babur.
— *Vever collection. Photo, Vever*

queror of the World, and the invincible Timur? — shows himself in his *Memoirs* to be the consummate ideal of a prince as conceived in the age of the Persian Renaissance. His Turco-Mongol origins made him the possessor of a dogged courage, and a methodical spirit which no mishap could discourage. But in his family the ruggedness of the Turkish temperament had long been moderated by the effects of Iranian environment. Moreover, as represented in his portraits, Babur resembles not so much the terrible Mongol conquerors of past days as some nobleman of Isfahān or Shīrāz, with the pure oval of his delicate Turco-Persian cast of countenance — in spite of the slightly oblique eyes, which tell of his Tartar forebears — his noble profile, his small, carefully trimmed beard and aristocratic elegance. He almost reminds us of one of Clouet's portraits of nobles at the Louvre (Fig. 194). And he is indeed a true Renaissance type — a gentleman of exalted lineage, with a passion for literature and art, anxiously observing all the forms of humanism, at once a dilettante, an adventurer, and a statesman. Possessing, to quote Renan, "great good sense and a certain intelligent and gentle quality free from fanaticism, a subtle, just, unprejudiced, and open mind — such was this descendant of Tamerlane and Jenghiz-Khan, who worthily inaugurated that series of philosopher princes who shed such a bright radiance upon the throne of the Moguls in the sixteenth and seventeenth centuries." He was at the same time a poet, and even on the imperial throne of India felt home-sick for the landscapes of Ferghāna, the grassy plains where he had been wont to dream in the days of his youth. "The violets are lovely in Ferghāna; it is a mass of tulips and roses," he says. Or he will quote verses full of an Epicureanism that is quite Persian, such as the following of Khaiyām's:

A book of verses underneath the bough,
A jug of wine, a loaf of bread and thou
Beside me singing in the wilderness
And wilderness were Paradise enow;

or some lines by Ḥāfiẓ: "Sweet is the coming of the new year, sweet is the juice of the grape, but how much sweeter is the voice of love!

Snatch, Babur, at all the pleasures of living, for life doth flee, never to return."

A figure which appeals to our sympathies equally strongly is that of Humayun — one day padishah of the Indies, on the next abandoned by all men, exposed to the treachery of his own family, and trembling for the life of his young son Akbar, who had fallen into his enemies' hands; next finding a fitting welcome at the court of the King of Persia, and finally recovering his throne and capital only in time to die. . . . Such was the melancholy destiny of a prince without reproach, for long unjustly unfortunate, but as great in misfortune as in his belated triumph, and at all times profoundly human (Fig. 194, 195).

But the greatest of the Mogul emperors is undoubtedly Akbar (Fig. 196). A captain and an administrator of genius, he may be regarded as the real founder of the empire of the Indies. His liberal and reforming government treated Hindus and Moslems on an equal footing. He placed particular reliance upon the native aristocracy of the Rajputs, which swore him the staunchest loyalty and provided him with his best generals. Though himself brought up as an orthodox Sunnite Moslem, he kept all his favours for the dissident Shī'ites, and among them for the liberal pietism of the Ṣūfīs. In consultation with his counsellors, such as the sheikh Mubarak Nagori (who died in 1593) and his sons, Faiḍi (who died in 1595) and 'Abu'l Faḍl (who died in 1602), he tried by a fusion of the various positive religions to arrive at a sort of higher syncretism: " O God," cries 'Abu'l Faḍl, who was the confidant of the prince's ideas, " in all the temples I see men seeking Thee. What is polytheism? It is Thou. What is Islam? It is Thou. . . . One day I attend the temple, the next day the mosque, but on either day it is alone Thou whom I seek." True to these maxims, Akbar deprived Sunnism of its privileged position as the state religion and promulgated an edict of tolerance and protection on behalf of the Hindu cults. He was in-

FIGURE 220

After the banquet.

— *Vever collection. Photo, Laniepce*

terested in Brahman philosophy and caused the Vedas, the Sanskrit epics, and the *darśana* (Hindu philosophical systems) to be translated into his two favourite languages, Persian and Hindustani. Ultimately he borrowed from the philosophy of Vishnuism and from Jainism their doctrine of universal charity: "Would to God," he said one day, "that my body were great enough to feed all men! Then they would cease to cause suffering to any animal." Here Akbar uses the same language as Aśoka had done in past days; and certainly it is not one of the smallest surprises in history to find on this ancient soil of India, which seems to be the very native land of speculation, a Buddhist emperor of the third century B.C. and a Moslem emperor of the sixteenth century of our era arriving at the same eternal principles in spite of the gulf that separates their ages and civilizations. This philosophical syncretism found expression in 1582 in an attempt to create a new creed, the *Tawḥīd-i ilāhī* or *Dīn ilāhī*, an eclectic theism expressed by the ancient Indian symbols of the sun (*sūrya*) and fire (*agni*), admitting of no priesthood and calling for no offering save that of a pure and simple life.

Jahangir abandoned his father Akbar's religious reforms and returned to Moslem orthodoxy, though on the whole he followed his father's policy. In spite of his vices of drink and opium, and though he did not possess his father's genius, he was not without talent, had a love of nature, and was a great patron of the arts. He was, above all, a connoisseur of painting, and we possess a number of miniatures which have immortalized his sensual physiognomy, at once delicate and bloated (Fig. 197, 198). This voluptuous prince was ravaged by one great passion, his love for the beautiful Nūr Jahan, whose energy of character saved him in more than one dangerous situation.

Shāh Jahan, the fifth of the Mogul emperors, also had his romance: his love for his favourite sultana, Mumtāz Maḥall, who died in childbirth in 1651, and as a mausoleum for whom he built the marvellous Tāj Maḥall. In fact, he too encouraged the arts; like his father he was a connoisseur of painting, and his delicate aristocratic features, with their expression indicating a stubborn will, were a frequent subject for artists (Fig. 199–204). His taste for luxury and magnificence

FIGURE 221

Party on a terrace. Mogul school, early eighteenth century.
— *Bibliothèque Nationale. Archives photographiques*

marks the culminating point of the material civilization of Mogul India.

With Aurungzeb, who ascended the throne after disposing of his elder brother, Dara Shikuh, decadence set in. Not that this prince was lacking in talent: on the contrary, he was one of the strongest personalities of the whole dynasty. He was an able soldier and annexed the remaining independent sultanates of the Deccan. He was an energetic statesman and a diligent administrator who drew closer the bonds of Mogul centralization. But his harshness, hypocrisy, and despotism alienated all hearts. He had seized the throne by getting rid of his brothers and imprisoning his father. His Moslem fanaticism put an end to the good understanding existing between the Hindu and Mogul elements, upon which the State had been based since the days of Akbar. He lived long enough to witness the revolt of the native peoples (the Mahrattas, Rajputs, etc.) and the first symptoms of the ruin of the empire. The miniaturists are fond of representing him, with his fine, delicately stubborn features, like his father, Shāh Jahan, but with a more unyielding quality in the profile; in their works we often see him as a bent old man with a white beard, telling his beads piously beneath the imperial parasol — while his armies were no doubt treacherously putting some rebellious people to the sword by his orders (Fig. 205).

In the early days of the Moslem domination the sumptuous qualities of Indian architecture and decoration had imposed themselves almost of necessity upon the conquerors from the north, who had yielded to the dazzling richness of such ornamentation. It was not till the fourteenth century that they began to react against it: the gate of 'Alā al-Dīn at Delhi is already more Iranian than the previous monuments; next, under the dynasty of the Taghlaq (Tughlaks) the overloaded Hindu ornamentation began to assume a more ordered character and Indo-Moslem architecture, without repudiating its deep-rooted native affinities, became more sober and severe. Finally, under the Moguls, this simplification was to lead to a harmonious fusion of Jain and Persian art, and to the birth of a new art which was of a genuinely original and classic nature.[1]

[1] Cf. Hermann Goetz: *Bilderatlas zur Kulturgeschichte Indiens in der Grossmoghul-Zeit* (Berlin, 1930).

At the outset the Mogul domination was marked by a fresh wave of pure Iranianism, as well as by the coming of Ottoman influence. Not that Babur had time to do much building: we owe him scarcely

FIGURE 222
Duet. Musée des Arts Décoratifs.
— *Photo, Giraudon*

anything but the mosque of Pānīpat, built upon the site of his chief victory, and the Jāmi' Masjid at Sambhal. But he sent to Constantinople for some pupils of Sinan, the celebrated Ottoman architect.[1] Tradition has it that under the reign of Akbar, Sinan's favourite pupil, Yusuf, built the palaces of Delhi, Agra, and Lahore. None

[1] See Vol. I of the present work, p. 397.

the less, Persian influence won the day. It has been observed that during the sixteenth century Persia plays the same part in relation to Indo-Moslem art as Renaissance Italy did in relation to that of France. But the first cause of differentiation which arose between them was the fact that the soil of India offered the architect richer materials than did that of Iran. What distinguishes Mogul mosques and palaces at the very first glance from similar buildings in Iran is the fact that, instead of faience, they made use of marble and hard stone, a fact which gave Mogul buildings a curiously more imposing appearance and secured them a far greater prospect of survival: while the mosques of Isfahān are crumbling into ruin, the Tāj raises its white marble splendours eternally on high beneath the dome of the blue heavens.

The earliest buildings of the age of Akbar display all the strong and sober elegance of the Iranian style (Fig. 176, 177). This is true of the tomb of Humayun, near Delhi, a structure which reminds us both of Isfahān and of certain mosques of Constantinople in the age of Soleiman the Magnificent, and which must, as a matter of fact, have been built by some pupil of Sinan; but here Mogul art is already distinguished from the Turco-Iranian schools by its use of white marble and the absence of all polychrome decoration. Subsequently, however, the reign of Akbar achieved a fusion of native traditions with those of Iran in the sphere of art as well as in that of thought. The twofold influence is revealed in the buildings at Fatḥpūr-Sīkrī, a town built by Akbar between 1570 and 1574, some twenty-four miles from Agra. The plan of the sanctuary of the Great Mosque at Fatḥpūr is copied from that of the Juma' at Isfahān. The triumphal entrance, too, or Baland Darwāza, dating from 1601–2, has a classic purity which is quite Persian, allowing for the different materials, which are pink sandstone and white marble; the cupolas which surmount it, however, display Jain influence. Indian and Turco-Iranian traditions are fused in similar fashion in another building at Fatḥpūr, the

FIGURE 223
Love-scene.
— Demotte collection. Photo, Laniepce

palace of the Turkī Sulṭāna, with the Pānch Maḥall, a pavilion with five storeys, "each smaller than the one below," and the Dīwān-i Khāṣṣ, an audience-chamber formed of a single apartment, "in the middle of which rises an octagonal column surmounted by a gigantic round capital, from the top of which five narrow corridors radiate towards the angles of the building." This touch of fancy, these pieces of sheer bravura, which are incompatible with Persian classicism, are directly derived from Hindu and Jain art. The same combination of elements is to be found in the Great Mosque at Agra. "The building is charming in its colour-harmony of red sandstone, rosy stone, and white marble and is surmounted by Jain cupolas curiously reminiscent of Mount Abū."

The reign of Jahangir is signalized by the mausoleum of his father, Akbar, at Sikandra, five miles from Agra, which was completed in 1612;[1] a most curious building, with its five terraces, one above the other, its polychrome materials of red stone and white marble, its balustrades, kiosks, and pyramid of buildings, which some have thought fit to compare with certain Buddhist *vihāras* or with the *rathas* at Māvalipuram. To the same reign belongs the tomb of I'timād al-Daula, near Agra, which was completed in 1628 — a magnificent white marble edifice decorated with coloured stones, half mosque and half kiosk, in which the Turco-Persian style is combined with strictly Indo-Mogul elements such as the two open-work pavilions at the sides and the "hat-shaped" roof crowning the central structure (Fig. 178, 179, 180).

Under Shāh Jahan, Mogul architecture reached its culminating point. The style of his reign is characterized by a new wave of Persian inspiration, but we should always bear in mind that the buildings which he constructed are distinguished from those of Isfahān and Constantinople by the use of white marble, enhanced by decoration in hard coloured stones — agate, onyx, jasper, cornelian, etc.

[1] See E. W. Smith: *Akbar's Tomb, Sikandarah*, Archæological Survey of India, 1908.

At the same time, the taste of these buildings tends in the direction of a noble simplicity and "a truly feminine elegance." The principal

FIGURE 224
Indo-Mogul lady.
— *Demotte collection. Photo, Laniepce*

monuments of this period are the Great Mosque (Jāmi' Masjid) in the city, and the palace of the Mogul emperors at Delhi, begun in 1638 and built of white marble, pink sandstone, and brick. We give here a few photographs of these marvels, the Dīwān-i 'Āmm and the

Dīwān-i Khāṣṣ (the halls for public and private audiences respectively), white marble galleries in which the pillars, arches, and ribs of the vaulting were completely encrusted with delicate Persian motives in jasper, onyx, and cornelian; in the middle stood the famous Peacock Throne, so called because the back of it represented a peacock's tail, glittering with rubies, pearls, and diamonds (Fig. 181–186). Equally elegant in the purity of its style is the delightful Mosque of the Pearl, or Mōtī Masjid, built by Shāh Jahan between 1646 and 1653, also of white marble, inlaid with precious stones in floral motives in the Persian style. But the masterpiece of Shāh Jahan's art remains the Tāj Maḥall at Agra, begun by that prince in 1646 as a tomb for his beloved wife Mumtāz Maḥall, and completed about 1653 (Fig. 190–192). Mumtāz died in the full bloom of her beauty, exacting an oath from Shāh Jahan that he would associate her memory with the construction of an immortal monument. The monarch kept his promise and built this marvel of grace and taste, this triumph of Indo-Persian classicism, "a marble mausoleum, dazzling in the whiteness of its exterior, wonderfully sculptured, and carved in open-work, inlaid internally with mosaics of porphyry, agate, cornelian, and lapis lazuli of amazing finish." The setting adds still further to the beauty of the work: "The graceful dome of the Tāj, its slender minarets, its trellises of fine marbles, as fine as lace-work, stand in the midst of a vast garden, where innumerable fountains play in cypress avenues and beneath groves of orange-trees." It is in this dream landscape that the young Moslem Empress, snatched from the love of the ruler of the world at the age of twenty, sleeps her last sleep.

The Tāj has such purity of line that one would incline to attribute it to the genius of a single master. It was, however, the work of a whole group of them, and its peerless harmony is due to a blend of the most varying influences. There has been much discussion of this question. The principal architect of the Tāj was really the Turk (or Shirāzī) Ustadh 'Isā, as had been supposed, but, for the dome in particular, this master had the assistance of Hindu architects, and perhaps for the decoration of the exterior, at least, that of European artists as well (among others the Venetian Geronimo Veroneo).[1]

FIGURE 225
On the terrace, at the riverside.
— *Bibliothèque Nationale. Archives photographiques*

The Mogul emperors played the part of patrons of the arts in the sphere of painting quite as much as in that of architecture. We may remember that the Moguls were the direct descendants of those

[1] But Veroneo was surely not the principal architect, as has erroneously been claimed (cf. Mr. T. W. Haig in *Encyclopædia of Islam*, *s.v.* "Tāj Maḥall").

proud Timurids at whose court Iranian painting had risen to such heights during the fifteenth century in the provinces of eastern Iran, Khorāsān, and Transoxiana. In the preceding volume we saw what an influence was exerted by the Timurid sultan Ḥusain Bāiqarā upon the development of the school of Herāt, and what a friend he was to the most illustrious master of that school, the great Bihzād. His cousin Babur shared this taste of his, for in his *Memoirs* he, too, informs us of his admiration for Bihzād. He brought these tastes with him when he won the throne of India, and it will be no surprise to us to see the last pupils of Bihzād, such as Khwaja (or Khvājah) Abd al-Ṣamad of Shīrāz, occupying the position of court painters under the reign of Akbar.

Thus, as Percy Brown remarks, in its origins Indo-Persian painting is merely a province of Iranian painting: we find in it the same conventional treatment of the figures (Fig. 214) and landscape, and the same mosaic of brilliant colours.[1] Later, as we shall see, the Mogul masters were to shake off these conventions, which belonged rather to miniature-painting than to painting proper. To their honour be it spoken, the only feature of it which they were to preserve—thus showing themselves true pupils of Bihzād to the end—was the quality of line and virtuosity of drawing which they inherited from the calligraphers of Herāt and Isfahān. This Iranian mastery of drawing was to lend the Mogul profiles something of the spirited quality of the Italian medals of the Renaissance, the clear-cut delicacy of the sketches of Clouet, and the power and purity of the pencil drawings of Ingres (see A. Coomaraswamy: *Indian Drawings*, London, 1910–12).

Again, as Percy Brown remarks, though Mogul painting betrays its Iranian origins in all its qualities, yet, like the dynasty itself, it was not slow to become naturalized. The tradition of Indian painting, the great tradition of Ajaṇṭā and Bāgh, was not extinct. It survived,

[1] See Vol. I of the present work, Fig. 226–288.

as we shall see below, in the Rajput miniature. It was the happy combination of Iranian traditions and Rajput influences which gave birth, as early as the reign of Jahangir, to Mogul art properly so called — a genuinely new art, which could be distinguished at a glance from the two schools that we have just mentioned: from the Iranian school by its love of realism, and from Rajput art by the calligraphic quality of the drawing.

This specifically Indian taste for realism constitutes the contribution of the Mogul school to Moslem painting. It comes out everywhere, whether in portrait or in landscape: in portraiture, where the faces, which, in accordance with the Iranian tradition, had always been a little too fine and elegant, suddenly acquired a psychological intensity and commanding power which made them comparable to those of a Titian or a Holbein (Fig. 196, 197, 212, 213), or, more simply, to those in the frescoes of Ajaṇṭā and the reliefs of Ellora;[1] and in landscape, where the blooming backgrounds of Herāt and Isfahān gained in breadth till the splendour of their noontide skies or the crimson of their sunsets give one a sense of the whole vastness of earth and heaven (see the backgrounds of Fig. 194, 196, 197, 212, 221, 225): in short, it was by this process that the Persian *miniature* developed into the great Mogul school of *painting*. What is more, it cannot be denied that this realism profited by lessons from the outside world. The comparative advance in the modelling of the faces, the effects of chiaroscuro in the landscapes, the progress in perspective, the sense of atmosphere, are all points that bear witness to the teaching of Italian art. On the other hand, again following Percy Brown, we have to note the limitations of this inspiration, which were those of the society of the time. Mogul art is an art of the court, the art of an aristocratic society which is only interested in scenes of everyday life in so far as they concern itself, and therefore reproduces none but the acts and gestures of sovereigns

[1] Cf. Ananda Coomaraswamy: *Indian Drawings.*

and nabobs, their receptions, their hunts, and their loves, ignoring the life of the Hindu people, which was the delight of Rajput art. But, with this reservation and within these limitations, we are henceforth in the presence of a directness of inspiration, an art based on observa-

FIGURE 226
Lady and attendants.
— *Vever collection. Photo, Pivot*

tion, and a naturalistic spontaneity which transcend Iranian canons and bring Mogul art into harmony with the eternal spirit of India.

This realism found its first expression in portraiture, which was in many respects, the chief *raison d'être* of Mogul painting. The Moguls were a handful of noblemen of ancient lineage, all more or

FIGURE 227

Scene on a terrace.
— *Demotte collection. Photo, Laniepce*

FIGURE 228

Indo-Mogul ladies.
— *Demotte collection. Photo, Laniepce*

less descended from the noble houses of Jenghiz-Khan or of the Transoxianian dynasties and grouped round the glorious Timurid family, who, following in the train of that family, had succeeded in imposing themselves upon the vast and overpopulated Indian continent by their personal qualities and their superior talents and armaments — but also by their humanism. These great Renaissance nobles governed the empire of the Indies just as the Venetian aristocracy had once governed the empire of the Mediterranean and just as both the Dutch middle class and the British aristocracy were afterwards to govern their maritime empires. And in Venice, as in Amsterdam and England, the art of portraiture arose out of the aristocratic conditions of government. Titian, Rembrandt, and Lawrence are the products of an exclusive society. The conditions were similar at Agra and at Delhi. The Mogul princes, their courtiers, and their generals loved to have themselves immortalized by the art of the time.

Thus we have a whole gallery of portraits, a gallery of genuine contemporary history, in which a society as refined as that of Versailles under the French monarchy lives before us in all its splendour and reality. We see first Timur, the great ancestor of the house, represented oddly enough in the costume of the fourteenth century (Fig. 193);[1] then Babur, the royal adventurer, driven from his native Transoxiana and from the throne of his ancestors, the leader of a band of exiles, only afterwards, at their head, to become, by a stroke of genius, emperor of the greatest empire of the East and founder of a new Mongol dominion: a precise, vigorous Turkish face, and a singularly high-bred one, too, on which the Iranian environment has left its mark; the victor of Pānipat, the fastidious author of the *Memoirs*, lives again before us in a few touches of the brush (Fig. 104). Beside him is his son Humayun, with his more indeterminate

[1] See the same miniature in colour, in Mehta: *Studies in Indian Painting* (Taraporevala, Sons & Co., Kitāb Mahāl, 190 Homby Road, Bombay, 1926), Pl. 44, p. 102.

physiognomy, long and delicate, full of gentleness and distinction, philosophic resignation and melancholy, as befits the destiny of the man who lost his throne, endured the worst vicissitudes, and only won it back in time to die (Fig. 193). Akbar, that self-taught genius, who dominated and towered above his age, a powerful figure formed

FIGURE 229
Youth of Kṛishṇa.
— *From Percy Brown:* Indian Painting, *facing p. 52. By permission of the Oxford University Press*

of very human clay, himself illiterate, yet the promoter of a philosophical and literary syncretism which embraced all the sublimest productions of the human mind, the founder of an empire, a general always in the field, taking a personal share in his enterprises, yet at the same time a liberal-minded statesman, whose whole taste ran in the direction of philosophical speculation and lofty poetry: a genius with a heavy and strong-willed countenance (Fig. 196). His son Jahangir, a more complex personality, with a voluptuous temperament, sensual and indolent, an undoubted drunkard and a capricious and brutal administrator, but possessing a cultivated and inquiring mind, a patron of the arts and himself a dabbler in them, a connoisseur of painting and a student of natural history, whose face, though bloated with pleasure, none the less reveals a highly intellectual quality (Fig. 197, 198). Next Shāh Jahan, a colder and apparently more imperious countenance beneath the halo that surrounds him, with a profile of flawless Aryan purity, to which age has added the further majesty of his white beard, trimmed to a point; yet, in spite of all differences of fashion, having a touch of the hard and dazzling magnificence of his contemporary Louis XIV — a face, too, with a high-bred elegance, to which his love of the arts added a yet greater nobility — for in the background of his portrait we imagine the dome of the Tāj Maḥall (Fig. 199–204).

Moreover, this aristocratic taste for portraiture prided itself upon more than a spirited resemblance. As in Van Dyck and Titian, it delighted in the setting which surrounds its noble models: sumptuous garments, dazzling jewellery, splendid sashes, diaphanous gauzes and heavy brocades dotted with rosette patterns, priceless aigrettes and the massive jewellery with which these kings of the East glittered like the starry heavens.

From the imperial Timurid family the fashion for portraits spread to the great Mogul nobility (Fig. 206–210). Whether they are richly coloured, treated in sombre tones on faintly tinted neutral backgrounds or in light hues upon a dark background, or simply sketched in black and white, all these Mogul portraits are, in general, marvels of delicacy, finish, and psychological fidelity. In spite of the majesty of the attitudes and the sumptuousness of the costume, the racial and moral character represented in them is strikingly clear. The delicacy of the drawing, the subtlety of the modelling, and the keenness of the profile reveal the personality with a pitiless precision. Here again we are reminded of the greatest portraitists of the West. But in Titian, Rembrandt, Rubens, and Van Dyck the deliberate sumptuousness of the setting, the proud genius of the painter, often dominate the personality of the model. Here, as in Dürer or Clouet, in spite of the decorative treatment of the page in the style of an illuminated manuscript, we have nothing but the personality, nothing but the character of the nobleman represented, with his virtues or his vices, his good humour or his harshness, his honesty, his cynicism or his hypocrisy, his weakness or his boastfulness. There are portraits among them which are worth a page of Commines or of Saint-Simon.[1]

Side by side with these great nobles and courtiers, Mogul painting admitted another category of models: holy men, dervishes, fakirs, and *sannyāsi* (monks) (Fig. 211–213). In such subjects as these it discovered an original line of its own and has left us studies of remarkable psychological intensity. Certain of these portraits—grave, subtle, bearded doctors' heads, or hollow faces with great burning eyes and shaven crowns—live again before our eyes with a strange life of the spirit, in their faith, their mysticism, their self-sacrifice, fanaticism, or kindliness. At any rate, they are faces whose spiritual value is sometimes almost equal to those of Memling or Fra Angelico, with an added quality as well—the disquieting ardour of the old world of Islam, like a sombre Venetian flame.[2]

But in this connexion it should perhaps be recalled that India was already familiar with the spiritual quality of the painting of Ajaṇṭā. For the rest, as Percy Brown observes, the influence of earlier Indian

[1] See *Loan Exhibition of Antiquities, Delhi, Coronation Durbar* (Archæological Survey of India, 1911); Coomaraswamy: *Portfolio of Indian Art, Museum of Fine Arts, Boston*, Pl. LXXXVI; Coomaraswamy: *Les Miniatures orientales de la collection Goloubew, au Museum of Fine Arts de Boston* (*Ars Asiatica*, Vol. XIII, Paris, Van Oest, 1929), Pl. LXXII (the durbar of Jahangir, 1620), XXIII, XXV (Jahangir and courtiers), XXX, XXXI, XXXVIII, XXXIX.

[2] See Bodleian Library, Or. *a* I, fol. 34, the six Moslem doctors of law, reproduced by Stchoukine, Pl. L; *Rūpam*, January 1925 (Jahangir's festival, Rampur State Library).

schools seems to leave its stamp upon the Mogul paintings in the spiritual quality of the hands and the high æsthetic value of all these Moslem *mudrās*.

Portraiture found a further extension in the "divan" and "durbar" scenes, part of the heritage of Persian art, which they recall by

FIGURE 230

Kṛishṇa and his herd. Pahārī school, Kāngrā.
— *By permission of the Museum of Fine Arts, Boston*

their minuteness of detail and range of colour, which is in itself a delight to the eye. But as a rule they have greater warmth than the Persian scenes of the same sort, and a greater sumptuousness of tone, accompanied here, too, by a greater realism in the portraits of the courtiers, a more skilful treatment of the animation of crowds, more modelling in the body, and less conventional landscapes for their backgrounds. To the historian these works offer a still further interest. In them he sees displayed with unexampled magnificence, in all the pomp, regulated by a scrupulous etiquette, which is described by the travellers of the seventeenth century, the splendours of the richest court that ever existed, that fairyland which nowadays revives only for a few hours in the Anglo-Indian coronation durbars.

The hunting-scenes of the emperors or princes (Fig. 215, 216) recall the same splendours, for they serve as a pretext for the same display of luxury. In this respect, moreover, they hark back to the Persian taste of Herāt or of Isfahān. But here a different note is introduced by the art of the great Indian animal-painters and the realism of Mogul landscape. For in the representation of animals the Indian naturalistic tradition once more asserts its rights. There are certain subjects — for example, the treatment of the horse — which still remain Iranian in their delicate slenderness and excessive cleverness. But when it comes to painting the peculiar fauna of India, we find works of an originality full of zest. The powerful scenes of hunting the wild elephant or of hunting the tiger from the back of tame elephants bring us back into the full stream of the great Indian tradition. And this realism, which is the characteristic contribution of the eternal genius of India, is here exploited with a dramatic sense that even India herself had never known before in such a degree. For the same reasons, the country scenes in general display far greater power and breadth in Mogul painting than in Iran (Fig. 217). This realism in the representation of animals asserts itself even in the mythological scenes, as, for instance, in the painting in the Demotte collection showing Solomon amid the beasts of creation, the angels, and the demons — in which we may note the curious conception of the angels with downy bodies (Fig. 218).

The same remarks apply to the battle scenes, which are evidently inspired by the Timurid battles, but with an enormous advance in the composition of the landscape and in the realistic treatment of animals, as, for instance, in the battle elephants charging, in Fig. 219.

For the rest, the Moguls took a pleasure in the representation of animals for its own sake (see the marginal designs of Fig. 194 and

FIGURE 231

Kṛishṇa and the cowherds.
— *From Mehta:* Studies in Indian Painting.
By permission of Messrs. Taraporevala

201, and the detail of Fig. 216, 217, 218), so that in it they combine the fresh and powerful naturalism of Sāñchī, Ajaṇṭā, and Māvalipuram with a delicately decorative sense which is quite Persian. Thus we have works like the peacocks of Jagganātha in the British

Museum, which might have come either from Sāñchī or from Isfahān, or the powerful wild buffalo from Sarwān in the British Museum, dating from about 1600, which one cannot help comparing with the two fighting buffalo in Cave I at Ajaṇṭā. We have evidence of the taste of the Moguls for these subjects in the vogue enjoyed under Akbar and Jahangir by the animal-painter Manṣūr, who was famous for his paintings of birds.

In addition to this realism both in portraiture and in the representation of animals, the great characteristic of Mogul painting is its landscapes.[1] Not that landscape was treated for its own sake. For the most part, as in Iran, it only appears as a decorative motive. But the coldly conventional Persian tradition was suddenly thrown into the shade by a feeling for nature which was quite a new thing: Persian landscape-painting, even when it reproduced wild, rocky scenes, was always a beautiful garden, charming and precious; Mogul landscape was often nature itself.[2] The Moguls were the first of those inhabiting the Islamic lands who knew how to look at the outside world. They grasped the solidity of objects, the interrelation of places, the sense of towering mountains looming near at hand, the manifold life of the jungle, the brooding atmosphere of a solitary tree beneath which princes and dervishes found shelter for their meditations, the living softness of a rose-bush standing out against the golden depths of the sky. Above all, they had a feeling for space and for the living quality of atmosphere, a sense of immensity (Fig. 221, 225). Their luminous distances are as deep and quivering " as the very sky of India." They delighted to use as backgrounds to their court scenes or scenes of love or piety — or sometimes merely of their portraits of a prince

[1] Cf. I. Stchoukine: *La Peinture indienne à l'époque des grands Moghols* (Paris, Leroux, 1929), pp. 77–88; W. Staude: "*Le Paysage dans l'Akbar-Namah*," *Revue des Arts asiatiques*, V, ii, 102.

[2] See the transition stage marked by the "Miracle of the Prophet Elias" (the prophet rescuing Prince Nur al-Dahr, who had been thrown into the sea by a demon) in an *Amūr Ḥamzah* of the school of Akbar, British Museum, in Sir Thomas Arnold's *Painting in Islam* (frontispiece).

—wide, changing skies alive with clouds, now golden, now livid, or lent immensity by the crimson streaks of the setting sun. These Mogul sunsets, which stain the horizon with red, often lend an unexpected breadth to quite slight paintings, so that a mere miniature

FIGURE 232
Kṛishṇa and Rādhā playing at ball.
— *From Mehta:* Studies in Indian Painting.
By courtesy of Mr. Mehta

acquires the value of a vast canvas. Not to mention the fact that these reds, blues, and golds, trailing in broad bands across the horizon, are, as it were, a *Leitmotiv* in the harmony of colour, strengthening and enhancing the fairy-like effect of the costumes and flowers (Fig.

194, 196, 197, 201, 211, 212). Lastly, by their predilection for the play of light and shade and for effects of chiaroscuro the Mogul artists introduced a hitherto unknown novelty and ventured upon

FIGURE 233
Śiva and Pārvatī.
— *Kāngrā school. British Museum*

night scenes which would have brought the old masters of Herāt to a standstill.[1]

As we see, though Mogul art was a court art, it outgrew its original limits to a remarkable extent. Under princes so refined in their

[1] Cf. Stchoukine, op. cit., Pl. LIX, LX, LXI; Havell: *Indian Sculpture and Painting*, p. 228 (Indian impressionism: night scenes), Pl. LXIV–LXVI (Baz Bahadur and Rup Mate; Deer-hunting by night; Travellers round a camp-fire: all in the Calcutta Art Gallery); Blochet: *Peintures de manuscrits arabes, persans et turcs de la Bibliothèque Nationale de Paris*, Pl. 59 (painting of Faiz-Allah).

humanism as Babur or Akbar nothing human remained outside its province. What we have just said about landscape applies equally well to scenes of intimate life. The Mogul painters were not content with representing their princes or nobles on state occasions; they followed them even into the joys of their secret apartments. They borrowed from the Rajput artists the custom of painting the ladies of the court in the varied pastimes of the life of the harem. Hence our collections possess a whole series of charming paintings representing the contemporaries of Mumtāz Maḥall in that semi-undress the fashion for which had been borrowed by the Mogul court from the India of the rajahs. Here too we have subjects of a similar nature to those of the Ṣafawid miniatures, but, in our opinion, decidedly more voluptuous. It is not Sā'di who is suggested by these lovely bodies, tense or languid with an ardent tropical sensuality, but the pagan effusions of the *Gīta Govinda.* We reproduce a few of these works from the Vever or Demotte collections. In one a charming prince is retiring from a banquet amid the slight fumes of incipient intoxication, tenderly supported by his band of women (Fig. 220); in others we have love-scenes of striking frankness (Fig. 198, 223); or, again, we watch the fair Indo-Mogul ladies pass before us, full of coquetry, or surprise them in all the abandonment of intimacy (Fig. 224, 227, 228).[1]

After this general sketch it remains to say a few words about the internal development of Mogul painting, with the names of the principal artists, which we will now proceed to do, basing our account on the fine works of Messrs. Percy Brown, F. R. Martin, Coomaraswamy, Mehta, and Ivan Stchoukine.

For the reign of Humayun three names are mentioned, all of them Iranian: Shahim Muzahhib of Bokhara; Baljīd, who was painter at once to Humayun and to Shāh Ṭahmāsp, king of Persia; and, lastly,

[1] Cf. Stchoukine, op. cit., Pl. LVI, LVII, LIX, etc.

FIGURE 234

Śiva and Pārvatī on the bull Nandi. Miniature from a Hindu MS. of the eighteenth century.

— *Musée Guimet*

Abd al-Ṣamad. But the real founder of the Indo-Persian school was Akbar, who, as his historian Abul Faḍl remarks, encouraged the development of painting by every means in his power.[1] Setting an

FIGURE 235
Pārvatī on the Tiger. Miniature from a Hindu MS. of the seventeenth century.
— *Musée Guimet*

example to his courtiers, he expressed a desire to have the portraits of all the great men in his empire. He was even known to confer nobility upon the chief painters at his court, a custom followed by

[1] Cf. Anu Ghose: *Akbar as Painter* (*Roopa Lekha*, 1929), 2, 35.

his son Jahangir. As we have seen, he sent for masters from Iran to direct their work. Thus his favourite painters were Mīr Sayyid Alī of Tabrīz and especially Khwāja Abd al-Ṣamad of Shīrāz, nicknamed Shīrīnqalam, or " brush of milk," the pupil of Bihzād. Abd al-Ṣamad was both a poet and an artist and had already been a friend of the emperor Humayun when Akbar attached him to his person, conferred nobility upon him, and entrusted to him various official posts at Fatḥpūr and Multān. The names of other Moslem artists at the court of Akbar are known to us; for instance, Farrukh-bey the Kalmuck; but most of the artists there were Indian, such as Daswanth, Basāwan, the two Kēsū or Kēsāva, Mādhu, Muskīn, Mukund, Rāmdās, and Bhagvatī. This mixed character of the school of Akbar may well be borne in mind. The works of this reign, as we have seen, were no doubt still influenced exclusively by Iran, and at this period it is better to speak of Irano-Indian art than of Mogul art properly so called. But Mogul art was to arise out of this very association of Iranian masters with Indian works, and of Hindu painters with Persian works.[1] Nothing can be more instructive in this connexion than the case of Daswanth the Kahār, who died in 1584. At the court of Akbar this low-caste Hindu became a pupil of Abd al-Ṣamad — that is, of the last pupil of Bihzād, who taught him the style of the school of Herāt. By command of Akbar, who had recognized his talent and raised him from obscurity, he treated the old Indian subjects in the Persian manner, or, rather, he composed paintings " in which the chief figures were full of Indian reminiscences, but were surrounded by secondary figures or episodical details in the Iranian manner." His rival Basāwan, another pupil of Abd al-Ṣamad, was also an Indian of Iranian tendencies, whose Iranianisms did not, however, prevent him from painting works such as the " Rajah and the Frog Princess " in the Hudley collection

[1] See the scene from the *Mahābhārata*, of the school of Akbar, now in the Museum of Fine Arts, Boston, reproduced by Coomaraswamy: *Bulletin of the Museum of Fine Arts*, Vol. XVI, No. 93 (February 1918), p. 3.

(reproduced by Vincent Smith [1]), a delicious scene in which all the naturalistic feeling and polytheism native to the land find a happy survival. It seems, too, that Akbar took a pleasure in making Indian artists illustrate Moslem works, and Moslem artists picture scenes from Indian legend, just as he induced the Indian Kēsū to reproduce Christian paintings.[2]

Under Jahangir the fusion of the Iranian and Indian elements became complete, and this fusion, the way for which was prepared by Akbar, seems to have been really the work of the new sovereign. We have said above what an interest Jahangir took in painting; and we may add that he was a very well-informed connoisseur, with a taste which seems to have been quite remarkable. Under his influence Mogul painting emancipated itself from its servile imitation of Persia, and Western influence began to make itself felt. Jahangir was familiar with European art, and his private gallery contained Italian paintings as well as engravings by Dürer and Holbein. He seems also to have made certain borrowings from Chinese art. Above all, he had a deep feeling for nature. The naturalistic character and sense of direct observation that we can discern in the art of his reign seem, indeed, to have been to a large extent due to him personally. He paid particular attention to the resemblance and *life* of a portrait. The art of animal-painting was equally indebted to him: he caused rare animals and extraordinary plants and flowers to be copied for his albums. His interest in zoology and botany had as its result to give us some pages which are admirable both in drawing and in colour. The margins which served as a frame to the paintings also contained wonderfully accurate pictures of animals and flowers and especially some lifelike sketches of antelopes or zebras.[3] The full

[1] *History of Fine Art in India and Ceylon*, Pl. CXVII, p. 470.

[2] Cf. Stchoukine, op. cit., pp. 30–41, Pl. V–XIX; W. Staude: "*Muskīn*," *Revue des Arts asiatiques*, V, iii, 169.

[3] See the zebra attributed to Ustād Manṣūr in the Museum of Fine Arts, Boston; see *Bulletin of the Museum*, XVI, No. 93 (February 1918), p. 7.

value of this realism in the representation of flowers and animals, this scientific accuracy in the rendering of species and scientific families, can be estimated in the numerous hunting-scenes in which Jahangir caused his exploits in the chase to be immortalized, episode

FIGURE 236

Gadā-Vishṇu (Vishṇu with the club). Miniature from a Hindu MS. of the eighteenth century.

— *Musée Guimet*

by episode: these scenes are often very dramatic and, like the groups of portraits belonging to this reign, have a landscape setting which is full of quite a new feeling. In fact the life of the jungle, with its rocks, its thickets, and its wild beasts' lairs, is here rendered with striking lifelikeness. It is now, too, that those vast distances appear to which we referred above, with their effects of light and their impressions of storm or of evening.

But the triumph of the reign of Jahangir lay, above all, in its portraiture. Up to that time, even under Akbar, the figures had been represented in conventional attitudes, with the face always in profile, the right hand holding a flower, and the feet one before the other. Under Jahangir psychological intensity in portraiture came to be especially sought after; [1] hence those three-quarter-face portraits which enable the artist to seize the full moral complexity of his model with greater success. Hence, too, the more natural attitudes, which show humanity in all its sincerity of character. At a single stroke Mogul portraiture raised itself above the elegant accuracy of the pupils of Bihzād, which had always been a little hard and over-delicate, to a technical mastery, a character of authority, a pictorial power, and a psychological richness which, as we said just now, sometimes rise to the heights of the art of Titian.

The chief masters of the school of Jahangir were as follows: Abūl Ḥasan, known as Nāḍir al-Zamān, the son of Aqa Razā of Herāt, who was the Emperor's favourite. He was a portrait-painter first and foremost, but has also left us some admirably realistic elephants, and amused himself with painting various scenes of Indian life in the Rajput manner (see the car drawn by zebu reproduced by Mr. Mehta); [2] Ustād Manṣūr Naqqāsh, a very great animal-painter, who was also a favourite of Jahangir. We have some admirable drawings of birds and flowers from his hand in the albums; Muḥammad Murād of Samarqand, who has left us some elegantly drawn gazelles, a little in the Rajput manner, specimens of which are to be found in the Béhaigue collection and the Berlin Museum; Shafī Abbāsī, a native of Persia, who was a flower-painter; Manūhar, who was al-

[1] See the "Durbar of Jahangir, 1620," in the Museum of Fine Arts, Boston, reproduced by Coomaraswamy: *Les Miniatures orientales de la collection Goloubew, au Museum of Fine Arts, Boston* (*Ars Asiatica*, Vol. XIII, 1929), Pl. LXXII, p. 122.

[2] N. C. Mehta: *Studies in Indian Painting*, Pl. 27, p. 64.

FIGURE 237

Woman at her toilet.

— *Musée Guimet. Photo, Pivot*

ready known at the time of Akbar, and painted some splendid "divan" scenes representing embassies to the court of Akbar, besides being a great animal-painter; Farrukh-bey, who was already known under Akbar, and continued to paint hunting-scenes under Jahangir; Bhagvatī, also known under the reign of Akbar, who painted portraits — especially those of Humayun and of dervishes; Bishan Dās, who has left us the "House of the fakir Sheikh Fūl" reproduced by Mehta — a remarkable composition from a sure and sober brush, with some delightful half-tones.[1]

The reign of Shāh Jahan marks the "return to Persia," and realism falls into the background before the decorative style. "There is a return," so Goloubew notes, "to conventionalized foliage, gilding, and conventional designs with brilliant colour." The strength of the school of Jahangir to some extent disappears, and the psychological intensity of the figures is proportionately diminished. The silhouettes lose something of their life and animation. On the other hand, never did Mogul art achieve such supreme elegance. In short, the art with which we meet at this time is very rich, but rather cold, having at its disposal an incredible technical delicacy and astonishing refinements of execution.[2]

One outward sign of this partial retrogression is that the artists abandoned those three-quarter-face portraits which had been so dear to the age of Jahangir, and returned to mere profiles, as under Akbar.

We may hasten to add that, though Mogul painting ceased to make any progress, there was as yet no question of decadence in the strict sense of the word. This was only to set in with the pietistic reign of Aurungzeb. The age of Jahangir and that of the Tāj Maḥall were still to produce marvels.

One of the chief painters of this reign is Muḥammad Nādir Samarqandī, who in a few sure and sober strokes throws off a powerful,

[1] Cf. Stchoukine, op. cit., pp. 41–50, Pl. XX–XXXIII.
[2] Cf. Stchoukine, op. cit., p. 51 and Pl. XXXIV–L.

FIGURE 238

Woman at the spinning-wheel.
— *Musée Guimet. Photo, Pivot*

splendid portrait — for instance, his portraits of Shāh Jahan, Āṣaf Khān, and Khalīl Allāh Khān, which are like Clouets with the power of a Titian. For all their elegant simplicity, in fact, the elderly noblemen thus immortalized by Muḥammad Nadīr Samarqandī have a commanding majesty which reminds us of some doge of Venice or some great burgher of the United Provinces. We may note that the painter continues to draw three-quarter portraits — for instance, the Shēr Muḥammad Nawāl in the British Museum. Another leading painter of this reign is Mīr Muḥammad Hāshim, who has left us simple outline line drawings of figures at the Mogul court, which, again, have the clear-cut quality of the finest drawings of Clouet. Among his works we may draw attention to the group of Timur, Babur, and Humayun in the collection of the Comtesse de Béhaigue, a marvellous sketch of Ḥakīm Masīh al-Zamān in the British Museum, and a youthful portrait of Aurungzeb, drawn about 1660, which is reproduced by Martin. There is also Anūpchātar or Rāj Anūp, the favourite painter of Prince Dārā Shikūh, son of Shāh Jahan. One of the chief works from his hand is a Shāh Jahan seated among his emirs, dating from about 1640. The fifty or so line portraits brought together on this famous page, though only in profile, have a sureness of touch, a keenness of expression, and a psychological intensity which are still astonishing. Beneath the pomp and distinction of a princely life we can divine the dark passions of that troubled age, when all the treasures of India were to be at the mercy of intrigue and audacity at a court more divided and poisoned by hatred than any the world has known since the Rome of the Cæsars, the Italy of the Renaissance, and the France of the later Valois. And not only individual character and social blemishes, but racial characteristics too are thrown into brutal prominence by the cold and unerring elegance of line. In short, we have here an extraordinary page of history which helps us to understand the decline and fall of the Mogul domination.

Among Shāh Jahan's painters we may also mention two Indians,

Chitarman or Kalyān Das, who flourished about 1660, and Hūnhār, both of whom also drew elegant portraits of Mogul dignitaries, the former with more delicacy, and the latter with a more substantial realism.

And, lastly, side by side with Shāh Jahan, we should mention

FIGURE 239
Scene of adoration (*Śiva-pūjā*). Indo-Mogul school, end of the eighteenth century.
— *Musée Guimet. Photo, Pivot*

the patronage of art exerted by his son Dārā Shikūh (1615–59), who was unfortunately afterwards supplanted by his younger brother Aurungzeb. Unlike Aurungzeb, whose Moslem fanaticism prejudiced him against the pictorial arts, Dārā Shikūh proved himself a worthy follower of his father, showing an intelligent sympathy for things Indian, which was even more whole-hearted than his ancestor Akbar. We have seen how he sought to reconcile Hinduism and liberal Muḥammadanism in a higher philosophic synthesis. Like his grandfather Jahangir, he displayed a passionate interest in painting. We have an album of his, dated from 1641 to 1642, and now in the India Office Library, which is one of the most precious records of Mogul art that have come down to us. Indeed, this album contains works bearing dates between 1605 and 1634 — that is, from the days of Akbar to those of Shāh Jahan. It is interesting to note that we find in it paintings of animals which are at once artistically marvellous and excellent as illustrations of natural history. We shall also find in it a few portraits showing a rare mastery, such as the portrait of Prince Salim — that is, of the young Jahangir — in the midst of a magnificent landscape.

RAJPUT PAINTING

IN SPEAKING OF MOGUL ART WE HAVE CONSTANTLY REFERRED TO Rajput painting. It might perhaps have been more suitable to speak of the latter first, for the Hindu painting known by the name of Rajput has native origins which go back to the remotest past.[1] Through the humble Gujerati school of the fifteenth century and the miniatures in Jain manuscripts,[2] it is the heir of the great art of Ajaṇṭā and Bāgh, as well as of the Bengali school of the Pāla and Sēna dynasties.[3] All the same, it cannot be denied that, however native it may have remained both in origin and in inspiration, Rajput painting was none

[1] Cf. E. Vredenburg: "Continuity of Pictorial Tradition in the Art of India," *Rūpam*, January 1920 (with coloured illustrations from a Nepalese MS. of the *Prajñāpāramitā*).

[2] Cf. A. Coomaraswamy: *Catalogue of the Indian Collections in the Museum of Fine Arts, Boston*, IV, *Jaina Paintings and MSS.* (1924); N. C. Mehta: "Indian Painting in the Fifteenth Century," *Rūpam*, Nos. 22–3 (1925); A. Coomaraswamy: *Portfolio of Indian Art, Museum of Fine Arts, Boston*, Pl. LX and LXI (Jaina MSS. of Gujerat, fifteenth and sixteenth centuries).

[3] We shall examine this most important Bengali school of the Pāla, Sēna, and Nepalese MSS. in Vol. IV, Ch. ii, of the present work. See Coomaraswamy: *Portfolio of Indian Art*, Boston, Pl. XXXIII–XXXVI (MS. of the *Aṣṭasahasrikā Prajñāpāramitā*, Nepal, A.D. 1136).

FIGURE 240

Indian ladies.

— *André Godard collection. Photo, Laniepce*

the less stimulated and even considerably influenced by Mogul art. While preserving its deeply original character, it can be fully explained only by its emulation of Mogul painting.

Rajput painting, which is now well known from the learned works of Ananda Coomaraswamy, Nānālāl Chamanlāl Mehta, and Percy Brown, is divided into two groups: the Rājasthānī and the Pahārī. The Rājasthānī and Bundēla group, as its name indicates, is connected with the provinces of Rajputana and Bundelkhand, in the former of which, at the Rajput courts of Jeypūr, Bīkanir, and Udaipūr, this style, known as "*Jeypūr qalam*," the style (literally "brush") of Jeypūr, was developed during the seventeenth and particularly during the eighteenth and early nineteenth centuries. The second school, known as the *pahārī* or mountain style (*Pahārī qalam*), was developed during the same period in the Himalayan states of the upper Punjāb, round Jammū, Chamba, Tehri Garhwāl, and, most of all, Kāngrā —whence its other name of Kāngrā style (*Kāngrā qalam*).[1] From this Pahārī school is derived the Sikh school of the beginning of the nineteenth century, which also flourished in the Punjāb under the reign of Ranjit Singh (1803–39), with Kapur Singh as its chief painter.

In spite of many affinities and mutual borrowings, Rajput art can be distinguished from Mogul painting at a glance. Mogul art, as we have seen, is in its essence an art of official portraiture, of court scenes and representations of historic occasions. In its technique it always remains more or less close to the miniature, in which it had its origins, and the illuminated manuscript and faithful to the precision of line and meticulous detail of Persian calligraphy. Rajput art, on the contrary, though inspired by the little native courts of Rajputana and the Punjāb, appears to be an infinitely more popular art. Its technique, as Percy Brown observes, is derived, not from the

[1] Cf. Coomaraswamy: "Rajput Painting. The Kāngrā Valley," *Bulletin of the Museum of Fine Arts, Boston*, August 1919; Lal Mukandi: *The Pahārī School of Painting* (*Roopa Lekha*, 1929), I, 24–35.

miniature, but from mural fresco, of which it possesses the breadth and rapid movement, as well as the "facile conventions." This art makes its appeal by a more intimate and at the same time more

FIGURE 241
Woman with antelope.
— *Musée Guimet. Photo, Pivot*

poetic note than Mogul art. It is connected, in fact, with the eternal themes of Indian national poetry, the epics, the Krishnaite poems (for which see Fig. 229–232), the Śivaite ones (see Fig. 233–235), and the Indian erotic poets. By reason of this, it remains in close touch with the Hindu religious life of modern days, with that profoundly human mysticism and passionate quietism of which Rāmānanda and Kabir made themselves the apostles. It is an art full of fervent piety, inspired by a religious exaltation — or, to use the Indian term, a *bhakti* — instinct with tenderness, whose material

FIGURE 242
Night scene.
— *Demotte collection. Photo, Laniepce*

expression has, however, never been divorced from an eroticism at once sophisticated and innocent. The Kṛishṇa celebrated by its schools appears to us as the friend who speaks to the heart, the divine consoler whose human existence, as we may remember, was spent amid the sports and occupations of village life, in a joyous, tender pastoral setting. This bucolic theme was always a main source of

FIGURE 243
Rajput nobleman.
— *André Godard collection. Photo, Laniepc*

inspiration to the Rajput painters. From this *Imitation* of the divine cowherd — as mystical and tender as our own mediæval *Imitation of Christ,* but with an added element of eroticism — the Rajput school drew its naïve freshness, sincerity, and emotion. Thus whole series of paintings were devoted to the subject of the Lover and the Beloved, a theme which, to religious souls, at once suggested the mystic communings between Kṛishṇa and the faithful believer, but which is none the less treated in these works in a strange, romantic spirit, with a freedom of detail and a sensuality which are curiously remote from our Western religious sentiment. We may also note, in the same vein, how works of Śivaite inspiration were sometimes humanized by the great tenderness of the pervading Krishnaite spirit, as in the painting of the dance of Śiva (*saṃdhya gāyatrī*) reproduced by Percy Brown (see Fig. 233, 234).[1]

In a similar spirit of tender humanity, Rajput painting delighted in scenes of popular life, intimate pictures of feminine occupations and motherhood, the various crafts of the artisans, bazaar scenes, the noontide rest of travellers, and the strange life of the highways of India. It approached the treatment of animals in the same spirit. Instead of the powerful realism of the Moguls, we have here, as Percy Brown remarks, a school of animal-painting full of tenderness and sweetness, in which, as in former days at Sāñchī and Māvalipuram, animals are treated with a brotherly sympathy and seem to bear the impress of humanity: this is true of the animal-paintings reproduced by Messrs. Coomaraswamy, Mehta, or Percy Brown, in which we find lovingly depicted the kindly monkeys of the *Rāmāyaṇa,* the charming cows of Kṛishṇa (Fig. 229, 230, 231), the gazelles and antelopes, with their human eyes, which follow legendary princesses about their fairy-like parks (Fig. 241, 242), or the peacocks,

[1] Cf. A. Coomaraswamy: *Catalogue of the Indian Collections in the Museum of Fine Arts, Boston,* Pt. V: *Rajput Painting* (1926), Pl. LI, CLXIX, CLXX, CCLIV, CCLXVI, CCLXVII; Coomaraswamy: *Portfolio,* Pl. LXXIV, LXXV, etc.; Gangoly: *Masterpieces of Rajput Painting,* Pl. XXXII, XLIV.

proudly conscious of their beauty, which drink out of the fair ladies' hands: see, for example, in Mr. Mehta's remarkable album the painting of the Kāngrā school in which a beautiful lady leans down from her terrace, amid a landscape of mountains and waters, to stroke the muzzle of a sacred bull.[1]

The Pahārī schools, and that of Kāngrā in particular, have left us works permeated with this spirit which date from the end of the eighteenth century and the beginning of the nineteenth — among others, some fine illustrations of the Krishnaite legend (*Kṛishṇa līlā* — the sport of Kṛishṇa), which, while profiting by the technical improvements due to Mogul art, remain marvels of Indian poetry. Among others we may single out from the series of masterpieces in the Coomaraswamy collection an episode from the *Gīta Govinda* which is a perfect idyll, and a representation of the *Kālīya Damana* (conqueror of the snake), with curious female serpent deities in which the classic theme of the siren assumes a strange charm, thanks to the contrast between the Indian costume in which the body of these water-creatures is attired and their fishes' tails.[2] Similarly, in the Boston Museum, there is a deliciously mischievous child Kṛishṇa who is already an object of admiration and desire to the milkmaids, and a youthful Kṛishṇa in the character of a cowherd leading his beasts to pasture, the latter of which has such a power of suggesting atmosphere that we might almost imagine we hear the "herd streaming forth" through the gates of the village (Fig. 230). Here that powerfully naturalistic treatment of animals, whose history we have followed since the days of Sāñchī, has the added charm of an idyllic sentiment, light, caressing, and tender, in which we feel, as it were, a refreshing waft of Krishnaite poetry. We also reproduce a few

[1] Cf. N. C. Mehta: *Studies in Indian Painting*, Pl. 54, p. 118; A. Coomaraswamy: *Catalogue of the Indian Collections in the Museum of Fine Arts, Boston*, Pt. V, *Rajput Painting*, Pl. XXVIII, LXX–LXXII, LXXV, LXXVIII, LXXIX, LXXXI; Coomaraswamy: *Portfolio of Indian Art*, Boston, Pl. LXXVI, LXXVII, LXXVIII, etc.

[2] Coomaraswamy collection. See Gangoly: *Masterpieces of Rajput Painting*, Pl. XLVI.

scenes of feminine life — women at the spinning-wheel, the bath, etc. — either Mogul or Rajput, from the Musée Guimet or the Godard collection, which will give an adequate idea of these pleasing scenes of intimate life (Fig. 237, 238, 245, etc.).

A place by itself in Pahārī art is assigned by Mr. Mehta to the school of Tehri Garhwāl, a little Himalayan state which produced two great artists, Chaitu and Mānaku.[1] Mr. Mehta reproduces in his fine work several paintings of this school inspired by the Purāṇas or the *Rāmāyaṇa*, in particular the rape of the Yādava women, a work of great purity of line and full of simplicity, nobility, and dramatic interest; [2] a scene of the *Dāna-līlā* (gift of the milkmaids to Kṛishṇa); and a delicious game of blind-man's-buff played by the Krishnaite cowherds in the woods by moonlight in the midst of their herds (Fig. 231).[3]

In these paintings we may observe the breadth and realism of the landscape, which are evidence of the extent to which the Pahārī school was inspired by Mogul models. We even find romantic moonlight effects — for instance, in those scenes of antelope hunts in which the darkness is illuminated both by the moon and by the torches of the hunters (see Fig. 231 and 242). One of these scenes, reproduced by Mr. Mehta, represents Kṛishṇa and Rādhā in amorous converse on the bank of a river at the edge of a wood in a solitary night landscape, illuminated by nothing but the reflected light of their bodies and garments: the great silence of the country-side, the delicate passion in the gestures of the two lovers, the effect of the deep-blue night contrasting with the luminous shimmer of the divine couple, remind us a little of the skill of a Burne-Jones or a Rossetti.[4] In fact, this art is to Ajaṇṭā what English pre-Raphaelitism is to Botticelli. But in this "neo-Ajantism" there is something that was lacking in the

[1] See N. C. Mehta: "Two Pahārī Painters of Tehri Garhwāl, Mānaku and Chaitu," *Rūpam*, No. 26 (October 1926).

[2] N. C. Mehta: *Studies in Indian Painting*, Pl. 18, p. 51.

[3] Ibid., Pl. 21 (in colour), p. 54.

[4] Ibid., Pl. 24 (in colour), p. 56.

FIGURE 244

Hunting-scene.

— *André Godard collection. Photo, Laniepce*

Rossetti coterie — that is, popular inspiration, freshness, and spontaneity. Even in the modern works, permeated by Mogul and European influences — such as the flirtation scene between Kṛishṇa and Rādhā, which we reproduce here, thanks to the courtesy of Mr. Mehta — the Krishnaite charm remains unimpaired: its association with Western technique has even given rise to a classicism of remarkable purity (Fig. 232).

In the Jeypūr school we meet with Krishnaite scenes which are frequently less influenced by Mogul art than are the Pahārī works, and are therefore treated in a fashion that is at once broader and more naïve. We may once more draw attention to the works reproduced by Mr. Mehta in his fine work *Studies in Indian Painting,* and in particular to a charming *Rāsa-maṇḍala* (dance of pleasure), an Indian "beatific vision," in the spirit of St. Francis of Assisi,[1] and a *Govardhana-dharaṇa* (Kṛishṇa holding up Mount Govardhana),[2] a scene treated in the style of the Song of Songs, in which, in spite of all the distance that separates the two types of mind, the grouping of the figures — whether love-lorn shepherdesses, enamoured dancing-girls, or little cows transported with divine love — suggests the paradises of Fra Angelico.

As Mr. Coomaraswamy remarks, in such works as these Rajput art has created a new type of feminine beauty, or, rather, has succeeded, after centuries of oblivion, in rediscovering the canons of Ajaṇṭā. With these *gopī,* at once modest and passionate, eager and timid by turns — with these creatures compact of tenderness and grace, we have gone far from the brutal sensuality of the Tamil baroque. Here the feminine ideal — whether Rajput or Mogul — finds sources of a greater freshness — the very well-springs of the great Sanskrit poetry, from Sītā and Damayantī down to the heroines of Kālidāsa (Fig. 232, 233, 237, 238, 245).

[1] N. C. Mehta: *Studies in Indian Painting,* Pl. 11, p. 33.
[2] Ibid., Pl. 10, p. 32.

FIGURE 245

Interior.

— *André Godard collection. Photo, Laniepce*

Rajput painting is sometimes characterized as " musical painting "; and the Pahārī paintings do, as a matter of fact, often serve as illustrations to those musical compositions which are known by the name of *Rāgmālās.*[1] In the eyes of native connoisseurs, their interest consisted precisely in this adaptation of painting to music, the work of the painter being obliged to harmonize with the theme of the music, evoking and suggesting it and transposing it into visual values. Thus in the Kāngrā school we meet with corresponding sets of melodies and paintings, in which " the melody is composed upon a pictorial theme, and the painting is composed in accordance with the psychological suggestion of the music." There are very many Rajput paintings which have no value to a European except for their own sake, but to an Indian at once suggest the melodies of the *Rāgmālā*, the *Rāsarāja* of the poet Matirām, the works of Kēshvada and of Bihari. Here we have an association of painting, poetry, and music to which Europe can as yet furnish no equivalent.

As we have said, Rajput art was too dependent upon the little native courts of Rajputana, Bundelkhand, and the Punjāb not to have responded in its turn to the demand for portraits. These Rajput portraits — busts of rajahs or equestrian portraits — are more or less influenced by Moslem models, those of Kāngrā being rather firmly delineated and richly coloured, in the Mogul manner, while those of Jeypūr are remarkable for their colour, which is " simple to the point of timidity." All the figures, without exception, are represented in profile. In spite of their absence of solidity, slight naïveté of technique, and lack of flexibility of line, which is in contrast with the calligraphic drawing of the Mogul style, these Rajput portraits often leave us with a remarkable impression of grandeur and spirit, due in

[1] "A *Rāgmālā* is a Garland of *Rāgas*, poems describing the thirty-six musical modes. The *Rāga* or *Rāgiṇī* consists of a selection of from five to seven notes, or rather intervals, distributed over the scale from C to C, the entire gamut of twenty-two notes being never employed in a single composition." (Coomaraswamy: "Rajput Painting, the Musical Modes," in *Bulletin of the Museum of Fine Arts, Boston*, August 1918.)

FIGURE 246

Indian fête.

— Musée Guimet. Photo, Pivot

part to the models themselves — those Rajput nobles who formed the most chivalrous aristocracy of the Orient; and partly, too, to the sincerity of their technique, that absence of calligraphic quality, or "chastity of line" — to adopt Percy Brown's felicitous expression — which lends them a charm the more. Among these portraits we may draw attention to the bust of the Rajah Pratap Singh (1778–1803), reproduced in Mr. Mehta's work, and the splendid equestrian figure acquired at Jeypūr by Monsieur and Madame André Godard, which we are enabled to reproduce here by their courtesy (Fig. 243).

And in conclusion we reproduce two more Rajput and Mogul paintings from the André Godard collection: a marvellous Rajput gazelle-hunt (Fig. 244); a Mogul "night-piece" of two lovers on a high terrace surrounded by the tree-tops of a silent park (Fig. 245); and, last of all, a festival in the palace of a Rajput prince, a painting from the Musée Guimet, the softness of whose ancient tones — its old golds, subdued pinks, and faded mauves — our photograph is powerless to reproduce (Fig. 246).[1]

[1] For contemporary schools of Indian painting, see the collections of *Rūpam* and *Roopa Lekha* and the series *Modern Indian Artists* (published by *Rūpam*, Old Post Office Street, Calcutta): Vol. I, *K. N. Mazumdar*, by O. C. Gangoly; Vol. II, *Asit Kumar Haldar*, by J. H. Cousins and Gangoly, etc.; *Abanindranath Tagore and the Renaissance of Indian Painting* (*Roopa Lekha*, 1929), I, 41.